Contents – Biology

Cell components 4.1.1.2

- Animal and plant cells share some, but not all organelles.

Plant cell

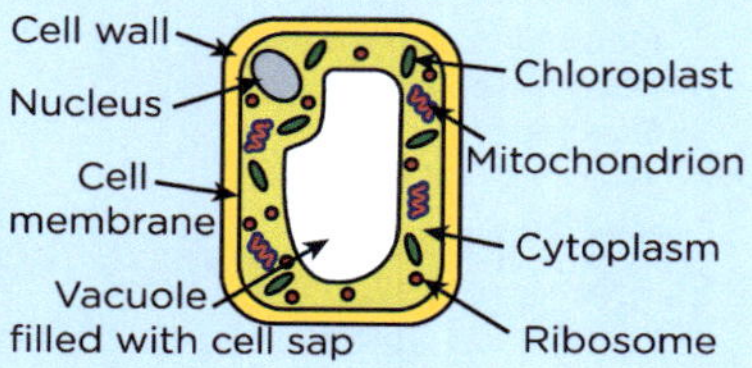

Animal cell

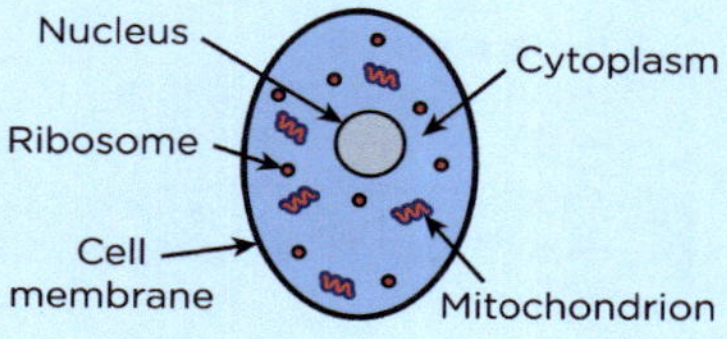

- Mitochondria are the site of aerobic respiration where energy is released from glucose.
- Cytoplasm is water-based and contains lots of the organelles. It is where most cell reactions take place.
- Nucleus contains deoxyribonucleic acid (DNA), which is the genetic information that controls the cell. DNA is organised into chromosomes.
- Cell membrane encloses the cell and controls which substances go in and out. Many simple substances travel by diffusion.
- Ribosomes are the site of protein synthesis.
- Chloroplasts (plant cells) contain the green pigment chlorophyll, which absorbs light for photosynthesis.
- Cell wall (plant and algal cells) made of cellulose, which strengthens the cell.

Bacterial cell

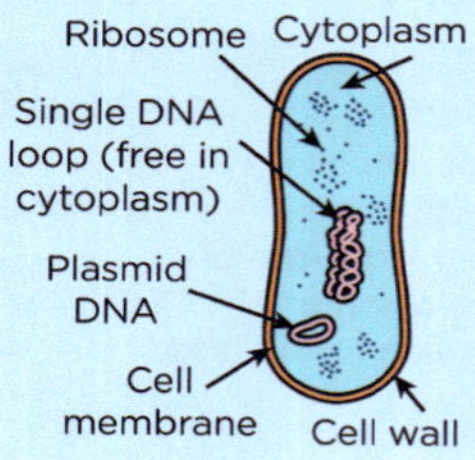

Eukaryotes and prokaryotes 4.1.1.1

Eukaryotic cells	Prokaryotic cells
Plant and animal cells	Bacterial cells
Cell membrane	Cell membrane surrounded by a cell wall
Cytoplasm	Cytoplasm
Genetic material enclosed in a nucleus	Genetic material is a single DNA loop and sometimes small rings of DNA called plasmids, not enclosed in a nucleus
Larger (5 µm - 100 µm)	Smaller (1 µm - 10 µm)

10^{-9} nano (n) → (× 1000) 10^{-6} micro (µ) → (× 1000) 10^{-3} milli (m) → (× 10) 10^{-2} centi (c)

Cell differentiation 4.1.1.4

- Cell differentiation is the specialisation of cells by acquiring different sub-cellular structures. This is required so cells can perform their specific functions.
- Cells differentiate to form different types of cells:
  - Most animal cells differentiate at an early stage. In mature animals, cell division is restricted to repairing and replacing damaged and old cells.
  - Many plant cells can differentiate throughout life.

Cell specialisation 4.1.1.

- Cells may have a specialised structure to carry out a particular function:

Cell	Function	Specialised structure
Sperm cell (animal) 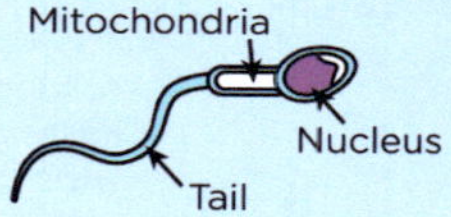	Travel through female reproductive system towards an ovum (egg cell) to fertilise it	• Tail to swim • Large number of mitochondria to release energy to swim
Nerve cell (animal) 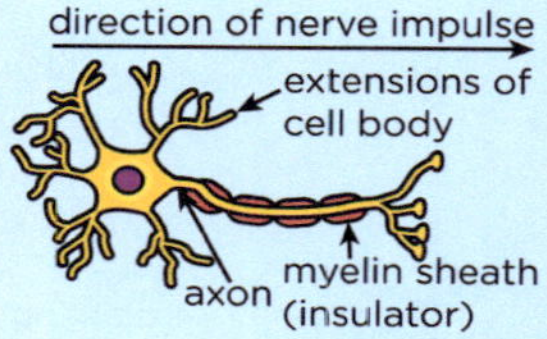	Transmit electrical signals quickly through nervous system	• Long cell extension (axons) • Myelin sheath insulator increases the speed of transmission of electrical impulses • Cell body has extensions to pick up signals from neighbouring cells
Muscle cell (animal) 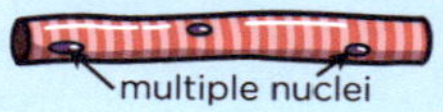	Contract and relax	• Large number of mitochondria to provide energy for contraction
Root hair cell (plant) 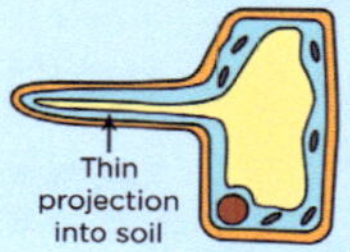	Absorb water and minerals from soil	• Small thin extension to increase surface area for absorption of water and minerals
Xylem (plant) 	Carry water and dissolved minerals upwards from roots up plant stems for transpiration	• Empty dead cells form long hollow tubes with no end walls • Lignin inside walls supports plant weight
Phloem cell (plant) 	Carry sucrose in cell sap from leaves to other parts of the plant via translocation	• Living cells form tubes • Contain few organelles so suga travels easily • End walls contain small holes (sieve plates)

Microscopy, cultures, mitosis, and human stem cells

SNAPREVISE

Microscopy 4.1.1.5

- Light microscopes were invented first, with a maximum resolution of 200nm.
  - Eyepiece lens often has x10 magnification.
  - Often 3 objective lenses of different magnifications (x5, x10 and x25).
  - Stage holds the specimen.
  - Specimen is on a microscope slide under a cover slip.
  - Course focus quickly moves the stage closer and further from the chosen objective lens to roughly focus the sample.
  - Fine focus moves the stage slowly to finely focus the sample.

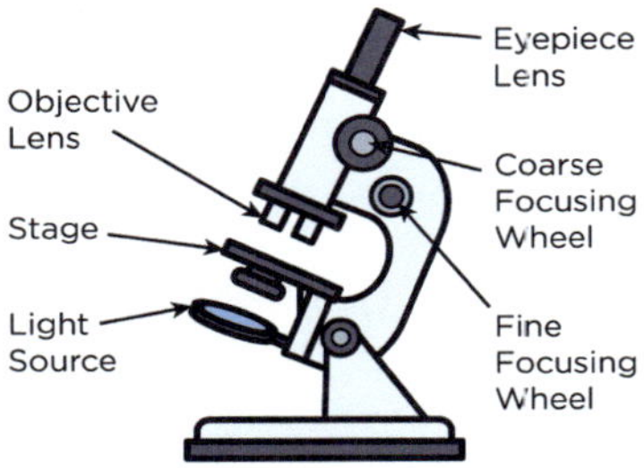

- Electron microscopes were invented later, with an increased maximum resolution of 0.1nm.
  - Transmission electron microscope (TEM) fires a beam of electrons through a thin slice of the specimen. Electrons that pass through the specimen are detected and used to make the image.
  - Scanning electron microscope (SEM) fires a beam of electrons across the surface of the specimen. Electrons scatter from the surface and are detected to make the image.
- Electron microscopes have a higher magnification and resolving power than light microscopes, increasing the understanding of sub-cellular structures.
- $magnification = \frac{size\ of\ image}{size\ of\ real\ object}$

Human stem cells 4.1.2.3

- A stem cell is an undifferentiated cell capable of replication and differentiation into other types of cell.
- In human embryos, embryonic stem cells can differentiate into any type of specialised human cell (totipotent). Once it has differentiated, it cannot change back or switch cell type.
- In adult bone marrow, adult stem cells can form many specific cell types, such as blood stem cells producing blood cells (multipotent).
- Human stem cells can be used in therapeutic cloning to help conditions such as diabetes and paralysis.
  - An embryo is produced with the same genes as the patient.
  - Stem cells from the embryo are not rejected by the patient's body.
  - Potential risks include transfer of viral infection and some people have ethical or religious objections.

Culturing microorganisms 4.1.1.6

- Bacteria multiply by cell division (binary fission) as frequently as once every 20 minutes.
- Bacteria only multiply if they have enough nutrients and a suitable temperature.
  - Bacteria can be grown in a nutrient broth solution.
  - Bacteria can be grown as colonies on an agar gel plate.
- Uncontaminated cultures of microorganisms are used to investigate the action of disinfectants and antibiotics. They are prepared using aseptic technique:
  - Petri dishes and culture media must be sterilised before use to prevent growing foreign microorganisms.
  - Inoculating loops must be sterilised by passing them through a flame before being used to transfer microorganisms to the petri dish.
  - The Petri dish should be stored upside down with the lid secured with adhesive tape to reduce the contamination risk from airborne microorganisms and stop condensation from pooling.
  - Cultures should be incubated at 25 °C to encourage growth of the microorganisms without growing contaminating microorganisms from humans (which grow best at 37 °C).
- $bacteria\ in\ population = initial\ total \times 2^{number\ of\ divisions}$
- $area\ of\ colony/clear\ area = \pi r^2$

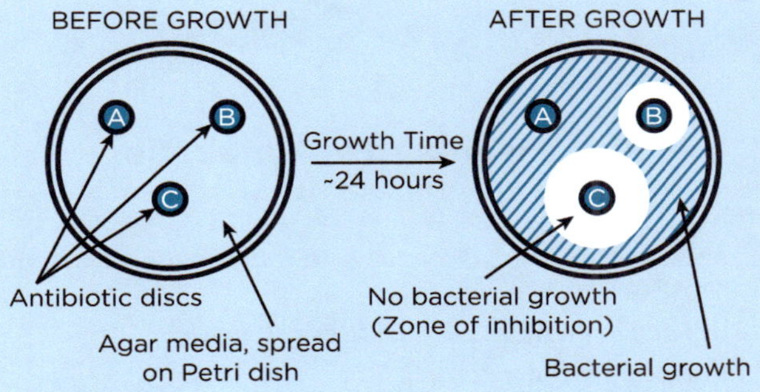

Effect of three antibiotics (A, B and C) on bacterial growth.

- A = No effect
- B = Inhibits growth weakly
- C = Inhibits growth strongly

Chromosomes 4.1.2.1

- Chromosomes are found in the nucleus. They are made up of DNA with each chromosome carrying a large number of genes.
- Chromosomes are usually found in pairs in body cells.
- Gene = section of DNA that codes for a specific protein.
- Alleles = Different versions of the same gene.

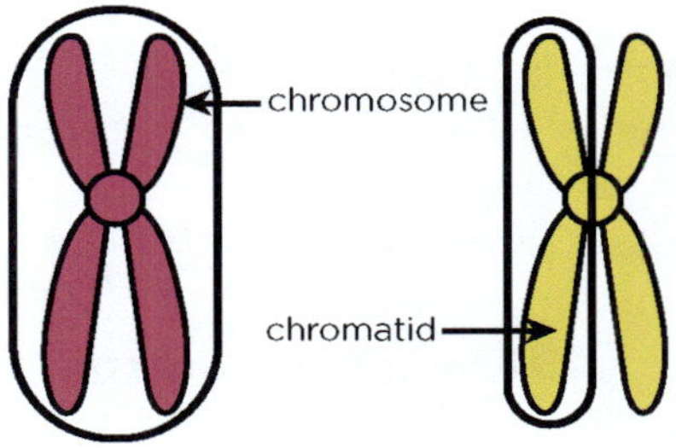

Mitosis 4.1.2.2

- Cells divide in a series of stages called the cell cycle.
  - Stage 1 – Interphase: cell growth, increase in number of organelles, DNA replicates so there are 2 copies of each chromosome (diploid).
  - Stage 2 – Mitosis: one set of chromosomes is pulled to each end of the cell and the nucleus divides.
  - Stage 3 – Cytokinesis: cytoplasm and cell membrane divide to form 2 identical daughter cells.
- Mitosis is important in the growth and development of multicellular organisms. It also replaces old or damaged cells.

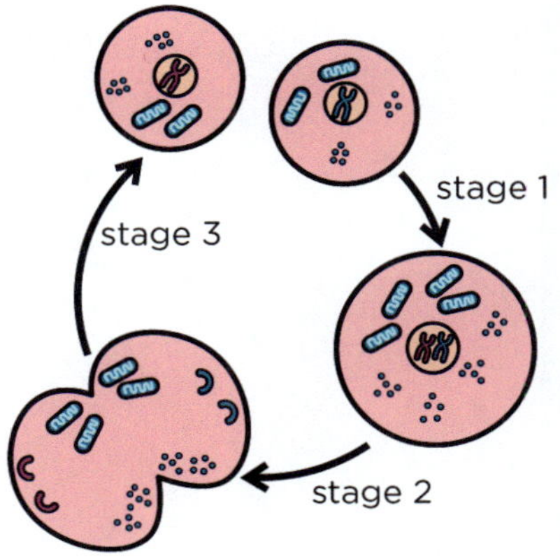

Plant stem cells, diffusion, and osmosis

SNAPREVISE

Diffusion 4.1.3.1

- Diffusion is the net movement of particles in solution or of a gas from an area of higher concentration to an area of lower concentration.
- Examples include:
  - Oxygen and carbon dioxide in gas exchange.
  - Waste urea from cells into the blood plasma for excretion in the kidney.
- Factors affecting diffusion rate:
  - Steeper concentration gradients increase diffusion rate.
  - Higher temperatures increase diffusion rate
  - Increasing surface area increases diffusion rate.

Diffusion in humans 4.1.3.1

- The effectiveness of exchange surfaces is increased by having:
  - A large surface area
  - A thin membrane (short distance for diffusion)
  - Efficient blood supply in animals
  - Well-ventilated in animals for gas exchange
  - Moist membrane in animals for gas exchange

Small intestine

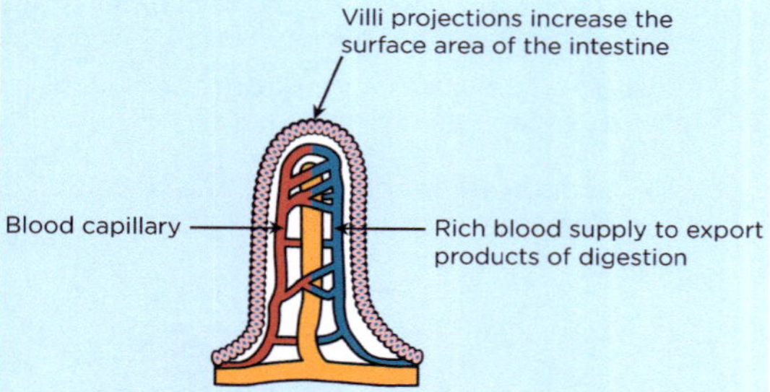

Lungs

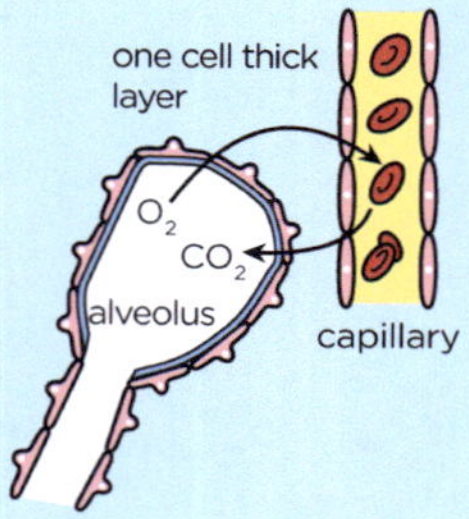

Diffusion in other organisms 4.1.3.1

Gills

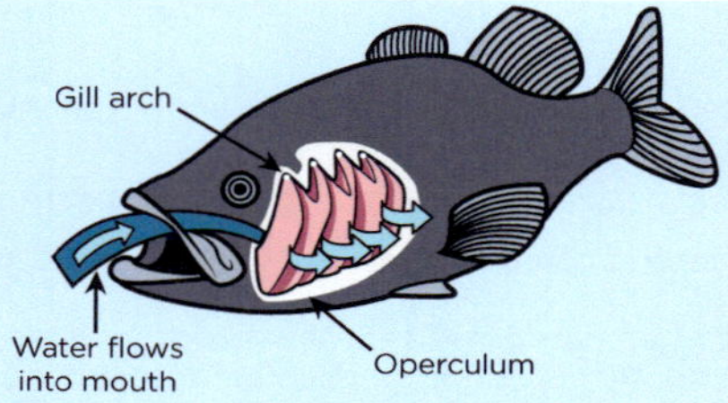

Roots

Leaves

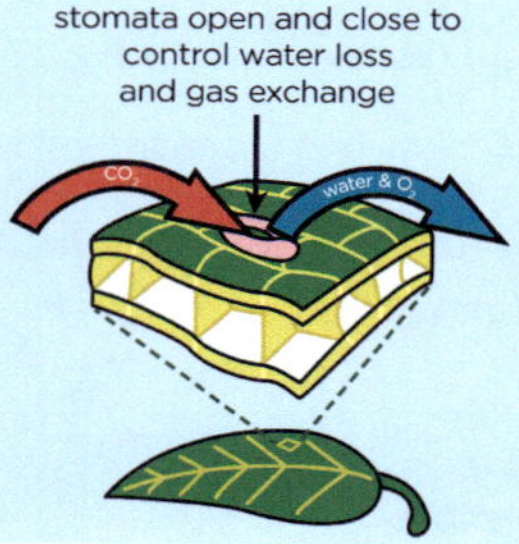

Surface area to volume ratio 4.1.3.1

- A large surface area to volume ratio increases the rate of diffusion.
- To calculate surface area to volume ratio, divide the surface area by the volume.
  - $\boldsymbol{Surface\ area\ of\ cube = 6\ sides \times length^2}$
  - $\boldsymbol{Volume\ of\ cube = length^3}$
- Single-celled organisms have a large surface area to volume ratio so molecules can move into and out of the cell to meet the needs of the organism.
- Multicellular organisms have a small surface area to volume ratio so require an exchange surface and transport system to sufficiently move substances around the organism.

Osmosis 4.1.3.2

- Osmosis is the diffusion of water from a dilute solution to a concentrated solution through a partially permeable membrane, such as the cell membrane.
- Cells can be placed in solutions with different relative concentrations.
  - Isotonic: concentration inside the cell is the same as the concentration of the solution. No net movement of water.
  - Hypertonic: concentration of the solution is higher than the concentration inside the cell.
  - Hypotonic: concentration of the solution is lower than the concentration inside the cell.

Solution	Animal cell	Plant cell
Hypertonic (e.g. salty brine)	Shrunken/shrivelled 	Flaccid → plasmolysed 
Hypotonic (e.g. pure water)	Swell and burst 	Turgid 

- $Percentage\ change = \frac{final\ value - initial\ value}{initial\ value} \times 100\%$
- $Water\ uptake\ rate\ (grams/hour) = \frac{change\ in\ mass}{time\ in\ minutes} \times 60$
- Linear graph has the equation $y = mx + c$
  - m is the gradient
  - c is the y-intercept

Plant stem cells 4.1.2.3

- In plant meristem tissue, stem cells can differentiate into any type of plant cell throughout the life of the plant.
- Plant stem cells are used to artificially produce clones of plants in a quick and economic way.
- Rare species can be cloned to prevent extinction.
- Crops with features such as disease resistance are cloned to make large numbers of identical plants for farmers.

Cell organisation, digestion, and enzymes

SNAPREVISE

The digestive system 4.2.2.1

- $rate\ of\ reaction = \frac{amount\ of\ reactant\ used\ or\ product\ formed}{time\ taken}$
- The digestive system is an organ system.
- Digestion is the breakdown of large, insoluble food into small, soluble molecules, which are absorbed into the bloodstream.
- The products of digestion are used to build new carbohydrates, lipids and proteins. Some glucose is used in respiration.

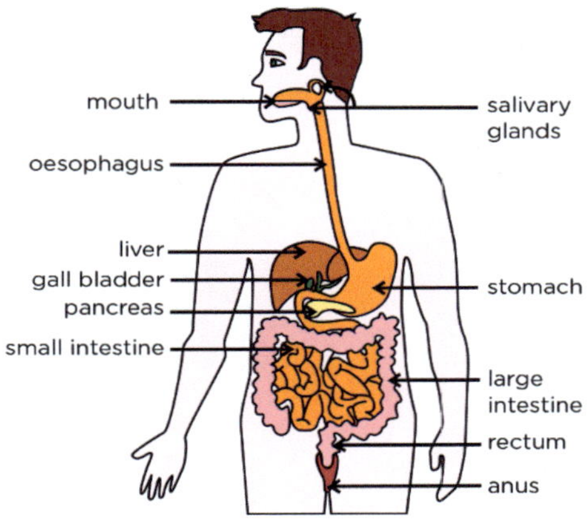

Structure	Function
Mouth	• Food ingested • Teeth chew food, breaking it into smaller pieces, increasing surface area for enzyme action
Salivary glands	• Produce slightly alkaline saliva containing enzymes that break down starch
Oesophagus	• Peristalsis (contraction and relaxation of circular and longitudinal muscles) moves food into the stomach
Stomach	• Churns the food with hydrochloric acid, killing microorganisms • Contains enzymes that break down protein
Small intestine	• Contains enzymes to break down food • Villi absorb the products of digestion • Glucose and amino acids are absorbed into the bloodstream (capillary) • Fatty acids and glycerol are absorbed into the lymph (lacteal)
Large intestine	• Absorbs remaining water, forming faeces
Rectum	• Stores faeces
Anus	• Egests faeces
Liver	• Produces bile
Gall bladder	• Stores bile
Pancreas	• Produces digestive enzymes

Cells, tissues, and organs 4.2.1

- Cells are the basic building blocks of all living organisms.
- Tissues are groups of cells with a similar structure and function.
- Organs are groups of tissues performing specific functions.
- An organ system is made up of organs.
- Organ systems work together to form organisms.

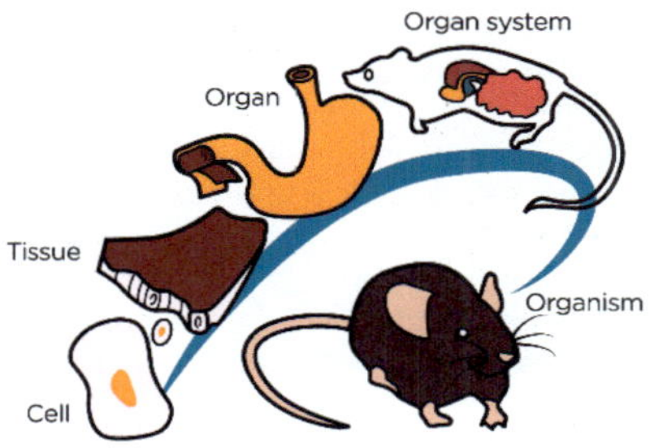

Digestive enzymes 4.2.2.1

- Saliva produced by salivary glands contains the carbohydrase enzymes amylase and maltase, which catalyses the breakdown of carbohydrates to simple sugars.
  - Amylase: *starch → maltose*
  - Maltase: *maltose → glucose*
- Proteases produced in the stomach begin the digestion of proteins into amino acids.
- Lipases break down lipids (fats and oils) into fatty acids and glycerol.
- The pancreas produces carbohydrase, protease and lipase enzymes and releases them into the small intestine.
- The liver produces bile, which is stored in the gall bladder.
- Bile neutralises the acid entering the small intestine from the stomach and emulsifies fats (breaks them up into small droplets, increasing the surface area for lipase action).

Lock and key theory 4.2.2.1

- Enzymes catalyse (speed up) specific reactions in organisms due to the shape of their active site.
- The substrate is the reactants of the reaction to be catalysed.
- The 'lock and key theory' proposes that the shape of the substrate is complementary to the active site so can bind to it, which allows the enzyme to break the bonds holding the substrate together.
- Enzyme-catalysed reactions contribute to metabolism.

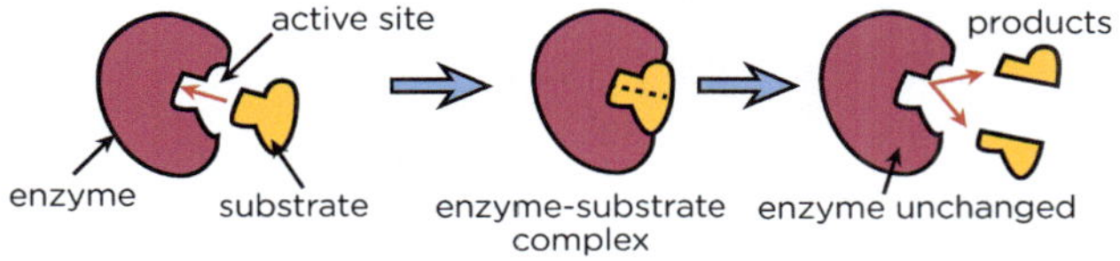

Denaturing enzymes 4.2.2.1

- Enzymes work at optimum conditions, and any movement away from these conditions lowers the enzyme activity and effectiveness.

Body part	Enzyme	Optimum pH	Optimum temperature
Mouth	Amylase, maltase	Alkaline	37 °C
Stomach	Protease	Acidic	37 °C
Small intestine	Lipase, protease, amylase, maltase	Alkaline	37 °C

- Enzymes are denatured by extremes of pH and temperature as the shape of the active site permanently changes so the substrate no longer fits.
- As temperature increases, enzymes and their substrate have more kinetic energy, so they will more frequently collide and enzyme activity increases.
- If temperature increases above the optimum temperature for an enzyme, it will denature because the bonds holding it together will break.

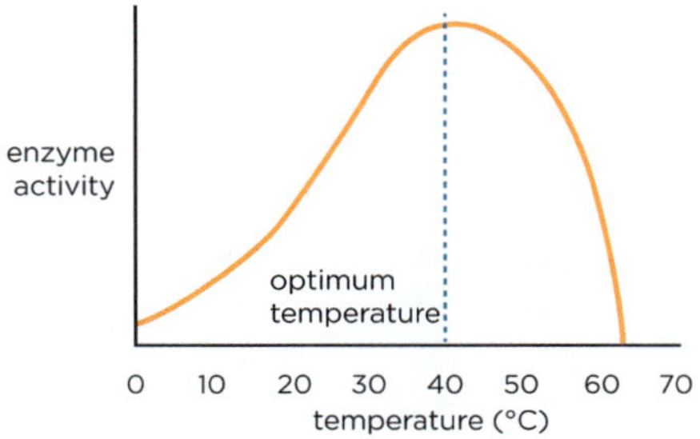

Active transport 4.1.3.3

- Active transport is the movement of substances from a more dilute solution to a more concentrated solution.
- As this movement is against a concentration gradient, it requires energy from respiration.
- Active transport facilitates:
  - The absorption of mineral ions from very dilute solutions in the soil into plant root hairs. Plants require ions for healthy growth.
  - The absorption of sugar molecules from lower concentrations in the gut into the blood, which has a higher sugar concentration. Sugar molecules are needed for cell respiration.

The circulatory system

Lung anatomy 4.2.2.2

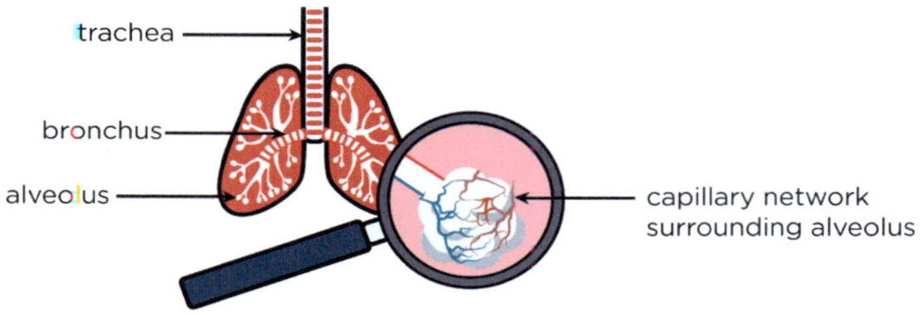

- Carbon dioxide is removed from the blood in the lungs to prevent the pH of the blood becoming too acidic.
- Lungs are adapted for gas exchange:
  - Alveoli have a thin wall only one cell thick so there is a short distance for diffusion.
  - Moist membrane accelerates the diffusion of gases.
  - Shape of alveoli provides large surface area for diffusion.
  - Extensive capillary network surrounding alveoli.
  - Well-ventilated to maintain a large diffusion gradient.

Heart anatomy 4.2.2.2

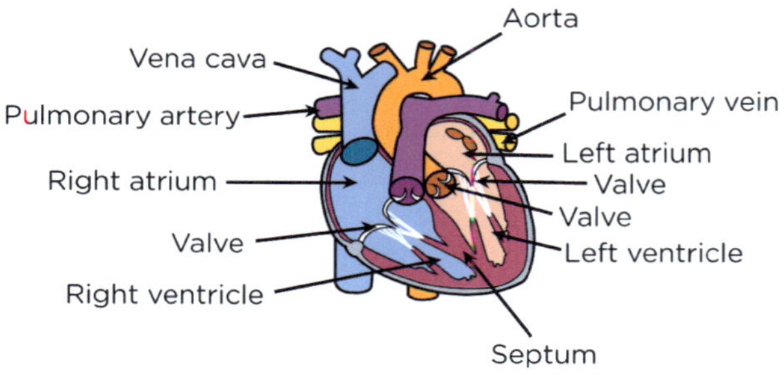

- Valves prevent the backflow of blood.
- The heart muscle cells are supplied by the coronary arteries, delivering oxygen for aerobic respiration to provide energy for the heart to contract.
- The resting heart rate is controlled by a group of pacemaker cells located in the wall of the right atrium.
- Irregularities in the heart rate are corrected using artificial pacemakers, which are electrical devices.

The circulatory system 4.2.2.2

- The heart is an organ that pumps blood around the body in a double circulatory system (blood passes through the heart twice in one complete circuit of the body):
  - The right ventricle pumps deoxygenated blood to the lungs for gas exchange. Oxygen enters the blood and waste carbon dioxide leaves the blood.
  - The left ventricle pumps oxygenated blood around the rest of the body where body cells use the oxygen for aerobic respiration to provide energy.
  - Respiration also produces waste carbon dioxide, which is transported in the blood and exhaled via the lungs.

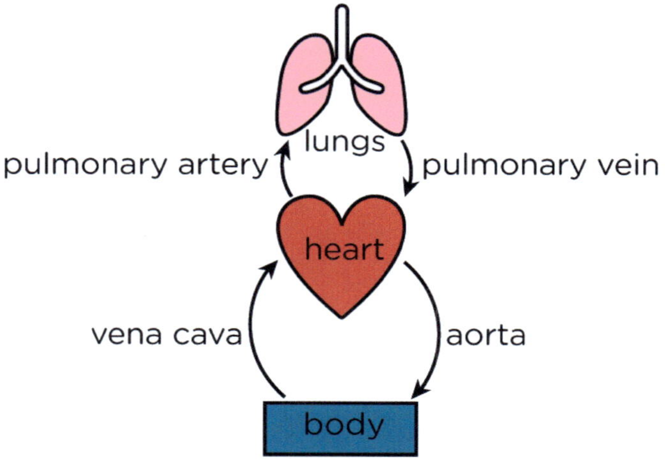

- Heart rate is the number of times the heart beats per minute.
- Stroke volume is the volume of blood ejected from the heart per heartbeat.
- Cardiac output is the volume of blood being pumped by the heart per minute.
- $\textit{cardiac output} = \textit{heart rate} \times \textit{stroke volume}$

Blood vessels 4.2.2.2

Blood vessel	Function	Structure
Artery 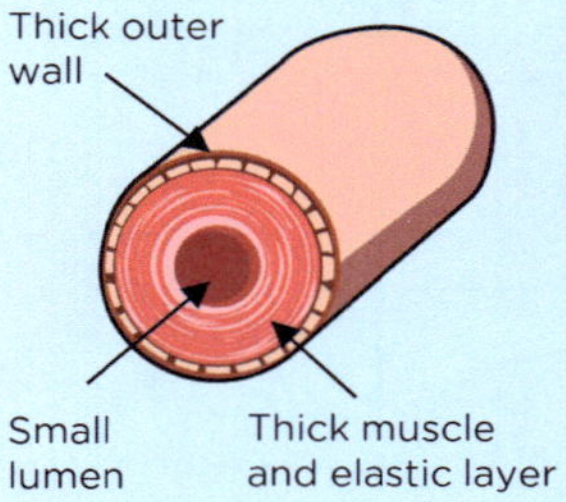	Transports oxygenated blood away from the heart at a high pressure so it can reach the rest of the body (apart from the pulmonary artery).	• Thick outer protective wall. • Thick muscle and elastic layer that can stretch to withstand high-pressure blood flow. • Small lumen to maintain high pressure. • Smooth lining to minimise friction.
Vein 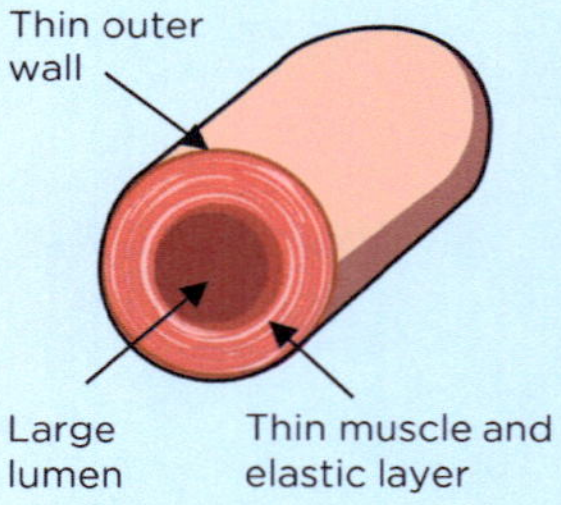	Transports deoxygenated blood back to the heart at a low pressure (apart from the pulmonary vein that carries oxygenated blood from the lungs).	• Thinner outer protective wall than artery as blood pressure is lower. • Thin layer of muscle and elastic. • Large lumen. • Smooth lining to minimise friction. • Valves to ensure blood flows one way.
Capillary 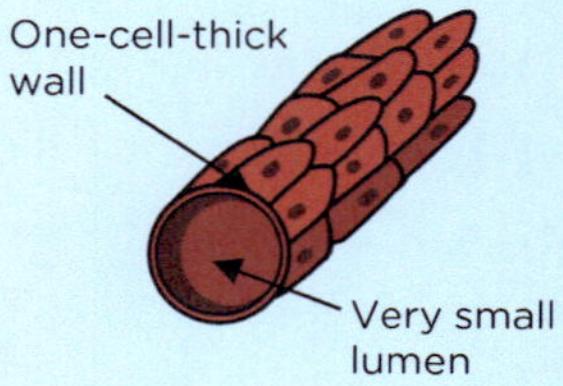	Surrounds respiring cells, transporting blood at a very low pressure so it moves slowly to allow time for gas exchange with neighbouring cells. Blood plasma passes through capillary walls into tissues where it is called tissue fluid.	• Very small lumen so blood is in contact with capillary wall to create a short distance of diffusion for gases. • Capillary wall is one cell thick so there is a short distance of diffusion.

Blood, heart problems, and human health

SNAPREVISE

Blood 4.2.2.3

- Blood is a tissue.

Blood component	Function	Structure
Plasma	Other blood components are suspended in plasma, and it transports glucose, amino acids, carbon dioxide and urea.	• Straw-coloured aqueous liquid, mostly made from water, which dissolves nutrients.
Red blood cells 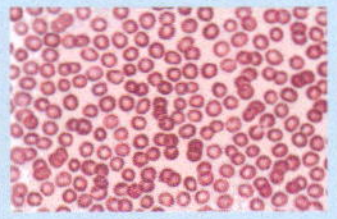	Transport oxygen around the body.	• Contain haemoglobin, which binds to oxygen. • Biconcave shape gives a high surface area to volume ratio • No nucleus to maximise space for more haemoglobin.
White blood cells 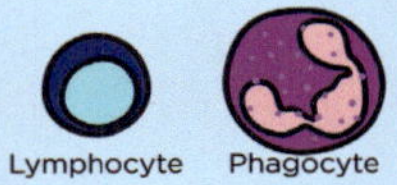	Part of immune system, which destroys pathogens. Phagocytes engulf pathogens and digest them using enzymes. Lymphocytes produce antibodies to clump pathogens together.	• Phagocytes have a lobed nucleus and a granulated cytoplasm (granules contain enzymes). • Lymphocytes are smaller, have a large nucleus and no granules.
Platelets 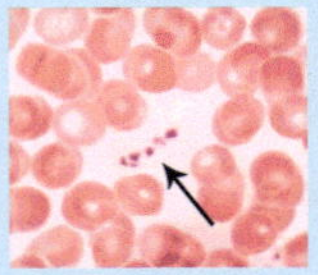	When the skin is wounded, they release clotting factors, which turn fibrinogen in the plasma into fibrin, forming a mesh that sticks platelets together to form a scab.	• Cell fragments containing chemicals called clotting factors.

Coronary heart disease 4.2.2.4

- Coronary heart disease can lead to a heart attack:
  - Fatty material (plaque) builds up in the coronary arteries, narrowing them and reducing the flexibility of the artery lining, which reduces blood flow (atherosclerosis).
  - Less oxygen is delivered to the heart muscle.
  - Heart muscle cells die.
- Treatments for coronary heart disease:
  - Stents are used to keep the coronary arteries open.
  - Statins are used to reduce blood cholesterol levels to slow down the rate of fatty material deposit.

Other heart problems 4.2.2.4

- Faulty heart valves:
  - Prevent the valve from opening fully, and can leak.
  - Blood flows backwards, reducing the efficiency at which blood flows around the body, meaning cells do not receive as much glucose and oxygen for respiration.
  - Breathlessness, tiredness, dizziness and chest pain.
- Treatment of faulty heart valves:
  - Replace with biological valves from donors.
  - Replace with artificial mechanical valves.

Treating heart problems 4.2.2.4

- A donor heart, or heart and lungs, can be transplanted in the case of heart failure.
- Artificial hearts are sometimes used to keep patients alive whilst waiting for a heart transplant or to allow the heart to rest during recovery.

Treatment	Advantages	Disadvantages
Drugs	• Cheap • Can reduce cholesterol or reduce clotting	• Not suitable if you have liver disease • Side effects • Must be taken for life • Anti-blood clotting drugs increase the risk of bleeding
Mechanical	• Less dangerous than transplants • Fast recovery	• Biological valves may need to be replaced • Mechanical valves may cause blood clots
Transplant	• Lifesaving • Life can return to normal	• Slow recovery • Expensive operation • Risk of rejection by the immune system means the patient must take immunosuppressants for life • Few donor hearts available • Risky operation

Lowering risk of heart disease 4.2.2.6

- Lifestyle factors can increase the risk of cardiovascular disease:
  - Poor diet (high in fat and cholesterol)
  - Smoking
  - Alcohol
  - Lack of exercise
- Pre-existing conditions can increase the risk of cardiovascular disease:
  - Type 2 diabetes (of which obesity is a risk factor).
  - High blood pressure
  - High cholesterol

Physical and mental health 4.2.2.5

- Health is a state of physical and mental well-being.
- Causes of ill health:
  - Communicable disease (can pass from one organism to another)
  - Non-communicable disease (cannot pass from one organism to another)
  - Diet
  - Stress and life situations
- Different types of disease may interact.
  - Defects in the immune system may mean an individual is more likely to suffer from infectious diseases.
  - Immune reactions caused by a pathogen can trigger allergies, such as skin rashes and asthma.
  - Viruses living in cells may trigger cancers.
  - Severe physical ill health can lead to mental illnesses, such as depression.

Lifestyle and risk 4.2.2.6

- Many diseases are caused by the interaction of multiple risk factors.
- Risk factors are linked to an increased rate of a disease, but a causal mechanism has not been proven for all of them. They include:
  - Lifestyle:
    - Alcohol is linked to degrading liver and brain function and can harm unborn babies.
    - Smoking is linked to lung disease and lung cancer and can harm unborn babies.
    - Obesity is a risk factor for Type 2 diabetes.
  - Substances in the body or environment (carcinogens, including ionising radiation, are linked to causing cancer).
- Non-communicable diseases are more common in poorer areas as inhabitants may be more exposed to negative risk factors, such as lack of fresh food, water, and shelter, and may be more exposed to substances such as pollutants.
- Non-communicable diseases have a human and financial cost at local, national, and global levels:
  - Decrease quality of life and life expectancy.
  - Emotional and financial strains on friends and family if a patient is unable to work or to provide additional support.
  - Patient less productive at work, causing strain on the employer.
  - Financial cost to health services to provide treatment and research.

SNAPREVISE

Cancer 4.2.2.7

- Cancer is the result of changes in cells that lead to uncontrolled growth and division.
- Benign tumours are not cancers:
  - Growth of abnormal cells, which are contained in one area, usually within a membrane
  - Do not invade other parts of the body
- Malignant tumours are cancers:
  - Invade neighbouring tissues
  - Spread to different parts of the body in the blood where they form secondary tumours (by metastasis)
  - Signs of cancer include tumorous lumps, a long-term cough and unexplained bleeding or weight loss
- Different cancers have different risk factors:
  - Smoking and alcohol
  - Obesity
  - Age
  - Infections, such as hepatitis and HPV
  - Ionising radiation (e.g. UV from the sun)
  - Environmental pollutants from industry
  - Genetic disorders inherited from parents
- Cancer can be screened (e.g. blood tests and X-ray images).
- Cancer may be treated with chemotherapy and radiotherapy; however, this can kill healthy cells too, with side effects including sickness and hair loss.

Xylem and phloem 4.2.3.2

- Xylem and phloem found together in the vascular bundle.
- Xylem tissue transports water and mineral ions up from the roots to the leaves via the stem.
  - Hollow tubes without end walls.
  - Tube walls strengthened by lignin.

- Phloem tissue transports dissolved sucrose from the leaves (made from glucose from photosynthesis) to the rest of the plant for use or storage. This is called translocation.
  - Tubes of living elongated cells.
  - Cell sap can move from one cell to the next through pores in the end walls.

Plant tissues 4.2.3.1

- The roots, stem and leaves form a plant organ system for transport of substances around the plant.
- The leaf is a plant organ made up of numerous plant tissues.

Tissue	Function	Structure
Epidermal tissues	• Protects against water loss • Regulates gas exchange in leaves • Regulates water and mineral uptake in roots	• Outermost layer one cell thick and transparent to allow light to easily pass through. • Contains stomata and guard cells on bottom of leaf.
Palisade mesophyll	Major site of photosynthesis	• Found towards upper surface of leaf so lots of light reaches it. • Tightly-packed cells containing lots of chloroplast to maximise photosynthesis.
Spongy mesophyll	Gas exchange	• Found towards bottom of leaves close to where gas enters through stomata. • Space between cells to allow gases to diffuse. • Cells have a large surface area in contact with air spaces to maximise gas exchange.
Meristem tissue	Stem cells are produced for plant growth	• Found at the growing tips of shoots and roots.

Root hair cells 4.2.3.2

- Root hair cells are adapted for the efficient uptake of water by osmosis and mineral ions by active transport:
  - Thin – short distance for osmosis and active transport.
  - Long – penetrate between soil particles to come into contact with water and mineral ions.
  - Large surface area – maximise osmosis and active transport.
  - Lots of mitochondria for active transport.

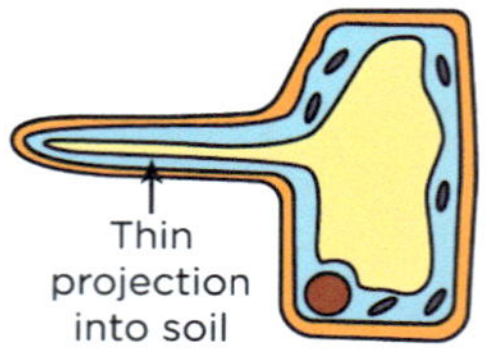

Transpiration and translocation 4.2.3.2

- The movement of water through a plant occurs through transpiration, where water is pulled through the plant as it is continuously released from the leaves through stomata.
  - Water enters the root hair cells by osmosis and travels through them to the xylem.
  - Water travels up the xylem in the stem into the spongy mesophyll of the leaf by osmosis.
  - Water evaporates out of spongy mesophyll cells, forming water vapour in the air spaces of the spongy mesophyll.
  - Water vapour diffuses out of the leaf through stomata.
- Stomata control gas exchange and water loss by opening and closing, which is controlled by guard cells.
  - When guard cells are turgid, the stomata are open, allowing water vapour to leave the leaf and carbon dioxide to enter for photosynthesis.
  - When dehydrated, guard cells are flaccid and the stomata are closed, preventing further water loss.
- $\textit{Transpiration rate} = \dfrac{\textit{decrease in mass or volume of water absorbed}}{\textit{time}}$

- Transpiration rate is affected by various factors:

Factor	Effect on transpiration rate
Temperature	Transpiration rate increases as temperature increases because molecules have greater kinetic energy, speeding up the rate of evaporation and diffusion.
Humidity	Transpiration rate decreases as humidity increases as the atmosphere has a higher concentration of water vapour, decreasing the diffusion of water vapour out of the leaf.
Air movement	Transpiration rate increases as wind increases as it carries water vapour from the leaf.
Light intensity	Transpiration rate increases as light intensity increases as the stomata open wider to allow carbon dioxide in for photosynthesis, allowing water vapour to escape.

Pathogens and non-specific immunity

Pathogens 4.3.1.1

- Pathogens are microorganisms (viruses, bacteria, protists, and fungi) that cause infectious disease.
- There are various ways a disease can be spread in animals and plants:
  - Direct contact – spread by physical contact.
  - Transfer of infected fluids, e.g. blood, saliva, and semen.
  - Contaminated water – travels in unsterilised water.
  - Airborne – propelled through the air in tiny droplets of water through sneezing and coughing.
  - Food – pathogens in uncooked or spoiled food.
  - Via another animal – the animal is called a vector.
- The spread of disease can be reduced or prevented by:
  - Sterilising water with chemicals or UV light.
  - Cooking food thoroughly and preparing it in hygienic conditions.
  - Disinfecting surfaces.
  - Treating infections, e.g. with antibiotics.
  - Vaccination.
  - Barrier method of contraception to prevent the spread of sexually transmitted diseases, e.g. condom.
- Bacteria and viruses can reproduce rapidly inside the body.
  - Bacteria can produce toxins that damage tissues and cause disease symptoms.
  - Viruses live and reproduce inside cells, causing cell damage.

Non-specific immunity 4.3.1.6

- Humans have non-specific defence systems to prevent pathogens from entering the body:
  - Skin – forms a physical barrier to prevent pathogens from entering the body, secretes antimicrobial compounds to kill pathogens, and sheds dead surface skin, which removes pathogens.
  - Tears and saliva – contain antibacterial lysozymes, which break down bacterial cell walls.
  - Nose – contains hairs acting as a filter, preventing large particles from passing through and producing sticky mucus that traps pathogens and is removed when you blow your nose.
  - Trachea and bronchi – lined with ciliated cells and goblet cells to prevent pathogens from entering the lungs. Goblet cells produce mucus to trap pathogens and cilia (tiny hair-like projections) rhythmically beat the mucus up the airway to the back of the throat where it is swallowed.
  - Stomach – contains hydrochloric acid, which destroys swallowed pathogens.

Viral diseases 4.3.1.2

Disease	Symptoms	Transmission	Details
Measles	Fever and red skin rash	Airborne: inhalation of droplets from sneezes and coughs	• Can be fatal if complications arise • Most young children are vaccinated against measles
HIV	Initially causes flu-like symptoms	Transfer of infected fluids: transfer of bodily fluids during sex or exchange of blood, e.g. in blood transfusion or when drug users share needles	• Unless controlled with antiretroviral drugs, the virus attacks immune cells • Damage to the immune system causes AIDS as it can no longer deal with other infections or cancers
Tobacco mosaic virus (TMV)	Distinctive 'mosaic' pattern of discolouration on leaves	Direct contact: rubbing of leaf against an infected leaf	• Affecting many species of plants including tomatoes • Affects growth of plant due to lack of photosynthesis

Bacterial diseases 4.3.1.3

Disease	Symptoms	Transmission	Details
Salmonella	Fever, abdominal cramps, vomiting and diarrhoea	Ingesting spoiled food or food prepared in unhygienic conditions	• Food poisoning. • In the UK, poultry are vaccinated against salmonella to control the spread
Gonorrhoea	Thick yellow or green discharge from the vagina or penis and pain when urinating	Sexual contact (STD)	• Was easily treated with penicillin until many resistant strains appeared • Treated with antibiotics and prevented by using barrier method of contraception

Fungal diseases 4.3.1.4

Disease	Symptoms	Transmission	Details
Rose black spot	Purple or black spots develop on leaves, which often turn yellow and fall early	Water or wind	• Affects the growth of the plant as photosynthesis is reduced • Treated using fungicides and removing and destroying the infected plant tissue

Protist diseases 4.3.1.5

Disease	Symptoms	Transmission	Details
Malaria	Recurrent episodes of fever, which can be fatal	Vector – protist carried by mosquito	• Can be fatal • Spread controlled by preventing mosquitos from breeding and using mosquito nets to avoid being bitten

The immune system 4.3.1.6

- If pathogens make it past the non-specific defence system and enter the body, the immune system will coordinate a response to destroy them.
- White blood cells defend against pathogens by:
  - Phagocytosis:

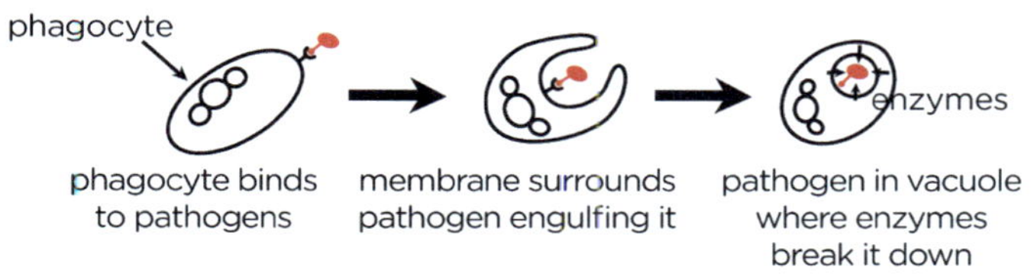

  - Antibody production – lymphocytes detect foreign antigens (proteins on surface of cells) on pathogens and respond by producing antibodies.
  - Antibodies are specific to each antigen and bind to the antigens of multiple pathogens to clump them together for phagocytosis.
  - If infected by the same pathogen again, memory lymphocytes recognise the antigens and produce a larger number of specific antibodies faster.

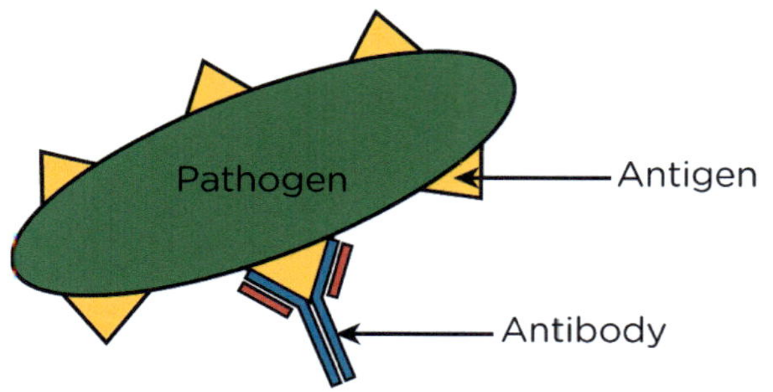

  - Antitoxin production – Lymphocytes form a special antibody called antitoxins, which bind to and neutralise harmful toxins produced by the pathogen.

Vaccination 4.3.1.7

- Vaccination introduces a small amount of dead or inactive forms of a pathogen into the body:
  - This stimulates the production of antibodies.
  - If the pathogen enters the body again, memory lymphocytes will recognise the antigens of the pathogen and produce a larger number of specific antibodies faster.
  - The pathogen is destroyed before the person becomes ill.
- Herd immunity is where the spread of pathogens can be reduced by immunising a large proportion of the population, meaning the disease is unlikely to spread.

Antibiotics 4.3.1.8

- Antibiotics are medicines used to treat bacterial diseases.
  - Penicillin is an antibiotic produced by a fungus, which kills bacteria by weakening their cell walls so they burst.
  - Some alter bacterial enzymes.
  - Some stop bacteria from reproducing.
- Specific antibiotics are used to kill specific bacteria, and they cannot kill viruses.
- Antibiotics have greatly reduced deaths from bacterial diseases.

Causes of antibiotic resistance 4.3.1.8

- Some strains of bacteria have evolved resistance to antibiotics.
- Drug companies are constantly researching new antibiotics or alternatives for resistant strains.
- Over-prescription of antibiotics has contributed to the emergence of these resistant strains.

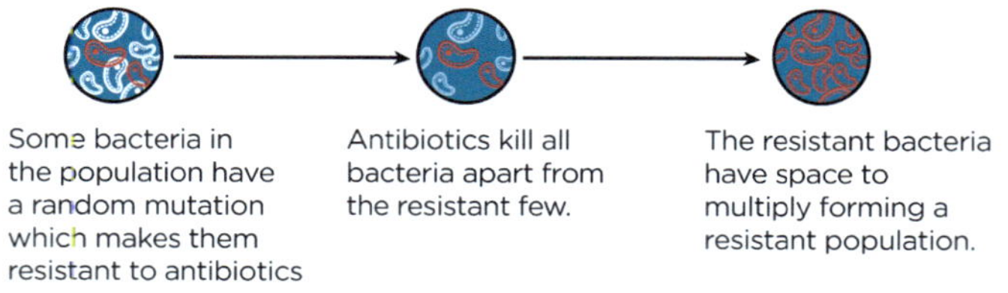

Painkillers 4.3.1.8

- Painkillers and other medicines treat the symptoms of disease but do not kill pathogens.
- It is difficult to develop drugs that destroy viruses without also damaging the body's tissues, as viruses are active within human body cells.

Historical drugs 4.3.1.9

- Drugs were traditionally extracted from plants and microorganisms:
  - The painkiller aspirin comes from the willow tree.
  - The heart drug digitalis comes from foxgloves.
  - Penicillin was discovered accidentally by Alexander Fleming from the Penicillium mould, which contaminated his petri dish of bacteria.

Modern drug development 4.3.1.9

- Most modern drugs are artificially synthesised by chemists in the pharmaceutical industry, e.g. paracetamol.

Stage in drug development	Description
Identifying potential drug	• May be a chemical extracted from another organism, e.g. plant
Computer modelling	• Modelling the drug's structure and potential interactions with substances in the body
Preclinical testing	• Done in a laboratory using live cells, tissues and live animals • Checks the drugs are safe and effective, with tests for toxicity and efficiency
Clinical trials	• First phase uses healthy volunteers to test toxicity • Very low doses of the drug are given at the start of the trial • If the drug is safe, it will be given to a small number of sick patients in phase two to test efficacy • Phase three trials use larger numbers of patients and finalise safe, optimum doses • In double-blind trials, some patients are given a placebo to test whether the drug is causing the improvement in patients or if it is just the placebo effect
Manufacturing	• The drug is produced on a mass scale and made available to the public

SNAPREVISE

Plant disease identification 4.3.3.1

- Symptoms of plant disease include:
  - Stunted growth
  - Spots on leaves
  - Rot (areas of decay)
  - Abnormal growths
  - Malformed stem or leaves
  - Discolouration
  - The presence of pests
- Plant disease can be identified by:
  - Research using a gardening manual or website
  - Taking the infected plant to a laboratory to identify the pathogen
  - Using monoclonal antibody testing kits

Plant disease examples 4.3.3.1

- Plants can be infected by viral, bacterial and fungal pathogens and insects.
- Aphids are insects that tap into the phloem of plant stems with very fine mouthparts (stylet) to ingest the sap.
  - This deprives the plant of its nutrient source.
  - Plant growth rate decreases and the plant wilts.
  - Can be prevented by increasing the number of ladybirds in your garden as they eat aphids, rather than spraying insecticides.

Disease	Type	Symptoms	Details
Tobacco mosaic virus	Viral disease transmitted by rubbing of leaf against the infected leaf	Distinctive 'mosaic' pattern of discolouration on leaves	• Affecting many species of plants, including tomatoes • Affects growth of plant due to lack of photosynthesis
Black spot	Fungal disease transmitted by water or wind	Purple or black spots develop on leaves, which often turn yellow and fall	• Affects the growth of the plant as photosynthesis is reduced • Treated using fungicides and removing the affected leaves

Plant nutrient deficiencies 4.3.3.1

- Mineral ions are absorbed from the soil by the roots.
- Nitrate ions are needed for protein synthesis and therefore growth. Hence, nitrate deficiency causes stunted growth.
- Magnesium ions are needed to make chlorophyll for photosynthesis. Therefore, magnesium deficiency causes chlorosis (yellow leaves).

Plant defences 4.3.3.2

- Plants have mechanical adaptations and physical and chemical defence responses to aid survival.
- Physical defence responses:
  - Cellulose cell walls act as a barrier to pathogens.
  - Tough waxy cuticle on leaves to control water loss also acts as a barrier to pathogens.
  - Layers of undigestible dead cells around stems (bark on trees) prevent plant being eaten by herbivores, and dead cells eventually fall off, taking pathogens with them.
- Chemical plant defence responses:
  - Antibacterial chemicals, such as in tea tree leaves.
  - Poisons to prevent being eaten by herbivores, such as in deadly nightshade.
- Mechanical adaptations:
  - Thorns and spines to prevent being eaten by herbivores.
  - Leaves that droop or curl when touched, knocking insects off.
  - Mimicry to trick animals, e.g. some species have spotted leaves that look like butterfly eggs, which prevents butterflies from egg-laying so as to avoid competition.

Producing monoclonal antibodies 4.3.2.1

- Monoclonal antibodies are a large population of identical antibodies.
- The antibodies are specific to one protein antigen and so target a specific chemical or cell in the body. Once the antibody is bound, the target can easily be detected or targeted for treatment.
- Monoclonal antibodies are produced from a single clone of cells.
  - An antigen is injected into a mouse. This stimulates the mouse lymphocytes to make an antibody specific to this antigen.
  - The lymphocytes are collected from spleen cells.
  - The lymphocytes are combined with myeloma tumour cells to make hybridoma cells.
  - The hybridoma cells are grown in a culture medium indefinitely, where they replicate and produce large amounts of the antibody.
  - The antibody is collected and purified by centrifugation, filtration and chromatography.

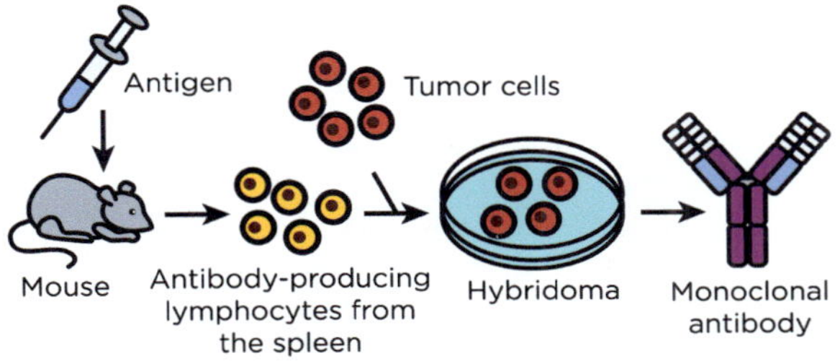

Using monoclonal antibodies 4.3.2.2

- Monoclonal antibodies have many uses

Use	Description
Pregnancy tests	• HCG is a hormone found in the urine of pregnant people. • The person suspecting pregnancy urinates on a small stick of paper containing a strip of monoclonal antibodies specific to HCG. • If the person is pregnant, HCG in the urine binds to the antibodies. The test then turns a different colour.
To detect pathogens or measure the levels of hormones and chemicals in blood, in a laboratory	• Antibodies are bound to a fluorescent dye. • When antibodies bind to the antigen and are viewed under UV light, they glow.
In research to locate or identify a specific molecule in cells or tissues	Antibodies are tagged with a fluorescent dye and are specific to the molecule to be identified/located.
To treat disease	• In cancer treatment, the monoclonal antibody is bound to a radioactive substance, toxic drug or chemical, which stops cancerous cells growing and dividing. • The antibody binds specifically to the cancer cells, delivering these substances without harming other body cells.

- However, monoclonal antibodies create more side effects than expected, so are not as widely used as people may have hoped.

Response to exercise 4.4.2.2

- During exercise, the human body reacts to the increased demand for energy:
  - Heart rate, breathing rate and breath volume increase to supply the muscles with more oxygenated blood so they can carry out maximum aerobic respiration to release energy for movement.
  - If insufficient oxygen is supplied, anaerobic respiration takes place in muscles to provide energy, causing a build-up of lactic acid, which causes cramps and muscle fatigue, so they stop contracting efficiently.
  - Blood flowing through the muscles transports the lactic acid to the liver where it is converted back into glucose.
  - Oxygen debt is the amount of extra oxygen required after exercise to react with lactic acid to remove it from cells.

Metabolism 4.4.2.3

- Metabolism is the sum of all the reactions in a cell or the body.
  - Conversion of glucose to starch, glycogen, and cellulose.
  - The formation of lipid molecules from a molecule of glycerol and three molecules of fatty acids.
  - The use of glucose and nitrate ions to form the amino acids needed to synthesise proteins.
  - Respiration.
  - Digestion (breakdown of carbohydrates, proteins, and lipids).
  - Breakdown of excess proteins to form urea for excretion.
- The energy released by cellular respiration is used by the organism for the continual enzyme-controlled processes of metabolism that synthesise new molecules.

Photosynthesis 4.4.1.1

- Photosynthesis is an endothermic reaction where light energy from the environment is transferred into the chloroplasts.
- Chlorophyll is the green pigment in chloroplasts, which absorb light energy for photosynthesis.
- Photosynthesis is carried out by the plant to produce glucose, which has many uses including plant respiration.
- Word equation:

$$carbon\ dioxide + water \xrightarrow{light} glucose + oxygen$$

- Symbol equation: $CO_2 + H_2O \xrightarrow{light} C_6H_{12}O_6 + 6O_2$

Rate of photosynthesis 4.4.1.2

- $rate\ of\ photosynthesis = \frac{volume\ of\ oxygen\ produced\ or\ carbon\ dioxide\ absorbed}{time}$
- There are various factors that can affect the rate of photosynthesis.

Factor	Effect on photosynthesis rate
Temperature	• Increases as temperature increases, as molecules have more kinetic energy, so they collide more often and react faster • Decreases at temperatures that are too high as the enzymes involved in photosynthesis denature
Light intensity	• Increases as light intensity increases, as light energy is needed for the reaction • If the distance between the plant and light is doubled, the rate is quartered (inverse square law): $light\ intensity \propto \frac{1}{distance^2}$
Carbon dioxide concentration	• Increases as concentration increases, as carbon dioxide is needed for reaction
Amount of chlorophyll	• Increases as chlorophyll amount increases, as chlorophyll absorbs light energy needed for reaction

- These factors interact and the one that limits the reaction rate of photosynthesis is known as the limiting factor, meaning the rate cannot increase further without changing that condition.

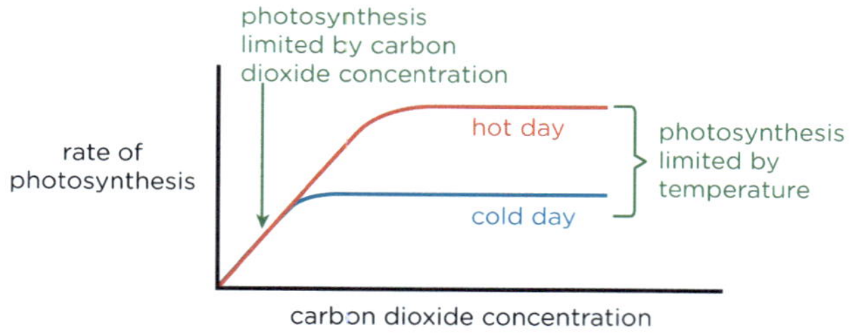

- Limiting factors are important in the economics of enhancing the conditions in greenhouses to gain the maximum rate of photosynthesis while still maintaining a profit.
  - For example, if the rate of photosynthesis is only limited by the current light intensity, increasing the temperature in the greenhouse will not have much of an effect.

Uses of glucose 4.4.1.3

- The glucose produced in photosynthesis may be:
  - Used for respiration to provide energy for the plant.
  - Converted into insoluble starch for storage for later use.
  - Used to produce fat or oil for storage.
  - Used to produce cellulose, which strengthens the cell wall.
  - Used to produce amino acids for protein synthesis and growth, which also requires nitrate ions from the soil.

Aerobic respiration 4.4.2.1

- Cellular respiration is an exothermic reaction as it releases energy. It is continuously occurring in living cells to provide all the energy needed for living processes.
- Aerobic respiration uses oxygen.
- Energy is released from glucose by completely oxidising it.
- Word equation: $glucose + oxygen \rightarrow carbon\ dioxide + water$
- Symbol equation: $C_6H_{12}O_6 + 6O_2 \rightarrow 6CO_2 + 6H_2O$

Anaerobic respiration 4.4.2.1

- Anaerobic respiration takes place without oxygen.
- As it is the incomplete oxidation of glucose, much less energy is released than in aerobic respiration.
- Anaerobic respiration takes place in muscles in humans.
  - Word equation: $glucose \rightarrow lactic\ acid$
  - The incomplete oxidation of glucose produces lactic acid.
- Anaerobic respiration takes place in plant and yeast cells.
  - Word equation: $glucose \rightarrow ethanol + carbon\ dioxide$
  - Anaerobic respiration in yeast cells is called fermentation and is used in the manufacture of bread and alcoholic drinks.

Uses of energy 4.4.2.1

- Organisms need energy for:
  - Chemical reactions to build larger molecules
  - Movement
  - Keeping warm

Homeostasis 4.5.1

- Homeostasis is the regulation of the internal conditions of a cell or organism to maintain optimum conditions for enzyme activity and all cellular functions in response to internal and external changes.
- In humans, homeostasis includes control of:
  - Blood glucose concentration (too low and you would not release enough energy in respiration, too high and you go into a coma).
  - Body temperature (too low and your enzymes will have a low kinetic energy and reactions would take place too slowly, too high and enzymes would denature and be unable to catalyse reactions).
  - Water levels (too low and your cells will shrink, too high and your cells will burst).
- Automatic control systems, involving nervous or chemical responses, are used to maintain homeostasis.
  - Responses involving the nervous system happen very quickly using electrical impulses.
  - Responses involving the hormonal system are slower as the hormones travel in the blood.
- Control systems include:
  - Receptor cells, which detect the stimulus (the change in the environment).
  - Coordination centres, which receive and process information from receptors (such as the brain, spinal cord, and pancreas),
  - Effectors, which bring about responses that restore optimum levels (muscles or glands).

The nervous system 4.5.2.1

- The nervous system enables humans to react to their surroundings and to coordinate their behaviour.

Stimulus → Receptor —neurones→ Coordinator (CNS) —neurones→ Effector (muscles/glands) → Response

- The stimulus is the change that the body must respond to.
- The receptor is the cell or part of a cell that detects the change and generates an electrical impulse.
- The information passes along neurone cells as electrical impulses to the central nervous system (CNS).
- The CNS is made up of the brain and spinal cord and coordinates the response involving effectors.
- The effector response may involve causing muscles to contract or glands to secrete hormones.

Nerves and neurones 4.5.2.1

- A bundle of neurones running parallel to each other forms a nerve.
- A fatty layer called the myelin sheath acts as insulation around sensory and motor neurones, speeding up the speed of electrical transmission.

Sensory neurones carry electrical impulses from the receptor to the CNS.

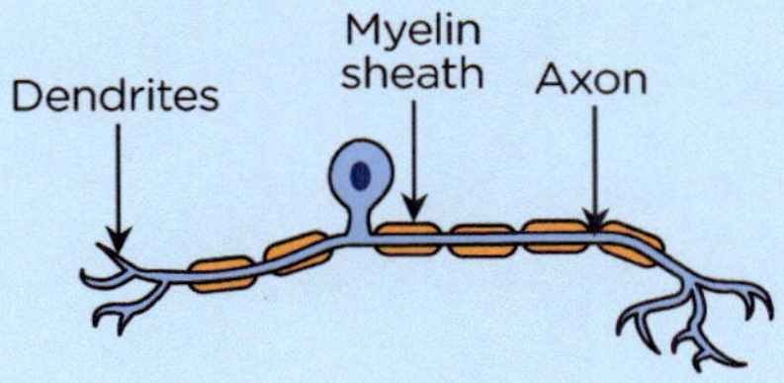

Relay neurones carry electrical impulses through the CNS.

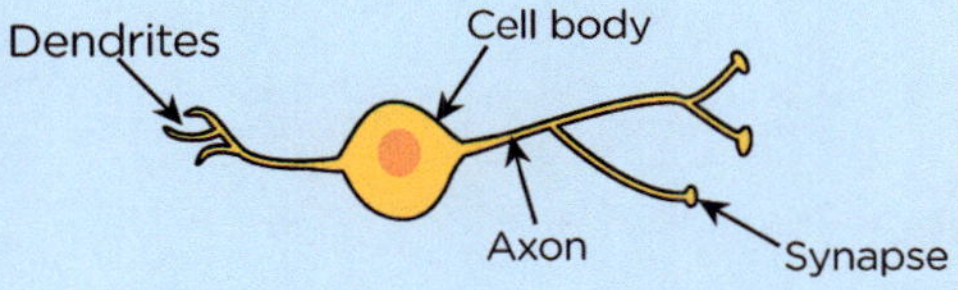

Motor neurones carry electrical impulses from the CNS to an effector (muscle or gland).

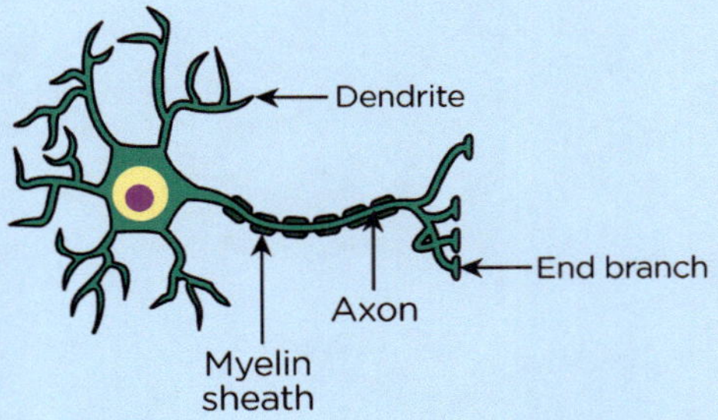

Synapses 4.5.2.1

- Electrical impulses move from one neurone to the next at junctions called synapses.
  - An electrical impulse reaches the end of an axon's branch.
  - The end branches convert the electrical impulse into a chemical signal called neurotransmitters, which diffuse across the synapse.
  - The neurotransmitters bind to the receptors on the dendrites of the neighbouring neurone, triggering the start of an electrical impulse in this neurone.
  - Once bound to receptors, the neurotransmitter is broken down by enzymes to prevent the second neurone from continually sending new electrical impulses.

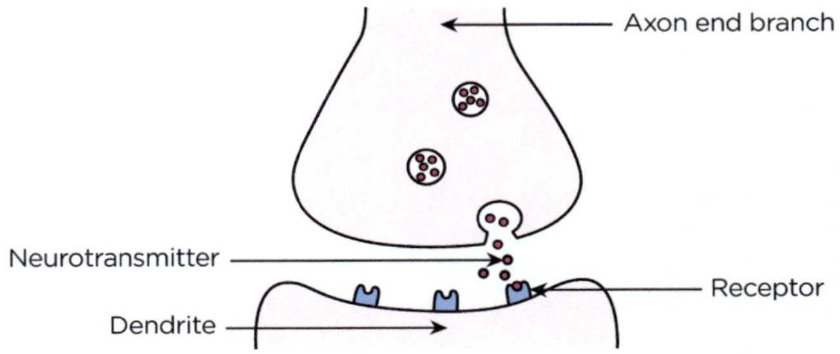

Reflex arcs 4.5.2.1

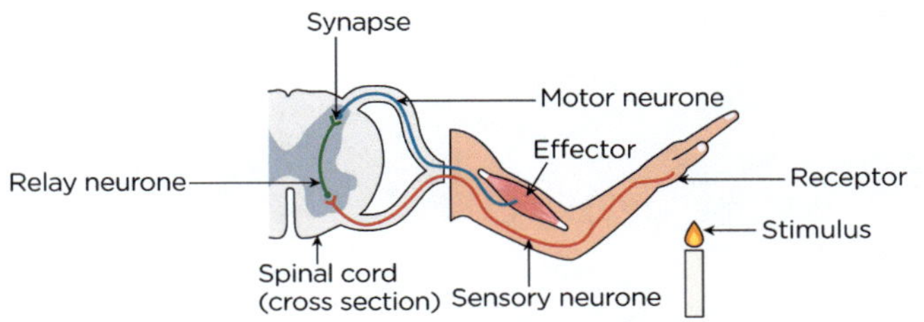

- Reflex actions take place to stop you damaging your body by mistake, in order to prevent or minimise damage, e.g. moving your hand away from a flame when pain and heat receptors sense burning.
- Reflex actions are automatic and rapid as they go through relay neurones in the spinal cord and do not involve the conscious part of the brain, meaning time is not taken sending the information there.
- Reflex responses also occur to coordinate internal processes without conscious thought, e.g. regulate heart rate and controlling pupil size.
- Reaction time is the time it takes to respond to a stimulus.

The brain 4.5.2.2

- The brain controls complex behaviour. It is made of billions of interconnected neurones and has different regions that carry out different functions.

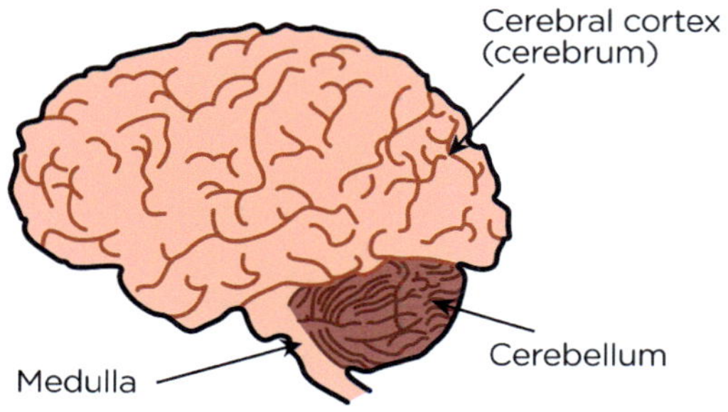

Brain region	Function
Cerebral cortex	Divided into left and right hemispheres, responsible for consciousness, memories, intelligence, and the ability to use language.
Cerebellum	Controls and coordinates the movements of muscles.
Medulla	Controls unconscious (automatic or involuntary) activities, e.g. heart rate and breathing.

Studying the brain 4.5.2.2

- The complexity and delicacy of the brain make investigating and treating brain disorders difficult.
  - Brain surgery is risky and may cause side effects or further damage.
  - Brain-damaged patients may not be able to consent.
- Neuroscientists have mapped the regions of the brain to particular functions by studying patients with brain damage, using non-invasive techniques, such as electrically stimulating different parts of the brain, and using MRI scanning techniques.

The eye 4.5.2.3

- The eye is a sense organ that contains receptors sensitive to light intensity and colour.

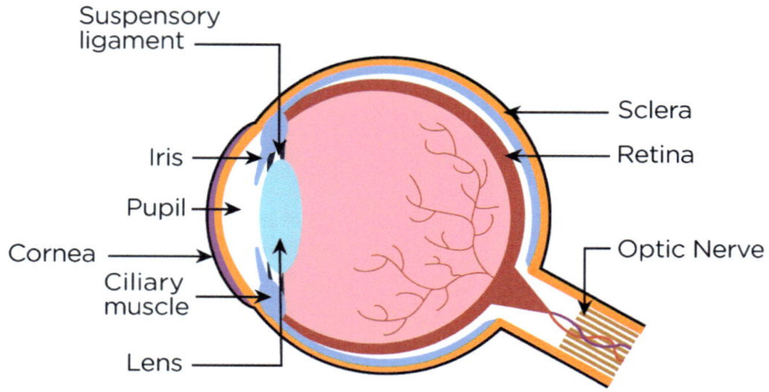

Structure	Function
Retina	Contains light-sensitive receptor cells: rods and cones that convert light into an electrical impulse. Cones allow you to see in colour when light intensity is high (daytime), while rods work in lower light intensities (night-time) but only enable black and white vision.
Optic nerve	Carries electrical impulses from the eye to the brain to generate an 'image'.
Sclera	Outer layer that protects the eye. White in humans.
Cornea	Transparent layer that refracts light through the pupil.
Iris	Muscles surrounding the pupil that control the size of the pupil. Muscles contract and relax to control how much light enters the eye.
Lens	Changes shape to focus light on the retina.
Ciliary muscles	Contract and relax to change the shape of the lens.
Suspensory ligaments	Loosen and pull tight to change the shape of the lens.

Accommodation 4.5.2.3

- Accommodation is the automatic process of changing the shape of the lens to focus on near or distant objects.
- To focus on a near object:
  - The ciliary muscles contract.
  - The suspensory ligaments loosen.
  - The lens becomes shorter and thicker, refracting light rays strongly.
- To focus on a distant object:
  - The ciliary muscles relax.
  - The suspensory ligaments are pulled tight.
  - The lens is pulled thinner and longer and only slightly refracts light rays.

Adaptation to dim light 4.5.2.3

- When light intensity is low (e.g. at night) the pupil becomes larger (dilates) in a reflex response to maximise the amount of light entering the eye.
  - The muscles in the iris increase the size of the pupil (dilated pupils).
  - Radial muscles contract.
  - Circular muscles relax.
- The opposite takes place in bright light, to prevent too much light from entering and damaging the eye.

Myopia and hyperopia 4.5.2.3

- Sometimes rays of light do not focus on the retina.
  - Myopia is short-sightedness.
  - Hyperopia is long-sightedness.
- These defects are treated with spectacle lenses (glasses), which refract the light rays so that they focus on the retina.
- New technologies include hard and soft contact lenses, laser surgery to change the shape of the cornea and a replacement lens in the eye.

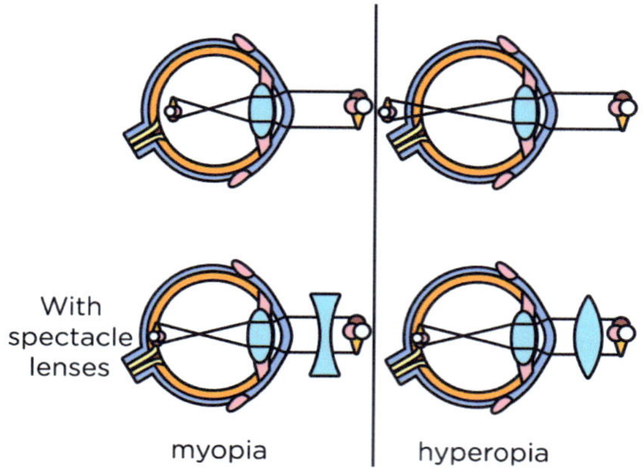

Thermoregulation 4.5.2.4

- Body temperature is monitored and controlled by the thermoregulatory centre in the brain.
- The thermoregulatory centre contains receptors sensitive to the temperature of the blood.
- The skin contains temperature receptors and sends nervous impulses to the thermoregulatory centre.
- If the body temperature is too high:
  - Arterioles near the skin's surface dilate (vasodilation), increasing blood flow so more heat is lost from the body via convection, conduction, and radiation.
  - Sweat is produced from sweat glands, so energy is taken from the body as it evaporates.
- If the body temperature is too low:
  - Arterioles near the surface of the skin constrict (vasoconstriction), minimising blood flow and heat loss.
  - Sweating stops.
  - Skeletal muscles involuntarily contract and relax quickly (shiver) to generate heat.

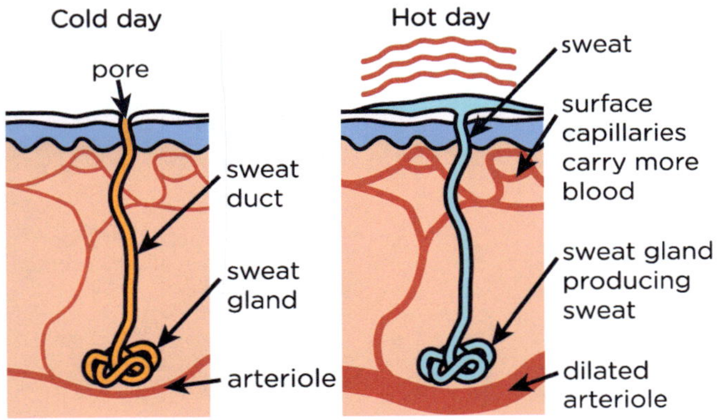

The endocrine system 4.5.3.1

- The endocrine system is composed of glands, which secrete chemicals called hormones directly into the bloodstream.
- The blood carries hormones to target organs where they produce an effect.
- Effects are slower but longer lasting than in the nervous system.

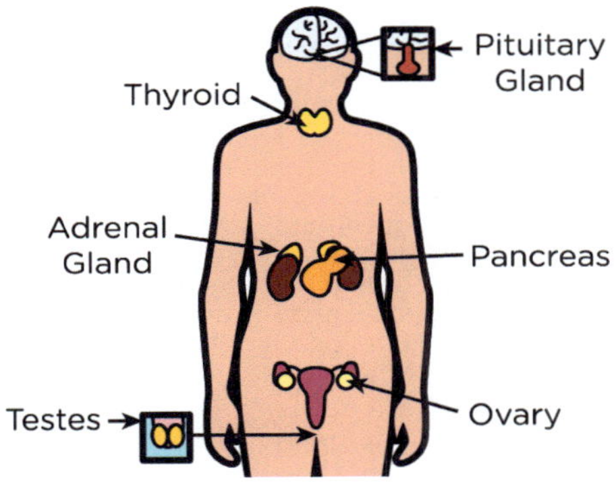

The pituitary gland 4.5.3.1

- The pituitary gland is a 'master gland' found in the brain.
- It secretes several hormones into the blood in response to body conditions.
- The hormones it secretes act on other glands to stimulate other hormones to be released to bring about effects.

Control of blood glucose 4.5.3.2

- Blood glucose concentration is monitored and controlled by the pancreas.
  - If the blood glucose concentration is too high, the pancreas produces the hormone insulin to return it to normal levels.
  - Insulin causes glucose to move from the blood into the cells, and excess glucose is converted to glycogen for storage in liver and muscle cells.
  - If the blood glucose concentration is too low, the pancreas produces the hormone glucagon, which causes glycogen to be converted into glucose to be released into the blood.
- Control of blood glucose concentration by insulin and glucagon occurs via a negative feedback cycle as the body detects a change from the optimum and makes an adjustment to return it back to normal.

Diabetes 4.5.3.2

- Type 1 diabetes is a disorder in which the pancreas fails to produce sufficient insulin. It is characterised by uncontrolled high blood glucose levels and is normally treated with regular insulin injections.
- In Type 2 diabetes, the body cells no longer respond to the insulin produced by the pancreas. A carbohydrate-controlled diet and an exercise regime are common treatments. Obesity is a major risk factor for Type 2 diabetes.

Water balance 4.5.3.3

- If body cells gain or lose too much water by osmosis, they do not function efficiently.
  - If body fluids become too dilute, cells can swell and burst as they take up more water by osmosis.
  - If body fluids are too concentrated, cells can shrink as more water leaves by osmosis.
- Uncontrollable water loss:
  - Via the lungs during exhalation.
  - Water, ions and urea are lost from the skin in sweat.
- The controlled removal of excess water (to maintain water balance), ions and urea takes place in the kidneys, which produce urine and maintain the water balance.

Protein removal 4.5.3.3

- The digestion of proteins from the diet results in excess amino acids, which need to be excreted safely.
- In the liver, excess amino acids are deaminated to form ammonia.
- Ammonia is toxic so it is immediately converted into urea.
- Urea in cells move into the blood plasma and travel to the kidney for excretion.

The kidney 4.5.3.3

- The kidneys produce urine by filtration of the blood and selective reabsorption of useful substances, such as glucose, water and some ions.
- The water balance in the body is controlled by the hormone ADH:
  - ADH is released by the pituitary gland when the blood is too concentrated.
  - ADH increases the permeability of the kidney tubules.
  - This causes more water to be reabsorbed back into the blood from the kidney tubules.
  - This is an example of control by negative feedback as more ADH is released when the blood is more concentrated.

Kidney failure 4.5.3.3

- Kidney failure happens when a person's kidneys are no longer able to filter their blood effectively and can lead to toxicity.
- Kidney dialysis can be used to treat kidney failure temporarily by the removal of high levels of urea.
  - The blood is filtered out of the body through a dialysis machine, an artificial kidney, before being returned to the body.
  - The blood flows past dialysis fluid, which is separated from it by a partially permeable membrane and contains no urea, but the same concentration of glucose and ions.
  - Urea diffuses from the highly-concentrated blood into the dialysis fluid with a lower concentration.
  - Dialysis takes several hours and must happen several times a week.

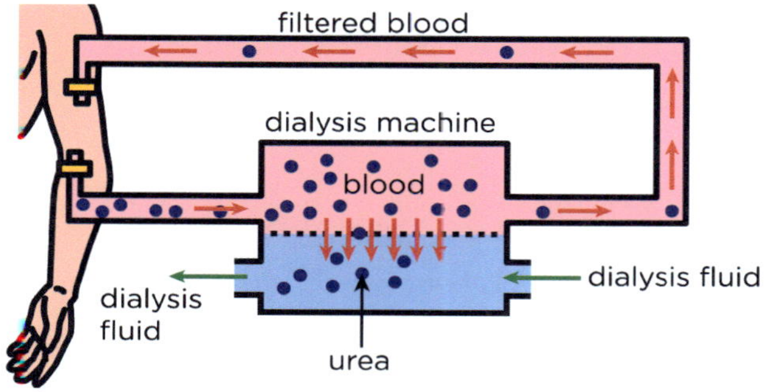

- An organ transplant can be used to treat kidney failure.
  - Humans have two kidneys and only require one to survive. Hence, a living person can donate a kidney for transplant.
  - The body may treat the kidney as foreign and the body's immune system may attack it.
  - Immunosuppressant drugs are given to the patient to reduce the chances of rejection; however, these weaken their immune system.
  - To minimise the chance of rejection, many donated kidneys come from close family members.
  - Tissue typing can be used to determine whether or not a kidney is likely to be rejected.
  - The operation is a permanent cure for kidney failure.

Hormones in reproduction 4.5.3.4

- During puberty, reproductive hormones cause secondary sex characteristics to develop, e.g. growth of pubic hair.
- Oestrogen is the main female reproductive hormone, which is produced in the ovaries. At puberty, eggs begin to mature, and one is released approximately every 28 days (ovulation).
- Testosterone is the main male reproductive hormone produced by the testes, which stimulates sperm production.

The menstrual cycle 4.5.3.4

- The menstrual cycle is around 28 days long.
- It requires oestrogen and progesterone from the ovaries and follicle-stimulating hormone (FSH) and luteinising hormone (LH) produced by the pituitary gland.
- Several hormones interact in the menstrual cycle to control it:
  - Follicle-stimulating hormone (FSH) causes maturation of an egg in the ovary and stimulates ovaries to produce oestrogen.
  - Oestrogen is responsible for thickening the uterus lining in preparation for a fertilised ovum, after menstruation.
  - High oestrogen concentration inhibits the release of FSH and stimulates the release of LH.
  - Luteinising hormone (LH) stimulates the release of the egg around day 14.
  - Progesterone maintains the thick uterus lining if a fertilised ovum embeds in it, preventing menstruation.
  - High progesterone concentration inhibits the release of FSH and LH.
  - If no fertilised ovum embeds in the uterus lining, less progesterone is produced, and the uterus lining shreds (menstruation). This starts on day 1, lasts approximately 5 days, and marks the start of the cycle.

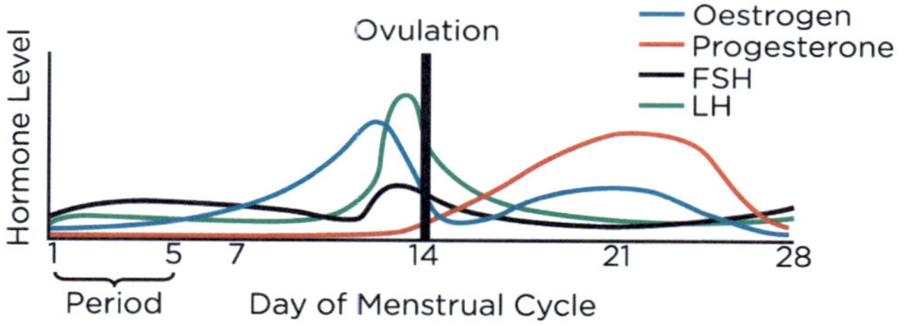

Infertility 4.5.3.6

- FSH and LH can be artificially provided in fertility drugs to support natural pregnancy through sexual intercourse.
- In Vitro Fertilisation (IVF) treatment:
  - FSH and LH are given to stimulate the maturation of several eggs.
  - The eggs are collected and fertilised by sperm in vitro (outside the body) in a laboratory.
  - The fertilised eggs develop into embryos.
  - When the embryos are a tiny ball of cells, one or two embryos are inserted into the uterus to develop.
- Fertility treatments allow people to have babies who otherwise might not be able to.
- Disadvantages of fertility treatment:
  - It is emotionally and physically stressful.
  - Low success rates.
  - It can lead to multiple births, which are a risk to both the babies and the person giving birth.
  - What happens to the unused fertilised embryos can be considered an ethical decision.

Contraception 4.5.3.5

- Fertility can be controlled by a variety of hormonal and non-hormonal methods of contraception.

Non-hormonal method	Description
Barrier method, e.g. condoms, femidoms, contraceptive sponges, diaphragms	Prevent the sperm from reaching an egg
Spermicidal agents	Often found coating barrier methods to kill or disable sperm
Intrauterine devices	Prevent implantation of an embryo
Abstaining from intercourse, especially during ovulation	No sperm enters the female reproductive system
Surgical methods of sterilisation	Vasectomy: sperm ducts are tied or cut Tubal ligation: fallopian tubes are tied or cut

Hormonal method	Description
Oral contraceptives	• Contain oestrogen and progesterone to inhibit FSH production so that no eggs mature • Thicken mucus in the neck of the uterus so it is harder for sperm to travel through • Thin the lining of the uterus so there is less chance of a fertilised ovum embedding
Injection, implant, or skin patch	Slow-release progesterone to inhibit the maturation and release of eggs over several months or years
Intrauterine devices	Release progesterone to prevent implantation

Adrenaline 4.5.3.7

- Adrenaline is produced by the adrenal glands in times of fear or stress, preparing the body for 'flight or fight':
  - Increases heart rate, blood pressure, and blood glucose levels, boosting the delivery of oxygen and glucose to the brain and muscles for respiration.
  - Suppresses immune system.
  - Levels are not controlled by negative feedback.

Thyroxine 4.5.3.7

- Thyroxine is produced by the thyroid gland:
  - Stimulates the basal metabolic rate.
  - Plays an important role in growth and development.
  - Levels are controlled by negative feedback, maintaining the levels within certain limits.

Tropisms 4.5.4.1

- Plants produce hormones called auxins to coordinate and control growth in response to light (phototropism) and gravity (gravitropism or geotropism).
- Auxins are produced in the tips of shoots and roots.
- Unequal distributions of auxin cause unequal growth rates in plant roots and shoots.
- **Phototropism**:
  - Plant shoots grow towards the light (positive phototropism) to maximise the light absorbed for photosynthesis.
  - In shoots, auxin causes cell elongation.
  - Auxins will concentrate on the shaded side of the shoot, causing unequal growth that makes the shoot bend towards the light.
- **Gravitropism**:
  - Plant roots grow downwards towards water (positive geotropism) in response to gravity, while plant shoots are negatively gravitropic.
  - In roots, auxin slows cell growth on the lower side, causing curvature downwards.

Other plant hormones 4.5.4.1

- Gibberellins:
  - Involved in plant growth.
  - Initiate seed germination and stem elongation.
  - Form flowers and fruit.
- Ethene:
  - Causes the ripening of fruit.
  - Controls cell division.
  - Involved in the opening of flowers and dropping of leaves.

Uses of plant hormones 4.5.4.2

- Plant growth hormones are used in agriculture and horticulture.
- Auxins:
  - Selective weed killers – broad-leaved weeds, such as dandelions, have a larger surface area to absorb more weed killer, which causes uncontrollable growth of some cells and inhibits growth in others, killing the plant.
  - Rooting powders – plant cuttings are taken, and the cut end of the stem is dipped in rooting powder and placed into the soil where auxin helps the cutting form roots.
  - Auxins are used to promote growth in tissue culture.
- Ethene:
  - Ethene is used to control the ripening of fruit.
  - Fruit is often picked before it is ripe to prevent rotting during the long journey to supermarkets.
  - Ethene is sprayed on fruit before arriving so it begins to ripen as it is placed on the shelves.
- Gibberellins:
  - Used to end seed dormancy to trigger germination.
  - Used to promote flowering.
  - Used to increase the size of fruit.

Meiosis 4.6.1.2

- Cells in reproductive organs divide by meiosis to form gametes, halving the number of chromosomes:
  - Copies of the genetic information are made.
  - The cell divides twice to form four gametes, each with a single set of chromosomes.
  - All gametes are genetically different from each other.
- Gametes fuse at fertilisation, forming a zygote and restoring the full number of chromosomes.
- The zygote divides by mitosis, increasing the number of cells to form an embryo.
- The cells differentiate as the embryo develops.

Sexual reproduction 4.6.1.1

- Meiosis leads to non-identical cells being formed.
- Gametes are formed using meiosis.
- Sexual reproduction involves the fusion of male and female gametes (fertilisation):
  - Sperm and egg cells in animals
  - Pollen and egg cells in flowering plants
- There is a mixing of genetic information from each parent, which leads to variety in offspring.

Asexual reproduction 4.6.1.1

- Asexual reproduction involves only one parent and no fusion of gametes, so there is no mixing of genetic information.
- Mitosis occurs, which produces cells that are genetically identical (clones) to the parent cell.
- Prokaryotic bacteria reproduce asexually.

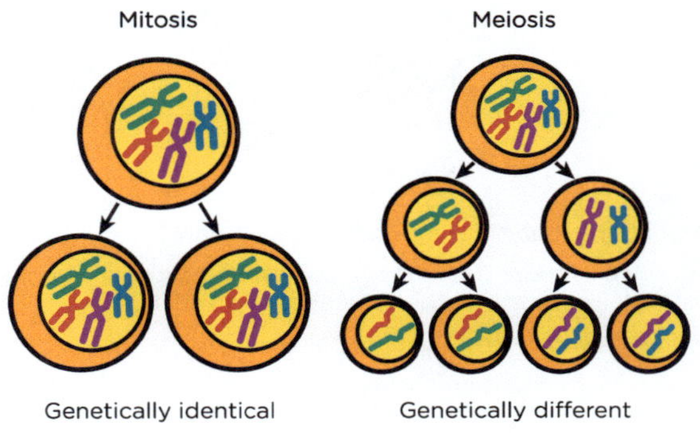

Sexual vs asexual reproduction 4.6.1.3

- Some organisms can reproduce by both sexual and asexual reproduction:
  - Malarial parasites reproduce asexually in the human host and sexually in the mosquito.
  - Many fungi can reproduce asexually by spores and sexually to give variation.
  - Many plants produce seeds sexually but can also reproduce asexually, e.g. runners in strawberry plants or bulb division in daffodils.

	Advantages
Sexual reproduction	• Produces genetic variation in offspring. • If the environment changes, variation gives a survival advantage by natural selection (if there is a change in the environment, some organisms may survive due to adaptations). • Natural selection can be sped up by humans through selective breeding (e.g. breeding the best plants to increase food production)
Asexual reproduction	• Only one parent needed. • More time and energy-efficient as individuals do not need to find a mate. • Faster than sexual reproduction. • Many identical offspring can be produced in favourable conditions.

DNA structure 4.6.1.5

- DNA is a long polymer made from repeating nucleotide units consisting of alternating sugar and phosphate groups with the sugar attached to one of four bases.

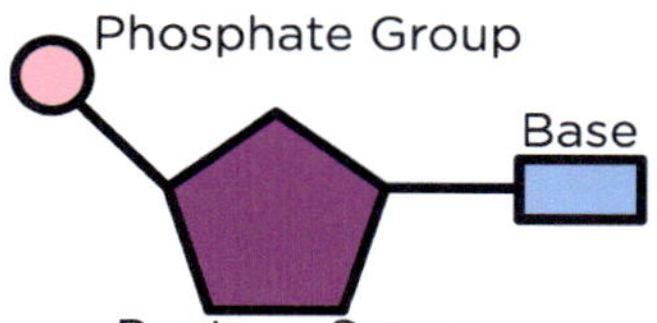

Nucleotide

- DNA contains four different bases: A, C, G and T.
- A sequence of three bases is the code for a particular amino acid, so the order determines the assembly of proteins.
- Two DNA strands form a double helix.
- The strands are complementary (the bases are the correct shape to bind to a specific base on the opposite strand via hydrogen bonds):
  - C always binds to a G.
  - T always binds to an A.

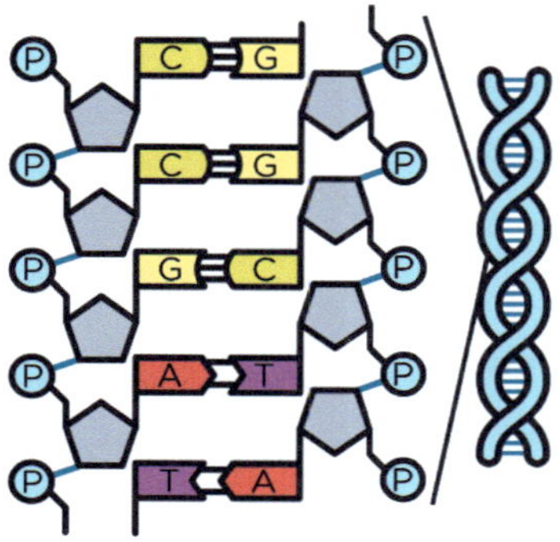

Uses of the Human Genome Project 4.6.1.4

- In the Human Genome Project, the sequence of all the bases in the entire human genome was identified using the DNA of male and female volunteers.
- Advantages of sequencing the human genome:
  - To link genes to different types of diseases.
  - To improve our understanding and treatment of inherited disorders
  - To trace human migration patterns from the past.

DNA 4.6.1.4

- The genetic material in the nucleus of a cell is made up of a chemical called DNA.
  - DNA is a polymer made up of two strands forming a double helix.
  - The DNA is contained in structures called chromosomes.
  - A gene is a small section of DNA on a chromosome.
  - Each gene codes for a sequence of amino acids that makes a specific protein.
- The genome is the entire genetic material of an organism.

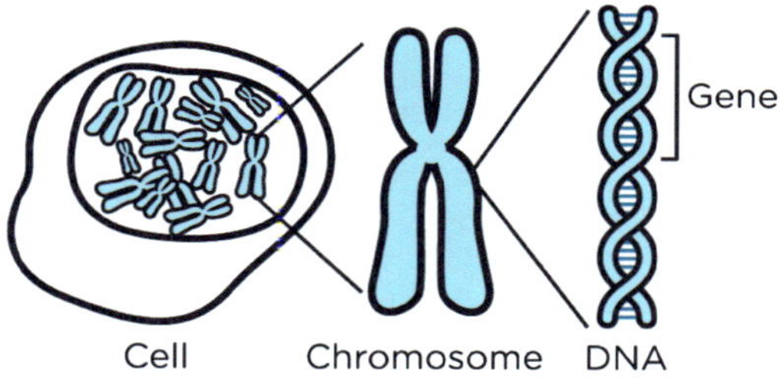

Transcription 4.6.1.5

- Transcription is the first stage of protein synthesis and takes place in the nucleus.
- An mRNA template is formed from a section of one of the nucleotide strands making up DNA.
- The template formed covers a section of DNA that codes for a particular protein (a gene).

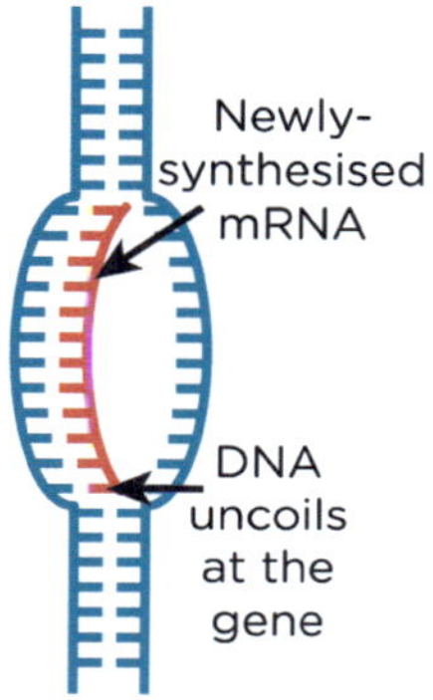

Translation 4.6.1.5

- Translation is the second stage of protein synthesis and takes place on ribosomes.
- tRNA carrier molecules bring amino acids that are specific to the template.
- A sequence of three bases on the template is the code for an amino acid. Therefore, the order of bases controls the order in which the amino acids are assembled and determines the protein that is made.
- The amino acids brought to the template bind to each other, forming a growing protein chain in the correct order.
- When the protein chain is complete, it folds up to form a unique shape.
- The shape of a protein enables it to do its job as an enzyme or hormone or allows it to form a structure in the body, e.g. collagen.

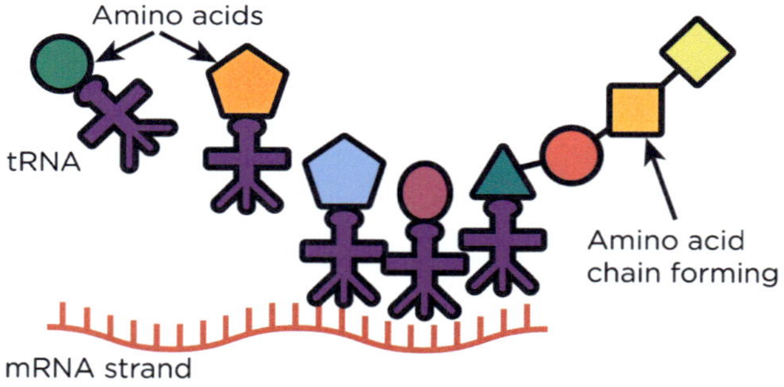

Mutations 4.6.1.5

- A mutation is a change in the DNA sequence; for example, an insertion of a nucleotide or a deletion of one.
- Mutations occur continuously.
- Most mutations do not alter the protein or only alter it slightly so that its shape and therefore function is not changed.
- A few mutations code for an altered protein with a different shape, altering the activity of a protein, e.g. an enzyme may no longer fit the substrate-binding site or a structural protein may lose its strength.
- Some mutations are advantageous and allow genetic variation.

Gene expression 4.6.1.5

- Not all parts of DNA code for proteins.
- Non-coding parts of DNA play a role in gene expression and can switch genes on and off.
- Variations in non-coding regions may affect how genes are expressed.

Inheritance and alleles 4.6.1.6

Term	Definition
Gamete	Sex cells that contain half the number of chromosomes of all other cells, with male and female gametes combining in fertilisation
Chromosome	Structures of DNA found in the nucleus of eukaryotic cells
Gene	A section of DNA that codes for a particular protein
Allele	Alleles are two versions of the same gene
Dominant	A dominant allele is always expressed and an organism will show a dominant characteristic if inherited from one or both parents
Recessive	Allele will only be expressed and show a characteristic if two copies are present, one from each parent
Homozygous	A genotype with two of the same alleles
Heterozygous	A genotype with two different alleles
Genotype	The collection of genes/alleles present in an organism
Phenotype	The physical characteristics of an organism, determined by the genotype and environment

- Some characteristics are controlled by a single gene:
  - Fur colour in mice.
  - Red-green colour blindness in humans.
- Most characteristics are a result of the interaction of multiple genes, rather than a single gene.

Phenotype and genotype 4.6.1.6

- 'B' is the brown eye allele. It is capitalised to signify it is dominant. If someone has a 'B' in their genotype, they will have brown eyes (Bb or BB).
- 'b' is the blue eye allele. It is lower case to signify it is recessive. Both alleles must be 'b' in someone's genotype for them to have blue eyes (bb only).
- If the genotype is 'BB', the phenotype would be 'brown eyes'.

Punnett squares 4.6.1.6

- A Punnett square is a grid used to determine the probability of an offspring's genotype based on the genotype of the parents.
- It shows the potential allele combinations offspring can inherit.
- Determining the inheritance of eye colour:
  - Both parents have the brown eye phenotype and the genotype Bb.
  - Punnett square:

		Parent 1	
		B	b
Parent 2	B	BB	Bb
	b	Bb	bb

  - Genotype ratio BB:Bb:bb = 1:2:1
  - Probability of offspring: BB = 25%, Bb = 50%, bb = 25%
  - Probability of offspring: Brown eyes = 75%, blue eyes 25%

Family trees 4.6.1.6

- Family trees show the inheritance of characteristics over several generations.
- The oldest members of a family are at the top of a tree.
- People with XY chromosomes are typically symbolised with squares and people with XX chromosomes are symbolised with circles, unless shown otherwise with a key.
- Individuals with a specific characteristic are symbolised by their shape being coloured in, unless shown otherwise with a key.

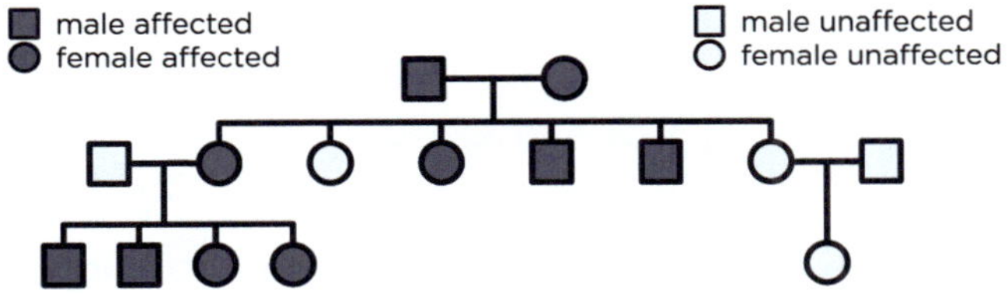

Inherited disorders 4.6.1.7

- Some disorders are inherited, meaning they are caused by the inheritance of certain alleles.
  - Polydactyly (having extra fingers or toes) is caused by a dominant allele.
  - Cystic fibrosis (a disorder of cell membranes) is caused by a recessive allele.
- Embryo screening involves looking for genetic disorders in embryos before they develop, allowing the parents to make an informed decision about continuing or terminating the pregnancy, which may alleviate suffering.
  - There is a possible risk to the embryo, and the person carrying the embryo.
  - It can be seen as unethical or against some religions.
  - It is expensive.

Determining sex 4.6.1.8

- Ordinary human body cells contain 23 pairs of chromosomes.
- 22 pairs control characteristics.
- 1 pair carries the genes that determine sex.
  - In females, the sex chromosomes are the same (XX).
  - In males, the sex chromosomes are different (XY).
- Determining the inheritance of sex:
  - Punnett square:

		Mother	
		X	X
Father	X	XX	XX
	Y	XY	XY

  - Genotype ratio XX:XY = 1:1
  - Probability of offspring: XX = 50%, XY = 50%

Variation 4.6.2.1

- Differences in the characteristics of individuals in a population are called variation.
- The phenotype of an organism is determined by the genome and the genome's interaction with the environment.
  - Some characteristics are determined purely from inherited genes (e.g. biological sex and blood group).
  - Some characteristics are determined purely by the environment (e.g. tattoos and scars).
  - Some characteristics are determined by genetics and the environment, where genetics predetermines the potential for a characteristic and the environment determines how much of this potential is reached (e.g. intelligence).
- There is usually extensive genetic variation within a population of a species.
- All genetic variation arises from mutations:
  - Most mutations have no effect on the phenotype.
  - Some mutations influence phenotype.
  - Very few mutations determine phenotype.
- Mutations occur continuously:
  - Very rarely a mutation will lead to a new phenotype.
  - If the new phenotype is better suited to an environmental change, it can lead to a fairly rapid change in the species.

Evolution 4.6.2.2

- The theory of evolution states that all species of living things have evolved from simple life forms that first developed over 3 billion years ago.
- Evolution is a change in the inherited characteristics of a population over time through a process called natural selection.
- Natural selection of variants in a population gives rise to phenotypes best suited to their environment.
- Natural selection may result in the formation of new species.
- If two populations of a species become so different from each other in phenotype that they can no longer interbreed to produce fertile offspring, they have formed two new species.

Selective breeding 4.6.2.3

- Selective breeding (artificial selection) is the process by which humans breed plants and animals for particular genetic characteristics.
- Humans have been doing this for thousands of years, e.g. the breeding of food crops from wild plants and the domestication of animals.
- Selective breeding involves:
  - Choosing parents with a desired characteristic from a mixed population and breeding them together.
  - Choosing the offspring with the desired characteristic and breeding them together.
  - Repeating the cycle over many generations until all offspring show the desired characteristic.
- The characteristic can be chosen for its usefulness or appearance:
  - Animals that produce more meat or milk.
  - Disease resistance or increased size in food crops.
  - Domestic dogs with a gentle nature.
  - Large or unusual flowers.
- Disadvantages of selective breeding
  - Can lead to 'inbreeding' when the parents are genetically very similar, where some breeds are especially prone to inherited defects or disease.
  - Reduced genetic variation means that a change in the environment or a disease is more likely to kill an entire population.
  - Physical problems in organisms, e.g. cows weighed down by large udders.
  - The breeding method (e.g. artificial insemination) can be seen as unethical.

GM crops 4.6.2.4

- GM stands for 'genetically modified'.
- GM crops generally show increased yields.
- Plant crops have been genetically engineered to:
  - Improve resistance to diseases and insect attacks.
  - Improve resistance to environmental conditions, e.g. drought.
  - Produce bigger and better fruit and vegetables.
  - Make crops resistant to the herbicides used on weeds.
- Concerns of GM crops:
  - Fears that the genes might spread into the wild gene pool, e.g. herbicide-resistant weeds.
  - Some people are cautious of the effects of eating GM crops on human health.
  - A higher yield of GM crops may cause a reduction in wildflowers and the insects that depend on them as a food source.

Genetic engineering 4.6.2.4

- Genetic engineering is a process that involves modifying the genome of an organism by introducing a gene from another organism to give a desired characteristic.
  - Enzymes are used to isolate the required gene by cutting it from the DNA.
  - The gene is inserted into a vector (a bacterial plasmid or virus). If the vector is a bacterial plasmid, the same enzyme is used to cut open the plasmid and a second is used to seal it.
  - The vector is used to insert the gene into the required cells.

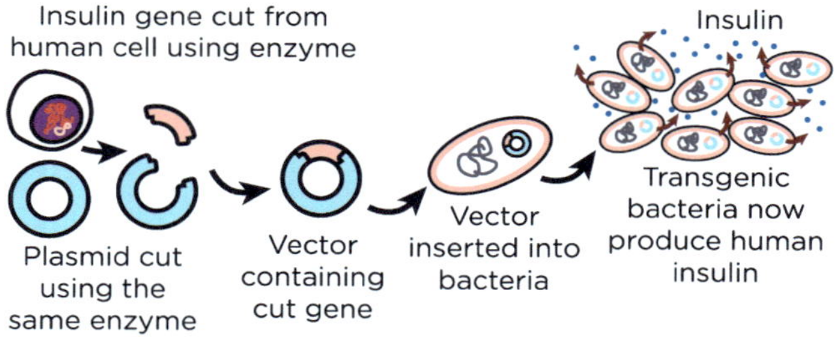

- Genes are transferred to the cells of animals, plants or bacteria at an early stage in their development (e.g. embryo in animals) so they develop with the desired characteristics; all cells produced via mitosis will then contain the same gene.
- Some people disagree with genetic engineering for religious or moral reasons.

GM animals 4.6.2.4

- Animals can be genetically engineered to produce molecules we need.
- Sheep have been genetically engineered to produce proteins used in medicine
- Modern medical research is exploring the possibility of genetic modification to overcome some inherited disorders.

GM bacteria 4.6.2.4

- Bacterial cells have been genetically engineered to produce useful substances, such as human insulin to treat diabetes.
- Benefits:
  - Produces insulin at a high yield.
  - Produces human insulin, which is safer to use than pig or cattle insulin.
- Some people are cautious of the effects of using GM medicines on human health.

Cloning 4.6.2.5

- Cloning is the asexual reproduction of an organism to produce genetically identical offspring, or the artificial cloning of an organism to produce a genetically identical organism.
- Plant cloning is used to grow identical new plants:

Method	Description
Tissue culture	• Takes small groups of cells from part of a plant and places them in a growth medium to grow identical new plants. • Used commercially in nurseries or to preserve rare plant species.
Cuttings	• Older and simpler method used by gardeners. • Cuttings are treated with plant hormones and placed directly into the soil where they develop roots.

- Animal cloning via embryo transplants:
  - Cells from a developing embryo are taken before they become specialised.
  - The cells are split from each other and transplanted into the wombs of multiple host animals.
  - The separated cells develop into identical embryos, forming multiple identical offspring.
  - This is illegal in humans.

Adult cell cloning 4.6.2.5

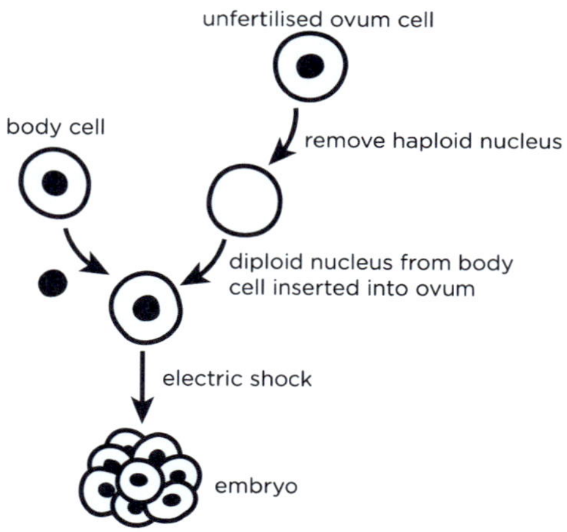

- Adult body cells, such as skin cells, are used.
- When the embryo is a ball of cells, it is inserted into the womb of an adult animal to continue its development.
- The embryo contains the same genetic information as the adult body cell whose nucleus was inserted into the ovum.

Theory of evolution 4.6.3.1

- Charles Darwin proposed his theory of evolution by natural selection based on:
  - Observations he made on a round-the-world expedition.
  - Developing knowledge of geology and fossils.
- Darwin published his theory in *On the Origin of Species* (1859).
- There was a lot of controversy about his theory.
  - The theory challenged the idea that God made all animals and plants that live on Earth.
  - There was insufficient evidence at the time the theory was published.
  - The mechanism of inheritance and variation was not known until 50 years after the theory was published.
- Jean-Baptiste Lamarck proposed an earlier theory of evolution:
  - Changes that occur in an organism during its lifetime can be inherited.
  - We know that in the vast majority of cases this type of inheritance cannot occur.

Natural selection 4.6.3.1

- The theory of evolution by natural selection:
  - Individual organisms in a species have a wide range of variation for a characteristic.
  - Individuals with characteristics most suited to their environment are more likely to survive long enough to breed successfully.
  - The characteristics that have enabled these individuals to survive are passed onto their offspring.
  - The cycle continues from one generation to the next.

Evidence for evolution 4.6.3.4

- Evidence for Darwin's theory of evolution by natural selection:
  - It has been shown that characteristics are passed on to offspring in genes
  - Fossil records
  - Antibiotic resistance has evolved in bacteria
- Because of this evidence, the theory of evolution by natural selection is now widely accepted.

Fossils 4.6.3.5

- Fossils are the 'remains' of organisms from millions of years ago, which are found in rocks.
- Fossils show us how much or how little different organisms have changed as life developed on Earth, providing evidence for Darwin's theory of evolution by natural selection.
- Fossils may be formed:
  - From parts of organisms that have not decayed because one or more of the conditions needed for decay are absent (e.g. warmth, air, and moisture).
  - When parts of the organism are replaced by minerals as they decay.
  - As preserved traces of organisms, such as footprints, burrows, and rootlet traces.
- Scientists cannot be certain about how life began on earth.
  - Many early forms of life were soft-bodied, meaning that they have left few traces behind.
  - The traces that have been left behind have mainly been destroyed by geological activity over time.

Speciation 4.6.3.2

- Though Darwin is more widely appreciated, Alfred Russel Wallace independently proposed a theory of evolution by natural selection as well.
  - He published joint writings with Darwin in 1858.
  - This prompted Darwin to publish *On the Origins of Species* in 1859.
  - Wallace worked worldwide gathering evidence for evolutionary theory.
- He is best known for his pioneering theory of speciation and his work on warning colouration in animals.
- More evidence over time has led to our current understanding of the theory of speciation, the gradual formation of a new species as a result of evolution.
  - A population of a species is isolated in a different environment to the rest of the species.
  - Different characteristics will be favourable for the survival of individuals in the isolated population as they are in a different environment to the rest of the species.
  - The isolated population will evolve different characteristics to the rest of the species thanks to natural selection.
  - Over time, the isolated population becomes so different from the rest of the species that they can no longer interbreed to form fertile offspring.
  - The isolated population has formed its own species.

Mendelian genetics 4.6.3.3

- In the mid-19th century, Gregor Mendel carried out breeding experiments on plants.
- He observed that the inheritance of each characteristic was determined by 'units' that were passed on to the descendants unchanged.
  - Mendel studied the inheritance of traits in pea plants to form the laws of Mendelian inheritance.
  - For example, crossing a yellow pea plant with a green pea plant always produced a yellow pea plant, so yellow was found to be dominant and green is recessive.
  - These laws are followed when we carry out Punnett squares to determine the potential genotypes of offspring.
- The importance of Mendel's work was not recognised until after his death as little was known about genetic information when his discovery was made; most scientists still believed in blended inheritance, where all characteristics are passed on.
  - Late 19th century – chromosome behaviour during cell division was first observed.
  - Early 20th century – Chromosomes and Mendel's 'units' observed to behave in similar ways, leading to the idea that the 'units', later known as genes, were located on chromosomes.
  - Mid-20th century - DNA structure and the mechanism of gene function were determined, leading to the development of gene theory.

Extinction 4.6.3.6

- Extinctions occur when there are no remaining individuals of a species still alive.
- Species that do not successfully adapt to environmental conditions or lack the genetic variation to survive changes in the environment are more likely to go extinct.
- Factors that may contribute to the extinction of a species:
  - Increasing population of humans increases human impact on the environment.
    - Cutting down rainforests.
    - Building bigger cities and urban areas.
    - Drilling for oil and materials.
  - Natural changes over time, e.g. end of the ice age.
  - Introduction of new predators.

Antibiotic resistance and interdependent organisms

Solving antibiotic resistance 4.6.3.7

- Bacteria reproduce at a fast rate, which means they can evolve rapidly.
  - Mutations of bacterial pathogens produce new strains.
  - Some strains might be resistant to antibiotics, so they are not killed.
  - The resistant strains survive and reproduce, increasing the population of resistant strains.
  - The resistant strain is more likely to spread because of the lack of immunity and of an effective treatment.
  - For example, MRSA is resistant to antibiotics.
- To reduce the rate of development of antibiotic-resistant strains:
  - Doctors should not prescribe antibiotics inappropriately, such as treating non-serious or viral infections.
  - Patients should always complete their course of antibiotics so that all bacteria are killed and none survive to mutate and form resistant strains.
  - The agricultural use of antibiotics should be restricted.
- The development of new antibiotics is slow and costly. It is unlikely to keep up with the emergence of new resistant strains.

Classification and Linnaeus 4.6.4

- Traditionally living things have been classified into groups depending on their structure and characteristics.
- This system was developed by Carl Linnaeus.
  - Linnaeus classified living things into kingdom, phylum, class, order, family, genus, and species.
  - Organisms are named by the two-part binomial system of genus plus species.
  - Scientists write binomial names in italics with a capital letter for the genus, e.g. for the organism *Homo sapiens*, Homo is the genus and sapiens is the species.

Evolutionary trees 4.6.4

- Evolutionary trees are a method used by scientists to show how they believe organisms are related.
- Evolutionary trees use current classification data for living organisms and fossil data for extinct organisms

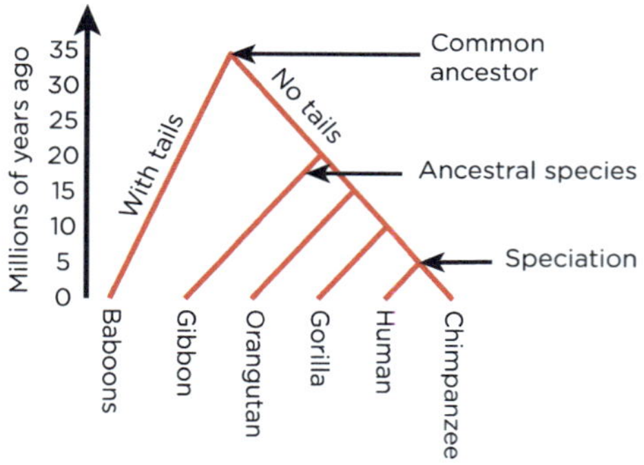

Updates to classification 4.6.4

- New models of classification have been proposed due to:
  - Developing evidence of internal structures due to improvements in microscopes.
  - Increased understanding of biochemical processes.
  - Development of techniques such as genome mapping.
- Due to evidence available from chemical analysis, there is now a 'three-domain system' developed by Carl Woese.
- In this system, organisms are divided into:
  - Archaea (primitive bacteria usually living in extreme environments).
  - Bacteria (true bacteria).
  - Eukaryota (including animals, plants, protists, and fungi).

Interdependence 4.7.1.1

- Within a community, each species depends on other species for food, shelter, pollination, seed dispersal, etc.
- A stable community is one where all the species and environmental factors are in balance with each other so that population sizes remain relatively constant.
- If one species is removed or added it can affect the whole community due to interdependence.

Abiotic factors 4.7.1.2

- Abiotic (non-living) factors that can affect a community are:
  - Light intensity – e.g. plants adapted to the shade may quickly wilt and die if they are moved into direct sunlight
  - Temperature – e.g. some organisms (e.g. reptiles) cannot regulate their own body temperature
  - Moisture levels
  - Soil pH and mineral content
  - Wind intensity and direction
  - Carbon dioxide levels for plants – a major limiting factor in photosynthesis
  - Oxygen levels for aquatic animals – required for respiration
- A change in an abiotic factor would affect a community, e.g. cacti are adapted to survive with little water and will die if overwatered, so species that depend on cacti for a habitat or a food resource would then also die.

Competition 4.7.1.1

- An ecosystem is the interaction of a community of living organisms (biotic) with the non-living (abiotic) parts of their environment.
- To survive and reproduce:
  - Organisms require a supply of materials from their surroundings and from the other living organisms there.
  - Organisms are adapted to the conditions in which they live.
- Organisms compete with each other for multiple factors:
  - Plants often compete for light, space, and for water and mineral ions from the soil.
  - Animals often compete for food, mates, and territory.
- Competition between organisms provides a struggle for existence, which drives evolution.
  - Only the organisms best adapted to their environment will survive and reproduce, forming offspring also adapted to their environment.
  - This is known as survival of the fittest.
  - Interspecific competition is between different species in a community.
  - Intraspecific competition is between organisms of the same species.

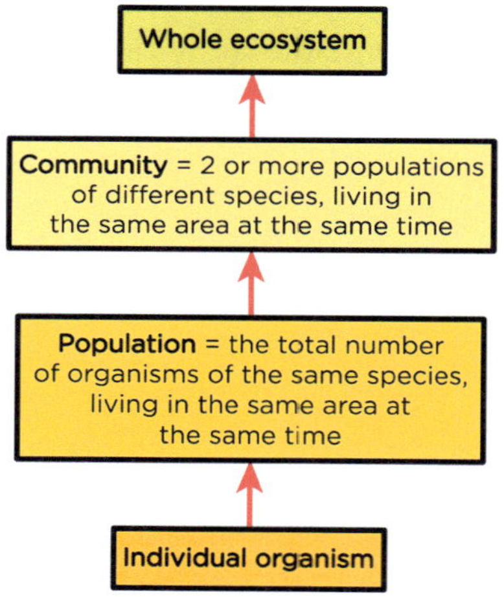

Food chains 4.7.2.1

- Feeding relationships within a community can be represented by food chains.

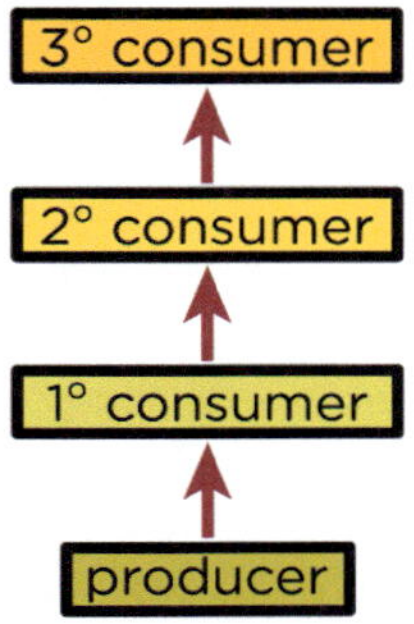

- All food chains begin with a producer, which synthesises molecules.
  - This is usually a green plant or alga.
  - They make glucose by photosynthesis.
  - They are the producers of biomass for life on Earth.
- Producers are eaten by primary consumers, which may be eaten by secondary consumers and then tertiary consumers.
- Predator-prey cycling:
  - Consumers that kill and eat other animals are predators.
  - Consumers that are eaten are prey.
  - In a stable community, the numbers of predators and prey rise and fall in interdependent cycles.
  - If the number of predators increases, the number of prey decrease after a short lag phase, as more are eaten.
  - As the number of prey decrease, the number of predators will decrease as there is less food.
  - This then causes the number of prey to increase, resulting in an increase in predators.

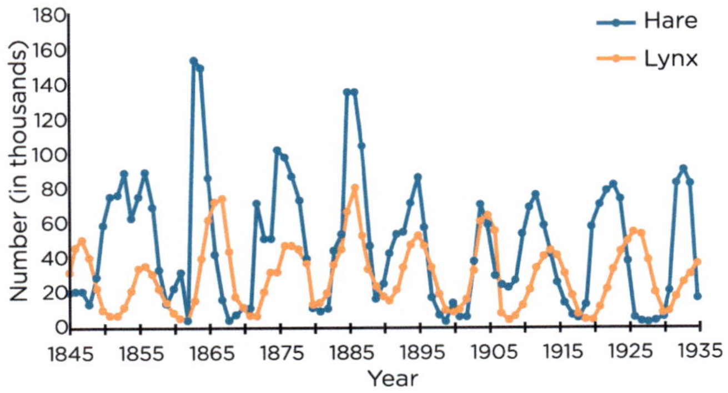

Biotic factors 4.7.1.3

- Biotic (living) factors that can affect a community are:
  - Availability of food
  - New predators arriving
  - New pathogens
  - One species outcompeting another so the numbers are no longer sufficient to breed
- A change in a biotic factor would affect a community, e.g. if a new pathogen appeared and killed an entire species, the organisms depending on this species for food or a habitat would also die.

Adaptations 4.7.1.4

- Organisms have features called adaptations that enable them to survive in the conditions in which they normally live.
  - Structural adaptations are physical features, e.g. tigers have sharp teeth to allow them to kill their prey.
  - Behavioural adaptations are behaviours that benefit an organism, e.g. a courtship display to attract a mate.
  - Functional adaptations are physiological processes organisms complete to aid survival, e.g. producing venom to deter predators from killing them.
- Adaptations allow organisms to outcompete others and provide them with an evolutionary advantage.
- Organisms called extremophiles live in environments that are very extreme.
  - Extreme conditions include extremely hot or cold temperatures, high pressure or salt concentration, and highly acidic or alkaline environments.
  - For example, bacteria living in deep-sea hydrothermal vents are extremophiles evolved to feed on the sulfur compounds released by the vents, toxic to almost all other life.

Sampling 4.7.2.1

- Sampling is the process scientists use to look at a section of a habitat and draw conclusions about the whole of it.
- The section of the habitat studied must be large enough to be representative of the whole of it for accurate predictions to be made.
- A range of experimental methods using transects and quadrats are used by ecologists to determine the distribution and abundance of species in an ecosystem.
  - A quadrat is a square frame separated into a grid. It is placed on the ground and the abundance of organisms within squares are recorded.
  - A transect is a straight line from one side of the habitat to the other.
  - Distribution and abundance can be determined by systematically recording all the organisms present along a transect, by placing a quadrat at fixed intervals along it.
- Methods of measuring the abundance of organisms:
  - Mode: The value that appears most frequently in a data set.
  - Median: The middle number in a data set when displayed in ascending order
  - $mean\ (average) = \frac{sum\ of\ terms}{number\ of\ terms}$

The carbon cycle 4.7.2.2

- Many different materials cycle through the abiotic and biotic components of an ecosystem.
- All materials in the living world are recycled to provide the building blocks for future organisms
- The carbon cycle is important so that living organisms can continually be supplied with carbon in forms suitable for use in making the molecules necessary for life, e.g. proteins, carbohydrates, lipids and nucleic acids.

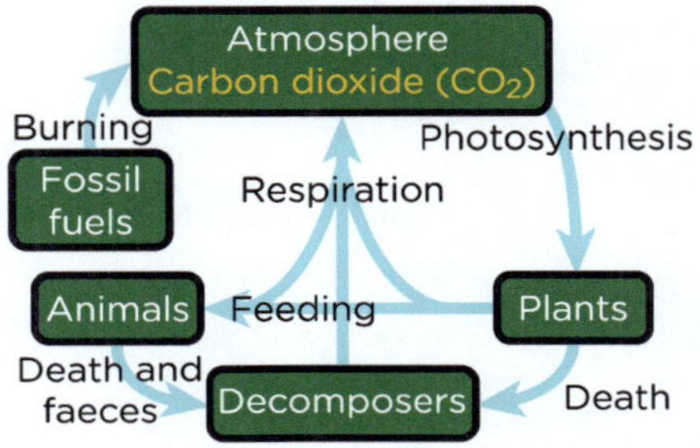

- The carbon cycle returns carbon from organisms to the atmosphere as carbon dioxide to be used by plants in photosynthesis.
- Microorganisms are important decomposers that cycle materials through an ecosystem by returning carbon to the atmosphere as carbon dioxide and mineral ions to the soil.

The water cycle 4.7.2.2

- The water cycle is important so that living organisms can continually be supplied with water, which is the major component of all cells and therefore necessary for life.
- The water cycle provides fresh water for plants and animals on land before draining into the seas.

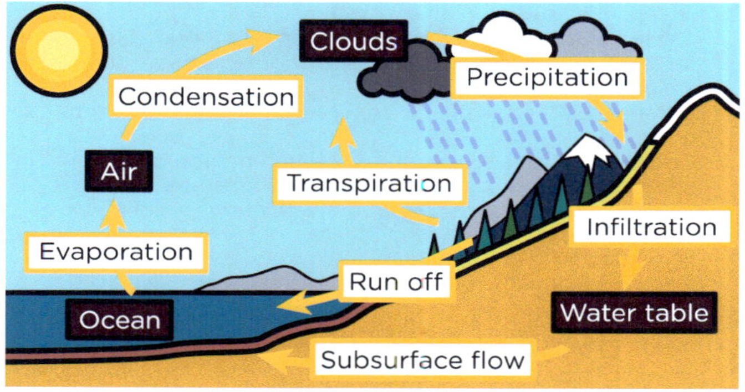

- Water is continuously evaporated and precipitated (as rain, snow, hail or sleet).
- Runoff is the movement of water across the surface.
- Infiltration is the movement of water into the ground to become groundwater.
- Subsurface flow is the movement of groundwater to the ocean.

Decomposition 4.7.2.3

- Decomposition is the breakdown of substances into smaller substances, carried out by bacteria and fungi.
- Increasing temperature, oxygen and water availability increases the rate of decay of biological material as bacteria and fungi grow faster.
- $rate\ change\ in\ the\ decay\ of\ biological\ material = \frac{change\ in\ value}{time}$
- Gardeners and farmers try to provide optimum conditions (e.g. neutral pH) for rapid decay of waste biological material to produce compost.
- Compost is used as a natural fertiliser.
- Anaerobic decay produces methane gas, which can be carried out in a biogas generator to produce fuel.

Effects of environmental change 4.7.2.4

- Environmental changes affect the distribution of species in an ecosystem.
- These changes may be seasonal, geographic, or caused by human interaction.

Change	Explanation	Example
Temperature	Enzymes have an optimum temperature at which they function.	Seasonal: seasonal decreases in temperature can cause migrations, e.g. towards winter, birds, such as swallows, migrate south from Northern Europe toward hotter temperatures.
Availability of water	No life can exist without water.	Geographic: in deserts, cacti and camels have adapted to survive with minimal water, and most life and green plants are found surrounding oases (where water rises from underground sources). The distribution of algal species also varies depending on the tide.
Composition of atmospheric gases	Combustion of fossil fuels release gases that can be toxic to organisms (e.g. oxides of carbon, sulfur and nitrogen).	Human interaction: most lichens will only grow in high numbers in clear air as they are sensitive to air pollution. The distribution of species can be a useful bioindicator of air pollution.

Biodiversity 4.7.3.1

- Biodiversity is the variety of all the different species of organisms on earth, or within an ecosystem.
- A great biodiversity ensures the stability of ecosystems by reducing the dependence of one species on another for:
  - Food
  - Shelter
  - Maintenance of the physical environment
- The future of the human species on Earth relies on us maintaining a good level of biodiversity.
- Many human activities are reducing biodiversity (e.g. deforestation) and only recently have measures been taken to try to stop this reduction.

Waste management 4.7.3.2

- Increasingly more resources are being used and more waste is being produced due to:
  - Rapid growth in the human population
  - An increase in the standard of living
- Unless waste and chemical materials are properly handled, more pollution will be caused.
- Pollution kills plants and animals, which can reduce biodiversity.
- Pollution can occur:
  - In water – from sewage, fertiliser, or toxic chemicals
  - In air – from smoke and acidic gases
  - On land – from landfill and toxic chemicals

Land use 4.7.3.3

- Humans reduce the amount of land available for other animals and plants by building, quarrying, farming, and dumping waste.
- The destruction of peat bogs and other areas of peat may occur to produce garden compost:
  - Peat is made up of partially decayed vegetation.
  - Destruction reduces the area of this habitat and the variety of different species living there (biodiversity).
  - The decay or burning of the peat releases carbon dioxide into the atmosphere.

Deforestation 4.7.3.4

- Large-scale deforestation in tropical areas has occurred to:
  - Provide land for cattle and rice fields.
  - Grow crops for biofuels.
- Environmental implications of deforestation:
  - Increase in carbon dioxide in the atmosphere as there are fewer trees to take in carbon dioxide for photosynthesis.
  - Burning of trees increases atmospheric carbon dioxide.
  - Reduces biodiversity as it destroys species of tree and removes habitat for several species of animals.
  - Causes drier climates as there is less transpiration by trees, resulting in drier soils, fewer roots, and greater risk of erosion and landslides.

Maintaining biodiversity 4.7.3.6

- Negative effects of humans on ecosystems and biodiversity:
  - Deforestation increases global warming and destroys species' habitats
  - Burning fossil fuels increases global warming
  - Industrial processes pollute air and habitats with waste chemicals
  - Build-up of plastic rubbish in the oceans
  - Overfishing, which damages wild food chains
  - Oil spills can kill aquatic organisms and species, such as sea birds, sea otters and seals
- Scientists and concerned citizens have put in place programmes to reduce the negative effects of humans on ecosystems and biodiversity:
  - Breeding programmes for endangered species to promote reproduction and safeguard the widest possible gene pool to increase the chances of survival of the offspring
  - Protection and regeneration of rare habitats, such as rainforests
  - Reintroduction of field margins and hedgerows in agricultural areas where farmers grow only one type of crop, providing habitats for wild species
  - Reduction of deforestation and carbon dioxide emissions by some governments
  - Recycling resources rather than dumping waste in landfills
  - Quotas on fishing

Trophic levels 4.7.4.1

- A trophic level is a level in a food chain.
- Trophic levels can be represented by numbers according to how far an organism is along the food chain.

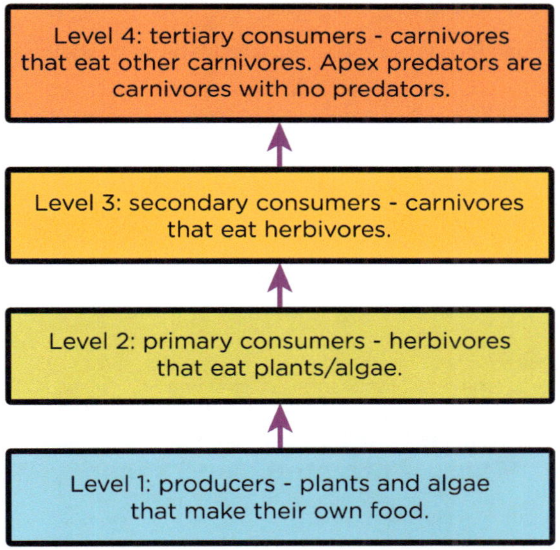

- Decomposers include bacteria, fungi and worms.
  - They break down dead plant and animal matter by secreting enzymes into the environment.
  - Small soluble food molecules then diffuse into the microorganism.
  - This also releases mineral ions and nutrients that plants can absorb from the soil.

Pyramids of biomass 4.7.4.2

- Biomass is the mass of any living or recently dead organism in grams or kilograms.
- Organisms can gain energy from consuming biomass and turn this energy into their body tissue (their own biomass).
- Dead organisms are first dried in an oven before biomass is recorded as different organisms contain different amounts of water.
- Pyramids of biomass can be constructed to represent the relative amount of biomass in each level of a food chain.
- Trophic level 1 is at the bottom of the pyramid.

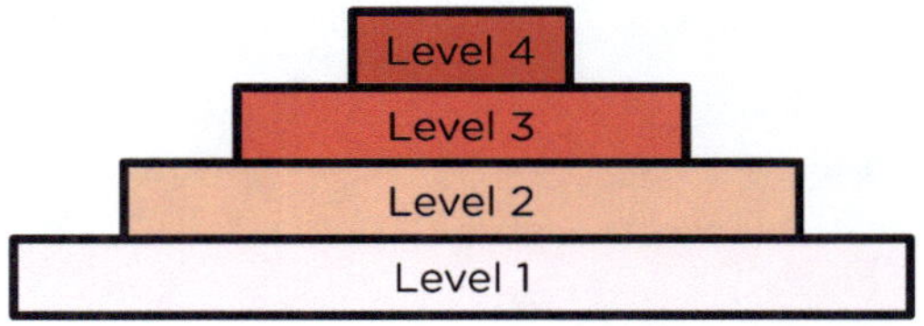

Global warming 4.7.3.5

- Global warming is the increase in the average temperature of the Earth.
- Levels of carbon dioxide and methane (greenhouse gases) in the atmosphere are increasing and contribute to global warming by trapping more heat.
- The increased emission of greenhouse gases in recent years is due to human activity, e.g. fossil fuel combustion.
- Biological consequences of global warming:
  - Glaciers are melting in the arctic, causing sea levels to rise and a loss of coastal regions and some islands.
  - Loss of suitable habitats for species, causing decreased biodiversity and decreased food security for humans.
  - Extreme weather conditions, e.g. flash floods and droughts.
  - Species are migrating as current conditions are no longer suitable for them.

Transfer of biomass 4.7.4.3

- A pyramid of biomass is largest at the bottom and decreases as we go up the levels as biomass is lost between the different trophic levels.
  - Not all ingested material is absorbed, some is egested as faeces.
  - A lot of absorbed material is lost as waste, such as carbon dioxide and water in respiration and water and urea in urine.
  - Large amounts of glucose are used in respiration.
- $Efficiency\ of\ biomass\ transfers = \frac{biomass\ in\ higher\ trophic\ level}{biomass\ in\ lower\ trophic\ level} \times 100\%$
- Producers transfer about 1% of the incident energy from light (from the sun) for photosynthesis.
- Only approximately 10% of the biomass from each trophic level is transferred to the level above it.
- As biomass and energy are lost at each level up the food chain, often the number of organisms decreases from one trophic level to the next.
- However, if level 2 was larger than level 1, then the herbivores may eat all of the plants, affecting the food chain.

Sustainable fisheries 4.7.5.3

- Fish stocks in the oceans are declining.
- It is important to maintain fish stocks at a level where breeding continues, or certain species may disappear in some areas.
- Introducing fishing quotas and regulating net sizes play important roles in the conservation of fish stocks at a sustainable level.
- Preventing overfishing promotes the recovery of fish stocks.

Farming techniques 4.7.5.2

- The efficiency of food production can be improved by restricting energy transfer from food animals to the environment.
- This can be done through intensive farming to maximise yields by reducing energy use and biomass loss:
  - Limiting movement by having animals packed together in small pens.
  - Controlling the temperature of their surroundings.
  - Some people have ethical objections to some intensive farming methods, for example restricting movement may affect an animal's quality of life.
- Some animals are fed high-protein foods to increase growth.
- Crop rotation can be done, which may provide less encouragement for pests and be less damaging to soil,

Factors affecting food security 4.7.5.1

- Food security is having enough food to feed a population.
- Sustainable methods must be found to feed all people on Earth.
- Biological factors that are threatening food security include:
  - The increasing birth rate in some countries.
  - Changing diets in developed countries means scarce food resources are transported around the world.
  - New pests and pathogens that affect farming.
  - Environmental changes that affect food production, such as widespread famine occurring in some countries if rains fail.
  - The cost of agricultural inputs.
  - Conflicts that have arisen in some parts of the world that affect the availability of water or food.

Biotechnology 4.7.5.4

- Possible biotechnical and agricultural solutions to the demands of the growing human population:

Demand	Solution
Meat substitute for vegetarians	• Modern biotechnology techniques enable large quantities of microorganisms to be cultured for food. • The fungus *Fusarium* is used to produce mycoprotein, a protein-rich food suitable for vegetarians. • The fungus is grown on glucose syrup in aerobic conditions, and the biomass is harvested and purified.
Insulin for diabetics	• Initially, purified pig insulin was used but some people have allergic reactions to it. • Now a genetically modified bacterium produces human insulin, which can be harvested and purified to treat people with diabetes.
More food or food with improved nutritional value	Genetically modified crops, e.g. golden rice, which reduces the chance of vitamin A deficiency.

Contents - Chemistry

SNAPREVISE

Atoms, elements, and compounds 4.1.1.1

- All substances are made of **atoms**. An atom is the smallest part of an **element** that can exist.
- Atoms of each element are represented by a **chemical symbol**, such as O for an atom of oxygen.
- There are a little over one hundred different elements, which are displayed in the **periodic table**.
- **Compounds** are formed from two or more elements.

Mass and isotopes 4.1.1.5-6

- The **atomic number** is the number of protons in an atom.
  - All atoms of the same element have the same number of protons.
  - In a neutral atom, the atomic number also equals the number of electrons.
- The **mass number** is the sum of the protons and neutrons in the nucleus of an atom.
  - Almost all of the mass of an atom is in the nucleus.
  - $\textit{Mass number} - \textit{atomic number} = \textit{number of neutrons}$
  - For example, atoms of sodium (Na) contain 11 protons, 12 neutrons and 11 electrons.

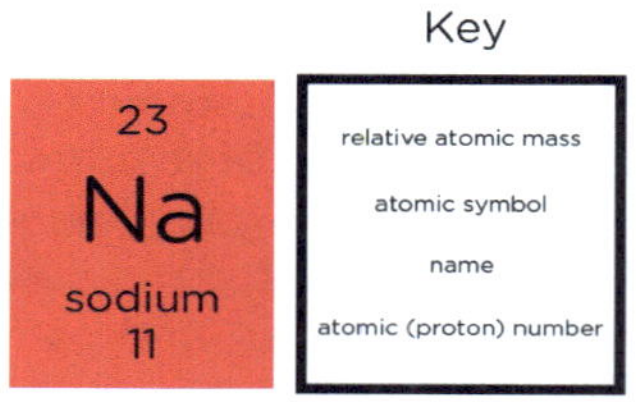

- **Isotopes** of an element are atoms of that element with different numbers of neutrons but the same number of protons.
- Isotopes of an element have the same atomic number but a different mass number.
- The **relative atomic mass**, A_r, of an element is the weighted average mass of all the isotopes of an element compared to 1/12th of the mass of a carbon-12 atom.
  - $A_r = \frac{[\textit{Sum of (Mass of each isotope} \times \textit{Abundance of isotope)}]}{100}$

Calculate the relative atomic mass of chlorine	
Chlorine contains 75% atoms with mass 35, and 25% of atoms with mass 37	
Step	**Example**
Substitute the values into the formula and solve.	$\frac{[(75 \times 35) + (25 \times 37)]}{100} = \frac{3550}{100} = 35.5$

Electrons and ions 4.1.1.7

- Electrons occupy **energy levels**, or **shells**, and move around the nucleus of an atom.
- Electrons occupy the **lowest** available energy levels.
  - The lowest energy levels are the innermost shells.
  - The lowest energy level, or the first shell, holds 2 electrons.
  - Consecutive shells hold up to 8 electrons.
- **Electronic structures** can be represented by diagrams or numbers. For example, the electronic structure of a sodium atom can be shown as 2,8,1.

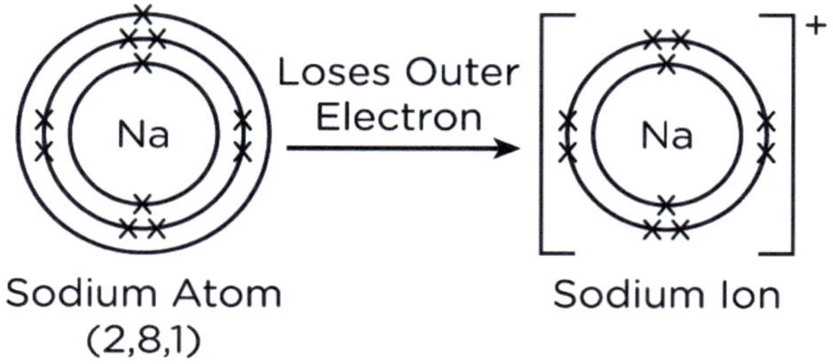

- **Ions** are particles with an electric charge because they do not contain the same number of protons and electrons.
  - **Positive ions** (such as Na^+, where one electron has been lost from the neutral atom) have more protons than electrons.
  - **Negative ions** (such as Cl^-, where one electron has been added to the neutral atom) have more electrons than protons.
  - Atoms react to form ions by **losing** or **gaining electrons**.
- **Simple ions** made from single atoms have a full outer shell as this is the most **stable** arrangement. They have the same electron structure as the highly stable **noble gases**.
- The atoms of more reactive elements readily gain or lose electrons to achieve a full outer shell.
- The **hydrogen ion** (H^+) has no electrons at all so has special properties. H^+ is the only simple ion that does not have the electron structure of a noble gas.

The structure of the atom 4.1.1.4

- Atoms are **very small** with a radius of about 0.1 nm, and the radius of the nucleus is less than 1/10,000 of that of the atom.
- The size of the nucleus relative to an atom is equivalent to the size of a pea relative to a football pitch.
- Atoms are made up of **subatomic particles**: protons, neutrons and electrons.
- Atoms have **no overall electrical charge** as the number of protons and electrons is the same.

	Proton	Neutron	Electron
Relative mass	1	1	Very small
Relative charge	+1	0	-1

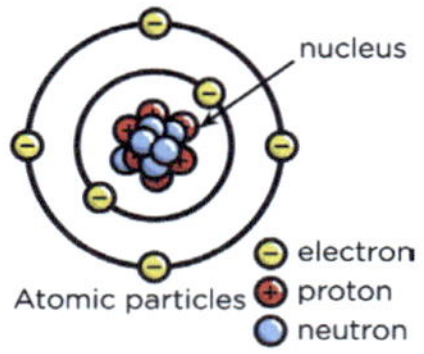

The periodic table 4.1.2.1

- Elements are arranged in order of atomic (proton) number in the periodic table.
- The table is called a periodic table because similar properties occur at regular intervals.
- Elements with **similar properties** are in columns known as **groups**.
  - Elements in the same group have the same number of electrons in their outer shell, giving them similar chemical properties.
  - The group number of an element is the number of outer electrons it has.
- The rows of the periodic table are called **periods**.
  - Elements across a period have an increasing number of electrons.
  - The period number of an element is the number of energy levels it has occupied with electrons.

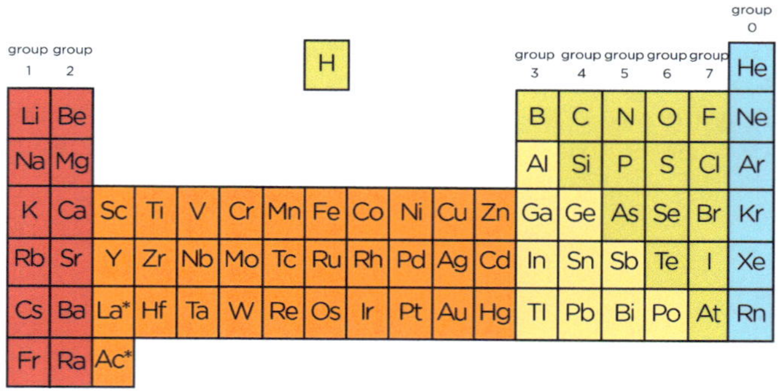

SNAPREVISE

Reactions 4.1.1.1

- **Compounds** are formed by **chemical reactions**, chemically combining two or more elements of fixed proportions.
- Compounds can only be separated into elements by chemical reactions.
- Compounds can be represented by **formulae**, using the **symbols** of the atoms from which they were formed.
- Chemical reactions always involve the formation of one or more new substances and often involve a detectable **energy change**.
- Chemical reactions are represented by **word equations** or **balanced symbol equations** with symbols and formulae:
  - $Oxygen + Hydrogen \rightarrow Water$
  - $\boldsymbol{O_2 + H_2 \rightarrow H_2O}$

Balanced equations 4.3.1.1

- The law of **conservation of mass** states that no atoms are lost or made during a chemical reaction so the mass of the products equals the mass of the reactants.
- A **balanced equation** balances the numbers of atoms of each element on both sides of the reaction equation.

Balancing equations	
$Oxygen + Hydrogen \rightarrow Water$	
Step	**Example**
Substitute the word equation for the molecular formula, where subscript is used to represent the numbers of atoms of an element.	$O_2 + H_2 \rightarrow H_2O$
Use multipliers, or coefficients, to balance the number of atoms.	$O_2 + 2H_2 \rightarrow 2H_2O$

Development of the periodic table 4.1.2.2

- Before the discovery of subatomic particles, scientists classified elements by arranging them in order of **atomic weights**.
- Early periodic tables were incomplete with some elements in inappropriate groups if the strict order of atomic weights was followed, though it was known that elemental properties seemed to repeat periodically.
- **Mendeleev** devised the basis for the modern periodic table by **predicting** the properties of **undiscovered elements**, leaving gaps for them, and not following strict weight order.
- Elements with properties predicted by Mendeleev were discovered and filled the gaps.
- We now know he correctly predicted an order based on atomic number rather than weight, as elements are made of a mixture of isotopes.

History of the atomic model 4.1.1.3

- Before the discovery of the electron, atoms were thought to be tiny spheres that could not be divided.
- **Plum-pudding model** – suggested the atom is a ball of positive charge with negative electrons embedded in it.
- **Nuclear model** - alpha particle scattering showed positive particles were deflected or reflected from the atom's core.
  - Suggests the mass of an atom was concentrated at the centre (nucleus) and the nucleus was positively charged as like charges repel.
  - Niels Bohr suggested that electrons orbit the nucleus at specific distances. The theoretical calculations of Bohr agreed with experimental observations.
  - Further experiments showed individual particles with equal positive charge in the nucleus, protons.
  - James Chadwick discovered uncharged neutrons in the nucleus. This was about 20 years after the nucleus became an accepted scientific idea.
- New experimental evidence may lead to a scientific model being changed or replaced.

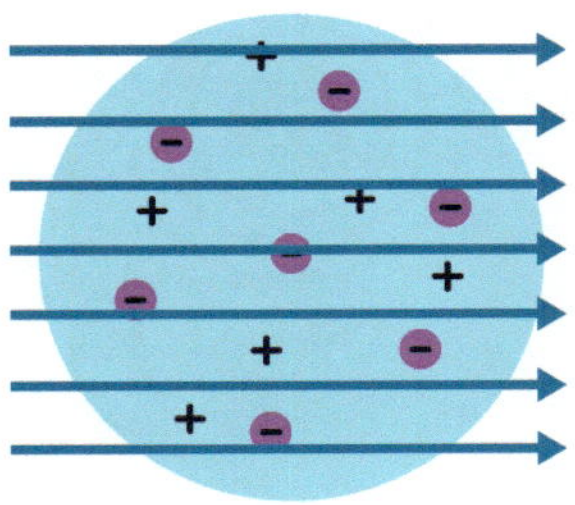

Expected result for plum-pudding model

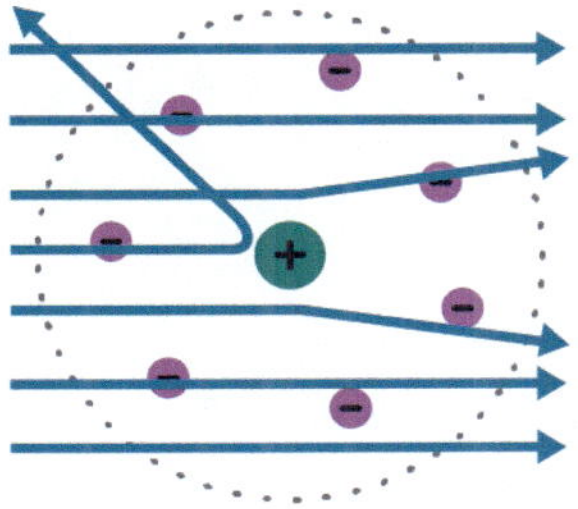

Alpha-particle scattering experiments support a nuclear model

Separating mixtures 4.1.1.2

- **Mixtures** consist of two or more elements or compounds mixed together that are **not chemically combined**.
  - The **chemical properties** of each substance in the mixture are unchanged.
  - Mixtures can be **separated** by **physical processes**.
  - These physical processes do not involve chemical reactions and no new substances are made.

Filtration separates insoluble solids from a liquid, such as sand from water.

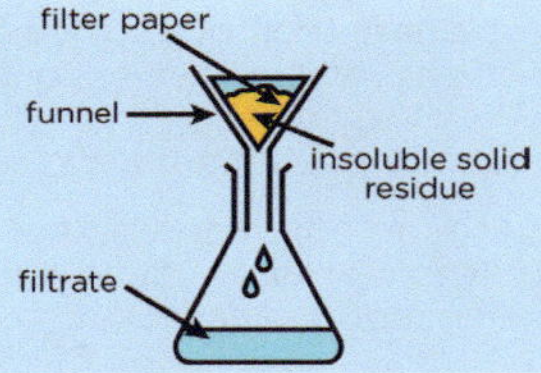

Crystallisation separates dissolved solids from a solvent, such as copper sulfate from water.

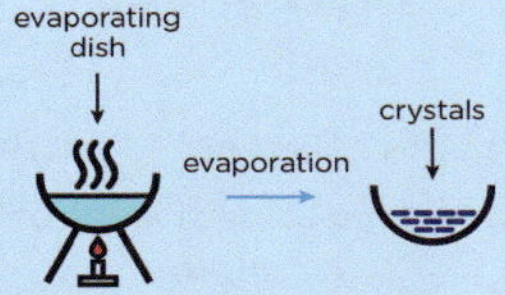

Simple distillation separates a vaporised solvent from a solution and condenses it for collection, such as water from salty seawater.

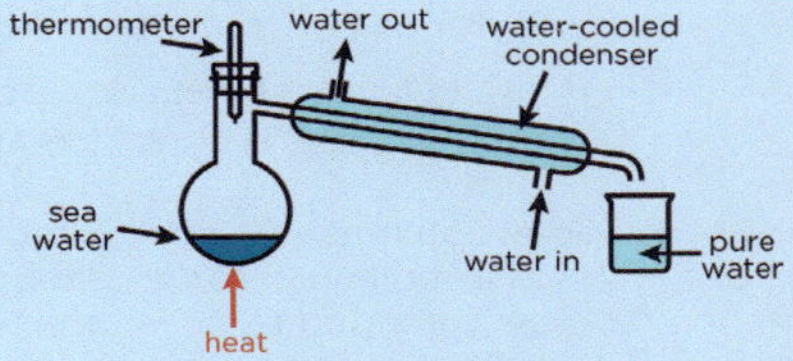

Fractional distillation separates miscible liquids by their different boiling points, such as water and ethanol. Immiscible liquids can just be separated using a separating funnel with a tap.

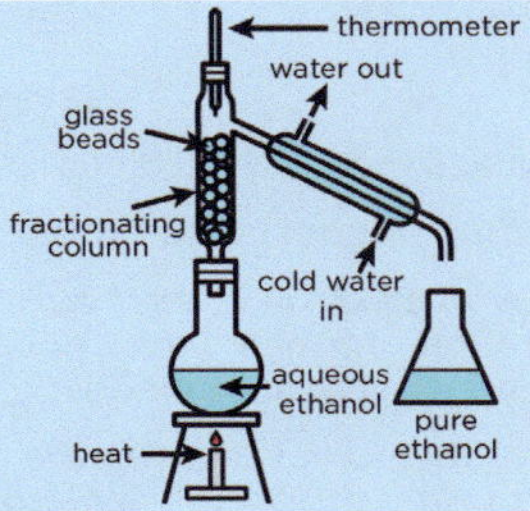

Chromatography separates mixtures of substances dissolved in solvent, such as different dyes in pen ink.

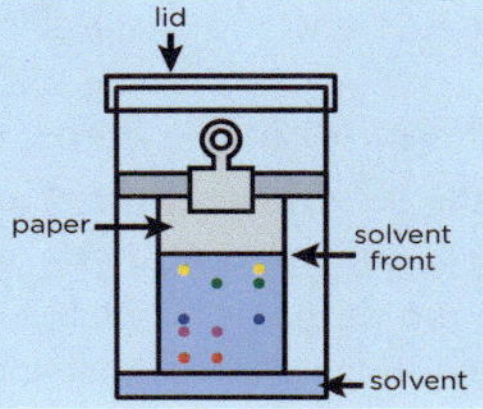

Properties of groups

Metals and non-metals 4.1.2.3

- Elements that react to form positive ions are **metals**, such as magnesium forming Mg^{2+} ions.
- Elements that do not form positive ions are non-metals.
- Metals are found to the left and towards the bottom of the periodic table while **non-metals** are found towards the right and top.
  - Being in lower group numbers, metals have fewer electrons in their outer shell and react by losing electrons to achieve a full outer shell.
  - Being in higher group numbers, non-metals have more electrons in their outer shell and often react by gaining electrons to achieve a full outer shell.
- The majority of elements are metals.
- Compared to non-metals, metals generally have higher melting and boiling points, are denser, malleable, shiny when polished, and can conduct electricity.

Group 0 4.1.2.4

- Non-metals called **noble gases,** e.g. argon (Ar) gas.
- **Colourless gases** with **low boiling points**.
- **Very unreactive** due to **stable electron structures** with **full outer shells**, so do not easily form molecules or ions.
  - Helium has 2 electrons in its outer shell
  - All other noble gases have 8 electrons in their outer shell.
- **Boiling points increase** going down the group. As the atoms get larger, the intermolecular forces between them grow stronger so more energy is needed to overcome these forces.

Group 1 4.1.2.5

- **Soft alkali metals**, e.g. lithium (Li) and sodium (Na).
- **Melting point decreases** down the group.
- All have **1 electron** in their outer shell so are **highly reactive** with non-metals, forming white powders containing **+1 ions** such as Na^+ and K^+, with stable noble gas-like electron structures.
- **Reactivity increases** down the group, so the reactions get more vigorous. As the atoms get larger, the force of attraction between the nucleus and the outer electron decreases, so it is more easily lost.
- ***Metal + chlorine → metal chloride***
- ***Metal + oxygen → metal oxide***
- ***Metal + water → metal hydroxide + hydrogen***
  - Lithium fizzes as it reacts with water.
  - Sodium melts into a ball and fizzes more rapidly.
  - Potassium fizzes the most and sets on fire with a lilac flame.

Group 7 4.1.2.6

- Non-metals called the **halogens**, e.g. chlorine (Cl), typically form **diatomic molecules** such as Cl_2.
- **Melting and boiling points increase** down the group as the relative molecular mass increases, which causes stronger intermolecular forces between halogen molecules.
- All have **7 electrons** in their outer shell, so they have similar reactions, are **reactive** and must gain 1 electron to form stable **-1 ions.**
- **Reactivity decreases** down the group. As the force of attraction between the nucleus and outer electrons decreases, it is harder to attract the extra electron.
- More reactive halogens **displace** less reactive ones from a halide compound. For example, ***chlorine + sodium bromide → sodium chloride + bromine***.
- Halogens react with metals to form **ionic compounds**.
- Halogens react with non-metals to form **covalent molecules**.

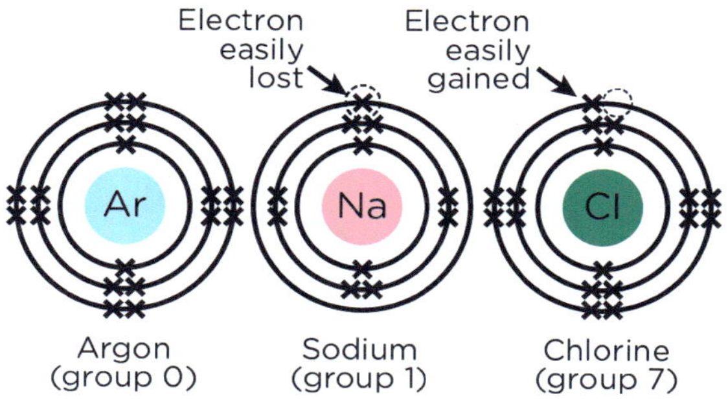

Properties of transition metals 4.1.3.2

- Many form **positive ions** with **different charges**. For example, iron can form 2+ ions or 3+ ions depending on the compound.
- Form **coloured compounds**, such as red copper oxide.
- Are useful as **catalysts** (e.g. nickel catalyst used to make margarine).
- **Thermal** and **electrical conductors** (e.g. copper used in electrical wires).
- **Shiny** when polished.
- Examples include chromium (Cr), manganese (Mn), iron (Fe), cobalt (Co), nickel (Ni) and copper (Cu).

States of matter 4.2.2.1-2

- Three states – **solid (s)**, **liquid (l)** and **gas (g)**.
  - Melting (solid to liquid) and freezing (liquid to solid) take place at the **melting point**.
  - Boiling (liquid to gas) and condensing (gas to liquid) take place at the **boiling point**.
- Can be represented by a **simple 2D model**.
  - **Particles** are represented by small solid spheres.
  - Particle theory can explain changes of state.

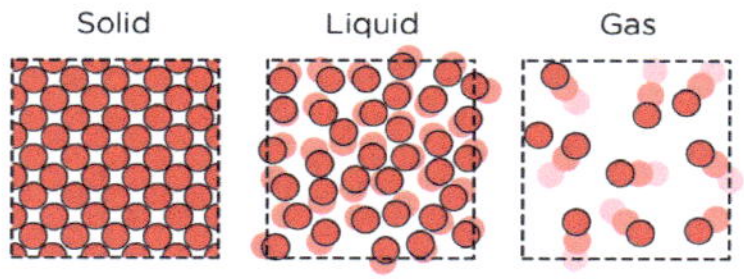

- The amount of **energy** needed to change state from solid to liquid and from liquid to gas depends on the **strength of the forces** between the particles.
  - The nature of the particles depends on the type of bonding between them and the structure of the substance.
  - The stronger the forces between particles, the higher the substance's melting and boiling point.
- **Limitations** of this model include that all the particles are represented as solid inelastic spheres and there are no forces shown between them.
- **Atoms** themselves do not have the bulk properties of materials.
- In chemical equations, **aqueous solutions** are signified with **(aq)**.

Comparing transition metals 4.1.3.1

- Compared to group 1 metals, the **transition metals**:
  - Have **higher melting points** (except mercury).
  - Have **higher densities**.
  - Are **stronger** and **harder**.
  - Have **lower reactivity** (e.g. with oxygen, water and halogens).

group 1	group 2											group 3	group 4	group 5	group 6	group 7	group 0
							H										He
Li	Be											B	C	N	O	F	Ne
Na	Mg											Al	Si	P	S	Cl	Ar
K	Ca	Sc	Ti	V	Cr	Mn	Fe	Co	Ni	Cu	Zn	Ga	Ge	As	Se	Br	Kr
Rb	Sr	Y	Zr	Nb	Mo	Tc	Ru	Rh	Pd	Ag	Cd	In	Sn	Sb	Te	I	Xe
Cs	Ba	La*	Hf	Ta	W	Re	Os	Ir	Pt	Au	Hg	Tl	Pb	Bi	Po	At	Rn
Fr	Ra	Ac*															

Properties of small molecules 4.2.2.4

- **Weak intermolecular forces** between the molecules are easy to overcome to cause a change in state. No covalent bonds are broken.
- **Low melting and boiling points**, so many are gases and liquids at room temperature.
- Larger molecules have stronger intermolecular forces and higher melting and boiling points.

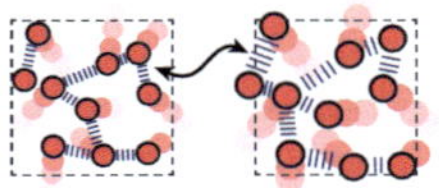

weak intermolecular forces are stronger for larger molecules

- Small molecules have no overall electric charge and do not conduct electricity.

Types of bonding 4.2.1.1

- Bonding between atoms depends on the **transfer** or **sharing** of **electrons**, which involves **electrostatic forces**.
- There are 3 types of strong chemical bonds:

Ionic bonding	Bonding that occurs in compounds formed from metals combined with non-metals.
Covalent bonding	Bonding that occurs in most non-metal elements and compounds.
Metallic bonding	Bonding that occurs in metallic elements and alloys, which share delocalised electrons.

Covalent bonding 4.2.1.4

- Atoms of non-metal elements share **pairs of electrons** in **covalent bonds,** which are very **strong**.
- Covalent bonds consist of the strong electrostatic forces of attraction between the **positive nuclei** of the atoms in the molecule and the shared pair of electrons between them.
- Covalently bonded substances may consist of small molecules, such as H_2O (water), large molecules, such as polymers, or giant covalent structures, such as diamond and silicon dioxide.
- Covalent structures, such as ammonia, can be represented in several forms:

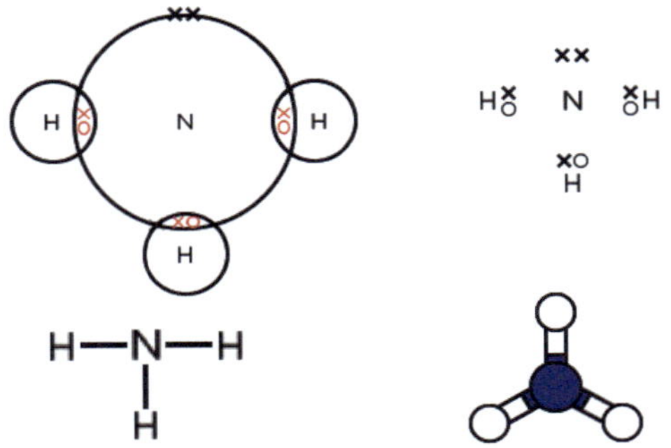

Ionic bonding 4.2.1.2

- Ionic compounds are formed from **electron transfer** from the outer shell of a metal to a non-metal.
- The ions produced by metals in Groups 1 and 2 and by non-metals in Groups 6 and 7 have the electronic structure of a noble gas (Group 0).
- For example, sodium forms sodium ions (Na^+) by donating an electron to chlorine, forming chloride ions (Cl^-).
  - These ions combine to form the ionic compound NaCl, sodium chloride, in a 1:1 **ratio**.
  - Electron transfer can be represented by a **dot and cross diagram**.
- The charge on the ions produced relates to the **group number** of the element.
  - Na is in group 1, so it has 1 outer electron. This electron is lost to achieve a full outer shell and forms +1 ions
  - Cl is in group 7, so it has 7 outer electrons. One electron is gained to achieve a full outer shell and forms -1 ions.

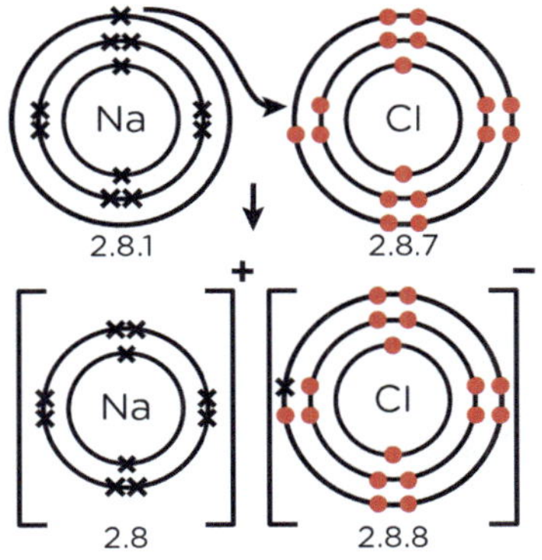

Ionic equations 4.1.1.1

- **Ionic equations** balance the atoms and the overall electric charges of the ions of the reactants and the products, then omit the unchanged **spectator ions**.

Writing an ionic equation	
Calcium chloride (aq) + Sodium carbonate (aq) → Calcium carbonate (s) + Sodium chloride (aq)	
Step	**Example**
Balance the atoms and the overall electric charges of the ions of the reactants and the products.	$Ca^{2+}(aq) + 2Cl^-(aq) + + 2Na^+(aq) + CO_3^{2-}(aq) \rightarrow CaCo^3(s) + 2Na^+(aq) + + 2Cl^-(aq)$
Remove the spectator ions that do not take part in the reaction.	$Ca^{2+}(aq) + CO_3^{2-}(aq) \rightarrow CaCo^3(s)$

Giant ionic structures 4.2.1.3, 4.2.2.3

- Ionic compounds form **giant ionic lattices** containing many positive and negative ions in a **regular structure** throughout the substance**.**
- **Oppositely charged ions** attract, so in ionic compounds, there are **strong electrostatic forces** of attraction between the negative ions and the positive ions acting in all directions in the lattice (ionic bonding).
- Ionic substances have **high melting** and **boiling points**, and all are **solids** at room temperature because of the large amounts of energy needed to break the many strong bonds.
- The ions cannot move when solid, but when **molten** or dissolved in water, they can move and carry charge as **electrical conductors**.
- The **empirical formula** is the simplest ratio of the ions in a compound. For example, Na^+ and Cl^- bind in a **1:1 ratio** giving sodium chloride the empirical formula NaCl.
- Giant ionic lattices can be displayed as a:
  - Dot and cross diagram (does not show arrangement in space).
  - 2D (does not show other layers) or 3D diagram
  - 3D or ball-and-stick diagram (gives no information about the electron structures).

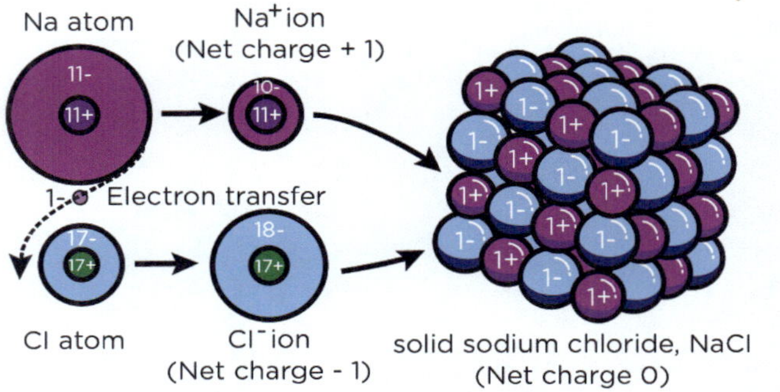

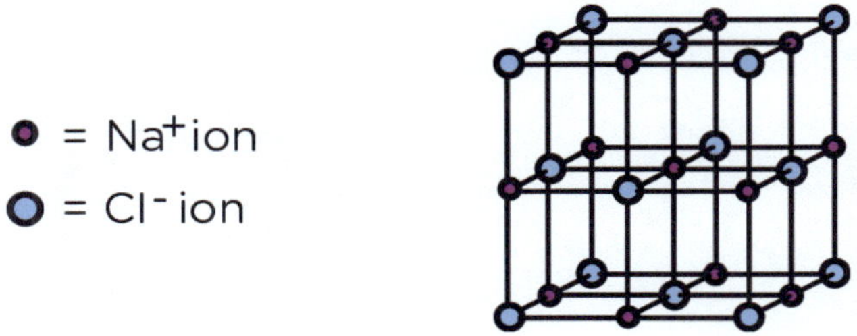

Giant covalent structures and fullerenes 4.2.2.6 4.2.3.1-3

- Some non-metals, such as **carbon (C)**, form **giant covalent structures**, where each atom forms **strong covalent bonds** with several other atoms.
- Other substances, such as silicon, can form giant covalent structures such as silicon dioxide (silica).
- These strong bonds cause **very high melting and boiling points**.

Diamond: each C atom forms four covalent bonds with other C atoms, so diamond is very hard, has a very high melting point and does not conduct electricity (as all outer electrons are involved in bonding).

Graphite: each C atom forms three covalent bonds with three other C atoms, forming layers of hexagonal rings that can slide over each other. One outer electron from each atom is delocalised as it is not involved in bonding, meaning graphite can conduct electricity. A single layer is called **graphene** and is useful in electronics and composites.

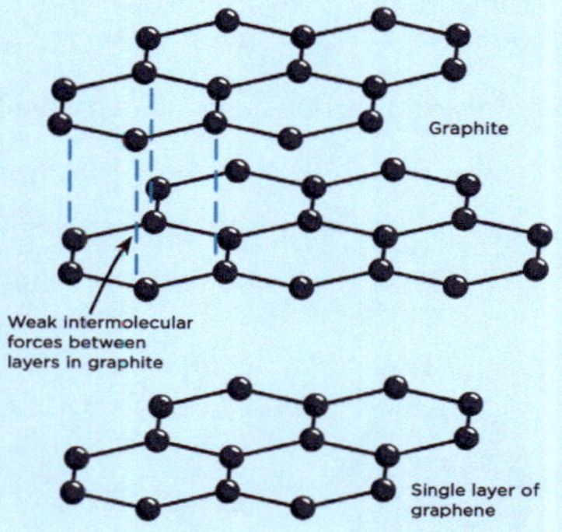

Fullerenes: non-giant, simple molecules made up of C atoms that form a hollow shape. Based on hexagonal rings but may also contain rings of five or seven atoms. May be used as catalysts, lubricants, or for carrying drugs.

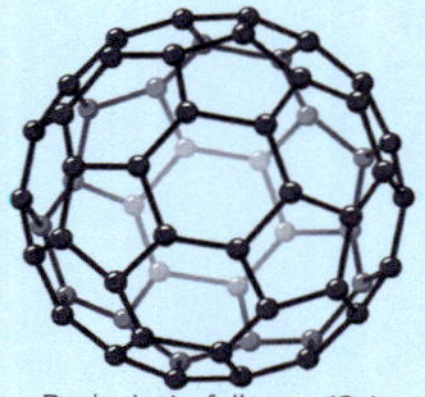
Buckminsterfullerene (C_{60})

Carbon nanotubes: hollow, cylindrical fullerenes with very high length to diameter ratios. High tensile strength and good conductivity. Useful for nanotechnology, electronics, and materials.

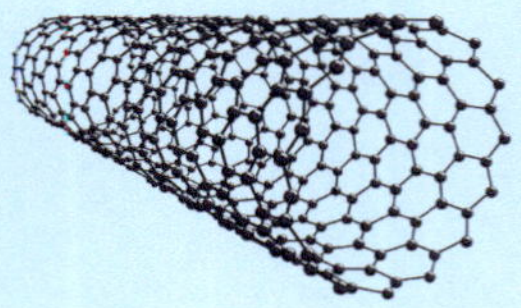

Metallic bonding 4.2.1.5, 4.2.2.7-8

- Metals form **giant metallic structures** of positively charged **ions** arranged in a regular pattern, which **share delocalised electrons**.
  - The electrons in the outer shells of metal atoms can freely move throughout the whole structure, forming a 'sea' of electrons.
  - This gives rise to **strong** metallic bonds: the electrostatic forces of attraction between the positive ions and delocalised electrons.
- **Pure metal** atoms are arranged in **layers**, allowing them to be cut, bent and shaped; however, they are too soft for most uses.
- Mixing pure metals makes **alloys**, containing differently sized atoms to **distort** the layers and make them harder.
- Metals **conduct electricity** due to delocalised electrons.
- Metals are good **heat conductors** as energy is transferred by the delocalised electrons.
- Most metals have high melting and boiling points due to their strong metallic bonds.

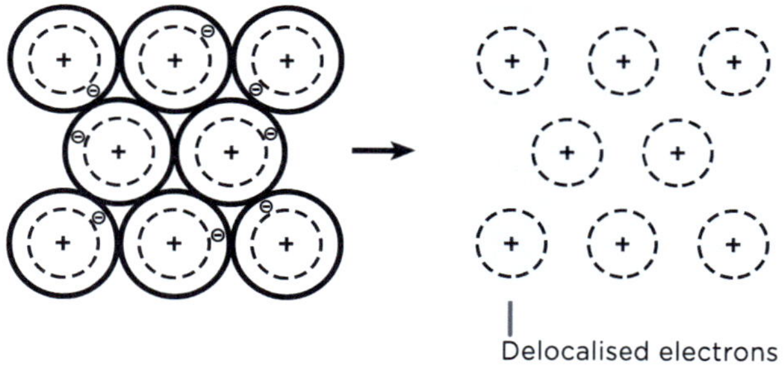

Polymers 4.2.2.5

- **Long-chain molecules** made from **repeating units** of smaller molecules joined together by **strong covalent bonding**.
- Polymers often contain hundreds or thousands of atoms.
- The **intermolecular forces** between different polymer chains are relatively strong, so they are **solid at room temperature**.
- **Plastics** are a type of polymer, including polyethene and PVC.

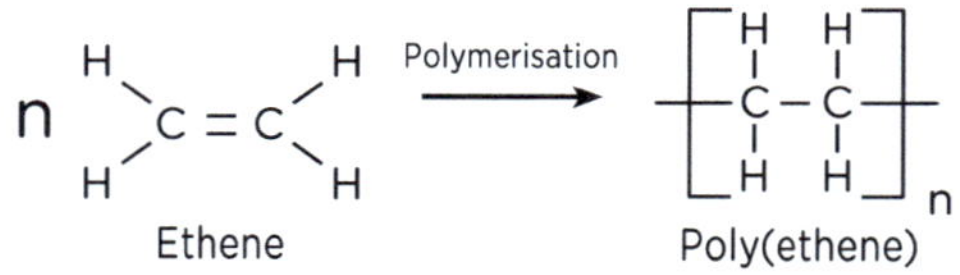

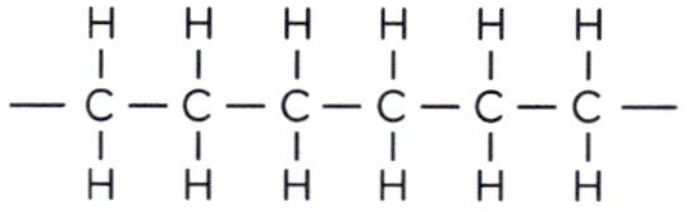

Bulk and surface properties 4.2.4.1

- **Nanoparticles** are structures 1-100 nm in size, of the order of a few hundred atoms.
  - **Atoms and molecules**: 0.05-1nm.
  - **Nanoparticles**: 1-100nm.
  - **Fine particles** such as soot ($PM_{2.5}$): 100-2,500nm.
  - **Coarse particles** such as dust (PM_{10}): 2500-10,000nm.
- As the side of a cube decreases by a factor of 10, the **surface area to volume ratio increases** by a factor of 10.

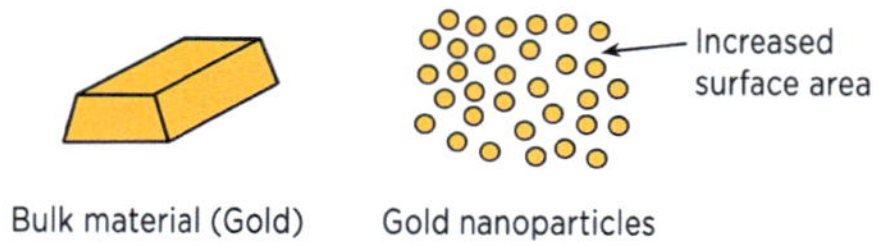

Uses of nanoparticles 4.2.4.2

- Applications in medicine, electronics, cosmetics, sun creams, as deodorants and as catalysts.
  - Higher fraction of the atoms available at the surface than in bulk form, so may be effective in smaller quantities and have different properties.
  - Could be harmful if they can penetrate living cells.

Reduction and quantitative chemistry

Reduction in terms of oxygen 4.4.1.4

- **Reduction** is the **loss of oxygen**.
- **Oxidation** is the **gain of oxygen**.

Reduction in terms of electrons 4.4.1.4

- **Reduction** is the **gain of electrons**.
- **Oxidation** is the **loss of electrons**.
  - Symbol equation: $Mg(s) + CuSO_4(aq) \rightarrow MgSO_4(aq) + Cu(s)$
  - Ionic equation: $Mg(s) + Cu^{2+}(aq) \rightarrow Mg^{2+}(aq) + Cu(s)$
  - Half equation: $\boldsymbol{Cu^{2+} + 2e^- \rightarrow Cu}$ (reduction)

    $\boldsymbol{Mg \rightarrow Mg^{2+} + 2e^-}$ (oxidation)

Relative formula mass 4.3.1.2

- The **relative formula mass (M_r)** is the sum of the relative atomic masses of all atoms in the numbers shown in the formula:

Calculate the relative formula mass of sulfuric acid (H_2SO_4)	
Ar of H = 1, S = 32, O = 16	
Step	**Example**
Multiply the Ar of each element by the number of atoms of each element.	$\boldsymbol{H_2 = 1 \times 2 = 2}$ $\boldsymbol{S = 32}$ $\boldsymbol{O_4 = 16 \times 4 = 64}$
Add the sums together.	$\boldsymbol{H_2SO_4 = 98}$

- In a balanced equation, the sum of the Mr of reactants equals the sum of the Mr of the products.
- $\boldsymbol{Percentage\ by\ mass = \frac{Total\ mass\ of\ element}{Relative\ formula\ mass} \times 100\ \%}$

Mass changes in gas reactions 4.3.1.3

- Some reactions may appear to involve a change in mass, but this can usually be explained because a reactant or product is a gas, and its mass has not been taken into account.
  - For example, when a metal reacts with oxygen, the mass of the metal oxide produced is greater than the mass of the metal alone.
  - $2Cu(s) + O_2(g) \rightarrow 2CuO(s)$
- Gases can escape in **non-enclosed reactions**, leading to an observed loss of mass.
  - For example, in the thermal decomposition of metal carbonates, carbon dioxide is produced and escapes into the atmosphere.
  - $CuCO_3(s) \xrightarrow{heat} CuO(s) + CO_2(g)$

Uncertainty in measurements 4.3.1.4

- Results from measurements always have some **uncertainty**, often recorded after a measurement as a **± value**, representing the **range** about the mean within which the true value can be expected to lie.
- **Anomalous results** that are significantly different should be excluded.
- The **resolution** of a piece of equipment is the smallest change it can measure.
- For liquids, always record the value from the **meniscus**.

Calculating uncertainty in a mean value	
The volume of a gas produced in a reaction was measured five times. The results are 81, 76, 77, 95 and 79 cm[3].	
Step	**Example**
Exclude any anomalous values when calculating the mean.	The anomalous value of 95 is excluded. $\boldsymbol{\frac{81 + 76 + 77 + 79}{4} = 78.25}$
Quote the mean to the resolution of the equipment.	$\boldsymbol{78.25 = 78}$
Calculate the uncertainty based on the range around the mean.	The uncertainty is ± 3 cm[3] as the highest and lowest values are within ± 3 cm[3] of the mean. $\boldsymbol{= 78 \pm 3\ cm^3}$

Moles and Avogadro's constant 4.3.2.1

- Chemical amounts are measured in **moles (mol)**.
  - The mass of one mole of a substance in grams is numerically equal to its relative formula mass.
  - One mole of a substance contains the same number of the stated particles (atoms, molecules, ions, electrons, formulae and equations) as one mole of any other substance.
  - For example, in one mole of carbon (C), the number of atoms is the same number as the number of molecules in one mole of carbon dioxide (CO_2).
- **The Avogadro constant** is the number of particles in one mole of a given substance.
  - The value of the Avogadro constant is 6.02×10^{23} per mole.

Amount of substance in equations 4.3.2.2-3

- The balancing numbers in an equation can be calculated from the masses of reactants and products by converting them to moles and then converting the number of moles into a ratio in its simplest form.
- Balanced symbol equations show how many moles react.
  - $\boldsymbol{Mg + 2HCl \rightarrow MgCl_2 + H_2}$
  - This shows one mole of magnesium reacts with two moles of hydrochloric acid to produce one mole of magnesium chloride and one mole of hydrogen gas.

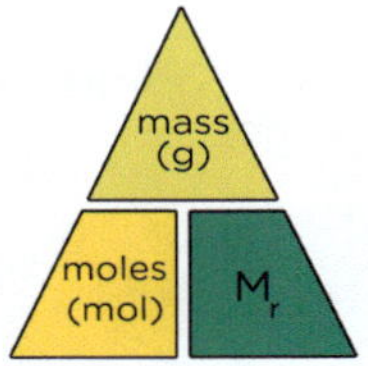

- Masses of reactants and products can be calculated from balanced symbol equations.

Calculate the amount of moles of water in 180g	
A_r of H = 1, O = 16	
Step	**Example**
Calculate the Mr of H_2O.	$\boldsymbol{H_2 = 1 \times 2 = 2}$ $\boldsymbol{O = 16}$ $\boldsymbol{H_2O = 18}$
Substitute the values into the formula.	$\boldsymbol{\frac{180}{18} = 10\ mol}$

Calculate the mass of sulfur dioxide that can be made from 16g of sulfur in this reaction	
$\boldsymbol{S_{(s)} + O_{2\,(g)} \rightarrow SO_{2\,(g)}}$ M_r of SO_2 = 64	
Step	**Example**
Calculate the moles of S.	$\boldsymbol{\frac{16}{32} = 0.5\ mol}$
Using the molar ratio, calculate the mass of SO_2 by substituting the values into the formula.	Molar ratio = 1:1:1 $\boldsymbol{64 \times 0.5 = 32g}$

Limiting reactants 4.3.2.4

- The reactant in a reaction that determines the amount of products that are formed.
- Any other reagents are in excess to ensure all of the limiting reactant is used up.
- E.g. In this equation, 2 moles of Mg react with each mole of O_2: $\boldsymbol{2Mg + O_2 \rightarrow 2MgO}$.
  - If 0.30 moles of Mg are reacted with 0.20 moles of O_2, then 0.30 moles of Mg can react with just 0.15 moles of O_2 to form 0.30 moles of MgO.
  - The other 0.05 moles of oxygen remain in excess and magnesium is the limiting reactant.

Concentration of Solutions 4.3.2.5, 4.3.4

- The **concentration** of a solution can be measured in **mass per given volume of solution** (grams per dm^3).
- The higher the mass per given volume of a solution, the **more concentrated** the solution.
- 1 dm^3 is the same volume as 1000 cm^3 or 1 litre.

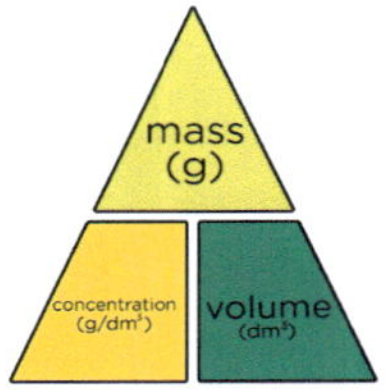

Calculating concentration using grams	
12g of the substance is dissolved in 200 cm^3	
Step	**Example**
Calculate the volume of the solution in dm^3.	$\frac{200}{1000} = 0.20\ dm^3$
Substitute the values into the formula.	$\frac{12}{0.20} = 60\ g/dm^3$

- Concentration can also be measured in **moles per given volume of solution** (moles per dm^3).
  - The amount in moles of solute or the mass in grams of solute in a given volume of solution can be calculated from its concentration in mol/dm3.
  - If the volumes of two solutions that react completely are known and the concentration of one solution is known, the concentration of the other solution can be calculated.

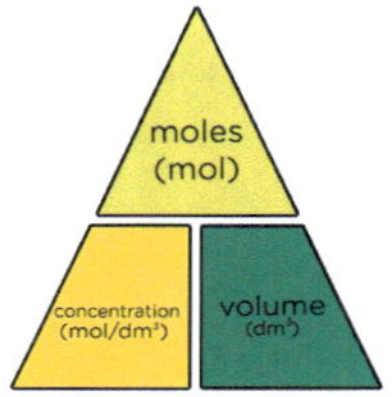

Calculating concentration using moles	
10 moles of the substance is dissolved in 4 dm^3	
Step	**Example**
Substitute the values into the formula.	$\frac{10}{4} = 2.5\ mol/dm^3$

What is the concentration of H_2SO_4 in 2 dm^3 of a solution?	
49g of H_2SO_4 is dissolved in 2 dm^3 of the solution	
Step	**Example**
Calculate the moles of H_2SO_4.	$\frac{mass}{M_r} = \frac{49}{98} = 0.5$
Substitute the values into the formula.	$\frac{0.5}{2} = 0.25\ mol/dm^3$

Percentage yield 4.3.3.1

- The amount of product obtained is called the **yield**.
- The higher the yield, the more **efficient** the reaction in industrial processes, reducing waste and increasing profits.
- Even though no atoms are gained or lost in a chemical reaction, it is not always possible to obtain the **maximum theoretical mass** of a product because:
  - The reaction does not go to **completion**, because it is **reversible**.
  - Some of the product is **lost** when it is separated from the reaction mixture.
  - The reactants may take part in other **undesirable reactions**, which are unexpected.
- $Percentage\ yield\,(\%) = \frac{Mass\ of\ product\ actually\ made}{Maximum\ theoretical\ mass\ of\ product} \times 100\%$

Atom economy 4.3.3.2

- A measure of the amount of starting materials that end up as useful products.
  - E.g. when ethene (C_2H_4) reacts with steam to make ethanol (C_2H_5OH), all of the reactant atoms end up in the desired product.
  - $C_2H_4 + H_2O \rightarrow C_2H_5OH$
  - This means the atom economy must be 100%.
- Reactions with high atom economy are more sustainable and better for economic purposes.
- $Percentage\ atom\ economy = \frac{M_r\ of\ desired\ product}{Total\ M_r\ of\ all\ reactants} \times 100\%$
- A particular **reaction pathway** may be chosen to maximise atom economy, yield, rate, equilibrium position and usefulness of by-products.

Volume of gas 4.3.5

- Varies with **temperature** and **pressure.**
  - Higher temperature = greater volume.
  - Greater pressure = smaller volume.
- Equal amounts in moles of all gases occupy the same volume under the same conditions of temperature and pressure.
  - **Volume** of **one mole** of **any gas** at **room temperature and pressure** (20°C and 1 atmosphere) is **24 dm^3**.
  - This is the same volume as **24 litres** or **24,000 cm^3**.
- Ratios in the balanced equation can be used to determine the volume of gaseous reactants and products from a given volume of gaseous reactant or product.

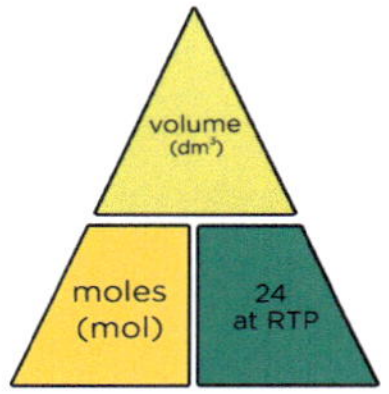

Calculating the volume of a gas	
10 moles of O_2	
Step	**Example**
Substitute the values into the formula.	$10 \times 24 = 240\ dm^3$

Calculating the moles of a gas	
48 dm^3 of CO_2	
Step	**Example**
Substitute the values into the formula.	$\frac{48}{24} = 2\ moles$

What volume of sulfur dioxide can be made from 5 dm^3 of oxygen?	
$S_{(s)} + O_{2\,(g)} \rightarrow SO_{2\,(g)}$	
Step	**Example**
Use the molar ratio to calculate the volume that can be made.	Molar ratio = 1:1:1 5 dm^3 O_2 = 5 dm^3 SO_2

Metal oxides 4.4.1.1

- Metals react with **oxygen** to produce **metal oxides.**
  - E.g. $Sodium + Oxygen \rightarrow Sodium\ oxide$
    - $4Na + O_2 \rightarrow 2Na_2O$
- This occurs through **oxidation** reactions because the metals **gain oxygen**.
- The mass of the metal oxide is greater than the mass of the original metal due to the added mass of oxygen.
- Metals with **very low reactivity**, such as gold, do not react with oxygen.

SNAPREVISE

The reactivity series 4.4.1.2

- When metals react with other substances, the metal atoms form positive ions.
- The **reactivity** of a metal is related to its **tendency to form positive ions**.
  - More reactive metals lose electrons more easily to form ions.
  - A more reactive metal can **displace** a less reactive metal from a compound:
  - E.g. $\textit{Zinc} + \textit{Iron oxide} \rightarrow \textit{Zinc oxide} + \textit{Iron}$
- Reactions with **oxygen**:
  - **Low reactivity** metals do not burn, but form oxide when heated or slowly oxidise over time, e.g. a layer of copper oxide forms on the surface of copper.
  - Metals in the **middle** of the reactivity series react with oxygen when **heated** and can burn if the metal is powdered.
  - **Reactive metals burn** when heated as they react with oxygen in the air.
- Reactions with **water**:
  - The more reactive metals above carbon in the reactivity series react with water:
    - $\textit{Metal} + \textit{Water} \rightarrow \textit{Metal hydroxide} + \textit{Hydrogen gas}$
    - E.g. $\textit{Calcium} + \textit{Water} \rightarrow \textit{Calcium hydroxide} + \textit{Hydrogen gas}$
      - $Ca\ (s) + 2H_2O\ (l) \rightarrow Ca(OH)_2(aq) + H_2\ (g)$
- Reactions with **dilute acids**:
  - Metals that are more reactive than hydrogen react with dilute acids:
  - $\textit{Metal} + \textit{Acid} \rightarrow \textit{Metal salt} + \textit{Hydrogen gas}$
    - E.g. $\textit{Lithium} + \textit{Hydrochloric acid} \rightarrow \textit{Lithium chloride} + \textit{Hydrogen gas}$
      - $2Li\ (s) + 2HCl\ (aq) \rightarrow 2LiCl\ (aq) + H_2\ (g)$
  - Hydrochloric acid (HCl) makes chloride salts.
  - Sulfuric acid (H_2SO_4) makes sulfate salts.
  - Nitric acid (HNO_3) makes nitrate salts.
- Metals can be arranged in order of their reactivity in a reactivity series, where the non-metals carbon and hydrogen are used for reference:

Most reactive ↑ Least reactive

Metal		Reaction with oxygen	Reaction with water	Reaction with acids
Potassium	K	Burns to form oxide	Reacts and gives off $H_{2(g)}$	Reacts violently and gives off $H_{2(g)}$
Sodium	Na			
Lithium	Li			
Calcium	Ca			Reacts and gives off $H_{2(g)}$
Magnesium	Mg			
Carbon	C			
Zinc	Zn	Forms oxide when heated (burns if powdered)	No reaction	Reacts slowly and gives off $H_{2(g)}$
Iron	Fe			
Hydrogen	H			
Copper	Cu	Forms oxide when heated	No reaction	No reaction
Silver	Ag	No reaction		
Gold	Au			
Platinum	Pt			

Extraction of metals 4.4.1.3

- Unreactive metals, such as gold, are found in the Earth as the metal itself.
- Most metals are found as **compounds** that require chemical reactions to extract the pure metal.
- Metals less reactive than carbon can be extracted from their oxides by **reduction with carbon**.
  - $\textit{Metal oxide} + \textit{Carbon} \rightarrow \textit{Metal} + \textit{Carbon dioxide}$
  - E.g. $\textit{Iron(III) oxide} + \textit{Carbon} \rightarrow \textit{Iron} + \textit{Carbon dioxide}$

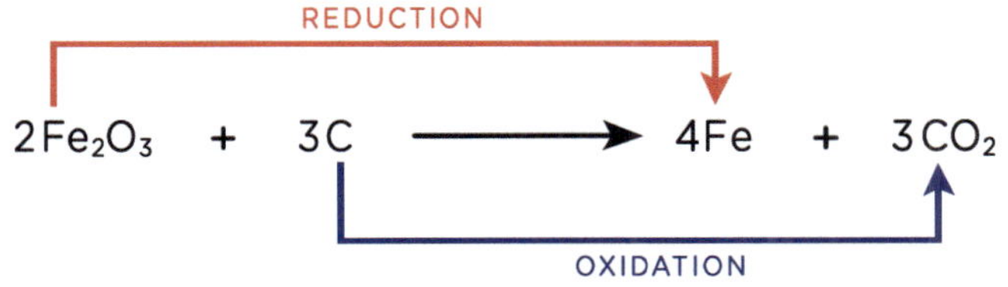

Reactions of acids and metals 4.4.2.1

- Acids react with some metals to produce **salts** and **hydrogen gas**, which causes the reaction to fizz.
  - $\textit{Metal} + \textit{Acid} \rightarrow \textit{Metal salt} + \textit{Hydrogen gas}$
  - Hydrochloric acid (HCl) makes chloride salts.
  - Sulfuric acid (H_2SO_4) makes sulfate salts.
  - Nitric acid (HNO_3) makes nitrate salts.
- The reaction is a **redox reaction** because the metal atoms lose electrons and so are **oxidised**. The H^+ ions in the acid gain electrons and are **reduced**.

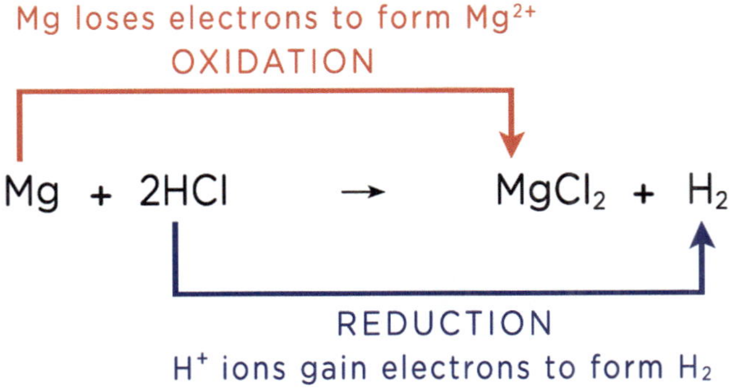

Neutralisation reactions 4.4.2.2-3

- Neutralisation of acids involves using up the H^+ ions from the acid.
  - $\textit{Hydrogen ions} + \textit{Hydroxide ions} \rightarrow \textit{Water}$
  - $H^+(aq) + OH^-(aq) \rightarrow H_2O(l)$
- Acids are neutralised by **alkalis** (e.g. soluble metal hydroxides) and **bases** (e.g. insoluble metal hydroxides and metal oxides) to produce **salts and water**.
  - **Soluble metal hydroxides** are **alkalis** as they release **OH^- ions** into the water.
  - **Insoluble metal hydroxides** are **bases** as they do not release OH^- ions into water.
  - $\textit{Metal hydroxide} + \textit{Acid} \rightarrow \textit{Metal salt} + \textit{water}$
    - E.g. $NaOH + HNO_3 \rightarrow NaNO_3 + H_2O$
    - Ionic equation: $H^+(aq) + OH^-(aq) \rightarrow H_2O(l)$
  - $\textit{Metal oxide} + \textit{Acid} \xrightarrow{heat} \textit{Metal salt} + \textit{water}$
    - E.g. $CaO + 2HNO_3 \rightarrow Ca(NO_3)_2 + H_2O$
- Acids are neutralised by **metal carbonates** to produce **salts**, **water and carbon dioxide**.
  - $\textit{Metal carbonate} + \textit{Acid} \rightarrow \textit{Metal salt} + \textit{water} + \textit{Carbon dioxide}$
    - E.g. $CuCO_3 + H_2SO_4 \rightarrow CuSO_4 + H_2O + CO_2$
- The particular salt produced by neutralisation depends on the acid used and the positive ion in the base, alkali or carbonate.
- **Soluble salts** can be made from acids by reacting them with solid insoluble substances, such as metals, metal oxides, hydroxides or carbonates.

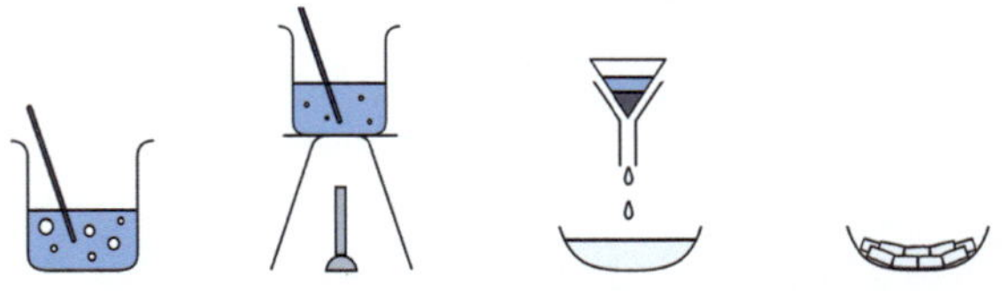

1) The solid is added to the acid until no more reacts and the solid is in excess
2) Heated to evaporate some solution
3) Filtered to remove excess solid and leave solution of the salt
4) Salt crystallises and can be dried by pressing between sheets of filter paper. A water bath or electric heater can be used to evaporate the solution

The pH scale 4.4.2.4

- Acids produce **hydrogen ions (H^+)** in aqueous solutions.
- Aqueous solutions of alkalis contain **hydroxide ions (OH^-)**.
- The **pH scale**, from 0 to 14, is a measure of the **acidity** or **alkalinity** of a solution and can be measured using a **universal indicator** or a **pH probe**.
    - A solution with pH 7 is **neutral**.
    - Aqueous solutions of acids have pH values of less than 7.
    - Aqueous solutions of alkalis have pH values greater than 7.
- In neutralisation reactions between an acid and an alkali, hydrogen ions react with hydroxide ions to produce water.
    - $H^+(aq) + OH^-(aq) \rightarrow H_2O(l)$

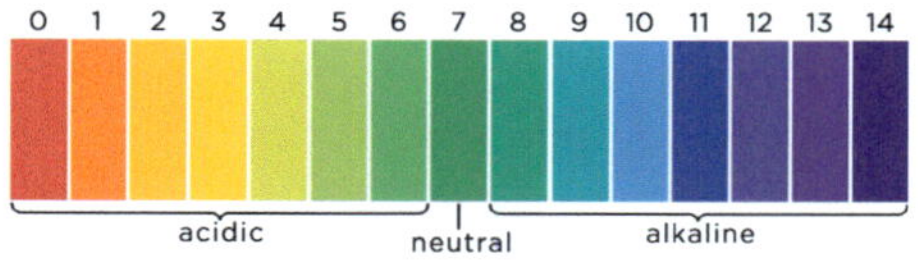

Strong and weak acids 4.4.2.6

- **Dilute** and **concentrated** refers to the **amount of substance** (the more substance present in a certain volume, the more concentrated the solution), while **weak** and **strong** refers to the **degree of ionisation**.
- For a given concentration of aqueous solutions, the stronger an acid, the lower the pH.
- A **strong acid** is **completely ionised** in aqueous solution; for example, hydrochloric, nitric and sulfuric acids.
- A **weak acid** is only **partially ionised** in aqueous solution; for example, ethanoic, citric and carbonic acids.
- Neutrality and relative acidity refer to the effect on hydrogen ion concentration and pH value.
    1. Neutral solutions have a pH value of 7, the H^+ concentration equals the OH^- concentration.
    2. As the pH decreases by one unit, the **hydrogen ion (H^+) concentration** of the solution increases by a factor of 10.

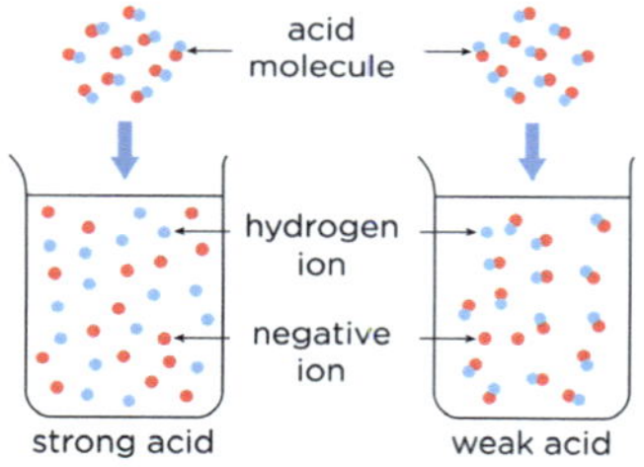

strong and weak acid

Titrations 4.4.2.5

- Titrations are used to find the **concentration** of a solution by reacting it with a solution of known concentration.
- The **reacting volumes** of acid and alkali solutions can be measured by **titration** using a **suitable indicator**, such as methyl orange or phenolphthalein.
- Titrations use apparatus including a **pipette**, **burette** and a **conical flask**, where the pipette is filled using a **pipette filler**.
    1. A **known volume** of a solution of an acid or alkali is measured out using a pipette into a conical flask.
    2. A few drops of a **suitable indicator** are added.
    3. The other **unknown concentration** of acid or alkali is added to the conical flask using a burette.
    4. When reaching the **end point** where the indicator changes colour, the solution is added dropwise to determine the exact volume required.
    5. The volume added from the burette is recorded.
    6. Repeat until **concordant results** are achieved to determine mean volume.

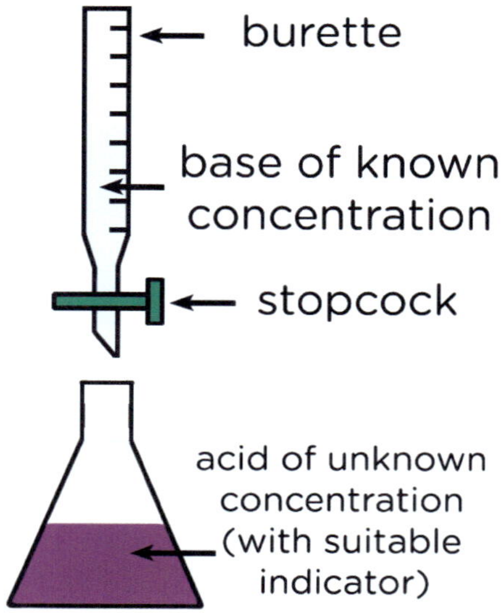

Calculations with titrations 4.4.2.5

- You can determine the **concentration** of one of the solutions (in mol/dm^3 or g/dm^3) from the reacting volumes and the known concentration of the other solution.

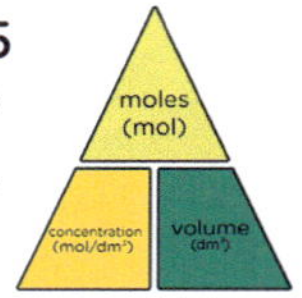

Calculate the concentration of the nitric acid solution in mol/dm^3.

$$HNO_3 + NaOH \rightarrow NaNO_3 + H_2O$$

25.0 cm³ of 0.500 mol/dm³ sodium hydroxide solution reacted with 20.0 cm³ of a solution of nitric acid.

Step	Example
Substitute into the formula to calculate the moles of the sodium hydroxide solution of known concentration.	$0.500 \times \frac{25.0}{1000} = 0.0125\ mol$
Use molar ratios from the balanced equation to work out the moles of the solution of unknown concentration.	$1\ mol\ NaOH : 1\ mol\ HNO_3$ $0.0125\ mol\ NaOH : 0.0125\ mol\ HNO_3$
Substitute into the formula to calculate the unknown concentration of the nitric acid solution.	$\frac{0.0125}{\left(\frac{20.0}{1000}\right)} = 0.625\ mol/dm^3$

Electrolysis 4.4.3.1

- Electrolysis is the **decomposition of ionic compounds** using **electricity**.
    1. When an ionic compound is melted or dissolved in water, the ions are free to move within the liquid or solution.
    2. These liquids and solutions can conduct electricity and are called **electrolytes**.
    3. Passing an **electric current** through electrolytes causes the ions to move to the electrodes.
    4. Positively charged ions move to the **negative electrode** (the **cathode**), and negatively charged ions move to the **positive electrode** (the **anode**).
    5. Ions are **discharged** (losing or gaining electrons to become neutral) at the electrodes producing **deposits** of elements.

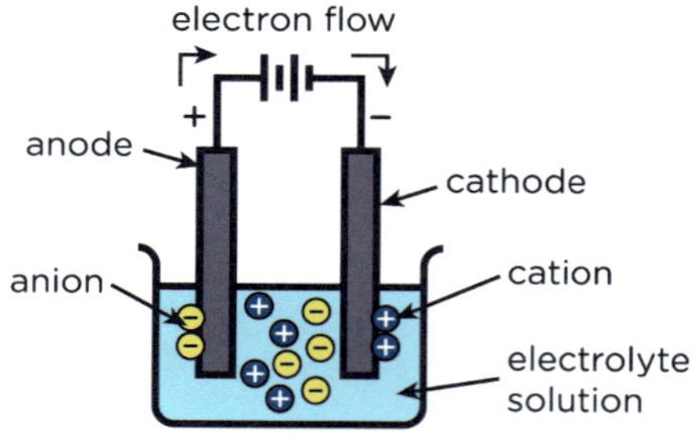

Application of electrolysis and reaction profiles

Types of Electrolysis 4.4.3.2, 4.4.3.4

- **Molten ionic compounds**:
  - When a **simple ionic compound** (e.g. lead bromide) is electrolysed in the molten state using inert electrodes, the **metal** (lead) is produced at the cathode and the **non-metal** (bromine) is produced at the anode.
  - **Inert electrodes** do not react themselves.
- **Aqueous solutions**:
  - In aqueous solutions, water molecules break down into **H^+ ions** and **OH^- ions**, which can be **discharged** instead of the ions from the ionic compound.
  - The ions discharged at an inert electrode depends on the **relative reactivity** of the elements involved.
  - At the negative electrode (cathode), **hydrogen** is produced by the discharge of H^+ ions if the metal is **more reactive** than hydrogen.
    - Sodium chloride (aq) discharges H^+ ions, which form H_2 gas.
    - Silver nitrate (aq) discharges Ag^+ ions, which form solid silver/Ag.
    - Copper (II) bromide discharges Cu^{2+} ions, which form solid copper/Cu.
  - At the positive electrode (anode), **oxygen** is produced by the discharge of OH^- ions unless halide ions are present, then the halogen is produced instead.
    - Potassium sulfate (aq) discharges OH^- ions, which form O_2 gas.
    - Sodium chloride (aq) discharges Cl^- ions, which form Cl_2 gas.
    - Copper (II) bromide discharges Br^- ions, which form Br_2.

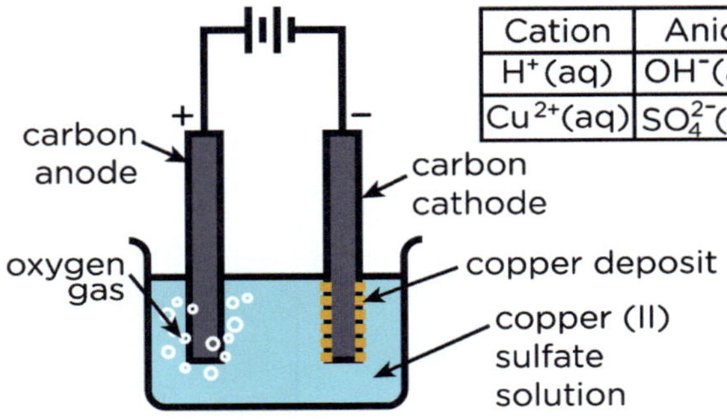

Cation	Anion
$H^+(aq)$	$OH^-(aq)$
$Cu^{2+}(aq)$	$SO_4^{2-}(aq)$

Electrode half equations 4.4.3.5

- At the **cathode**, positively charged ions **gain electrons** so the reactions are **reductions.**
- At the **anode**, negatively charged ions **lose electrons** so the reactions are **oxidations**.
- These reactions can be represented by **half equations**. **For example**:
  - $2H^+ + 2e^- \rightarrow H_2$
  - $4OH^- \rightarrow O_2 + 2H_2O + 4e^-$

Reaction profiles 4.5.1.2

- Chemical reactions only occur when reacting particles **collide** with each other and with **sufficient energy**.
- **The activation energy** is the minimum amount of energy that particles must have to react. It is the energy needed for a reaction to occur.
- **Reaction profiles** show the **relative energies** of **reactants and products**, the activation energy and the **overall energy change** of a reaction.

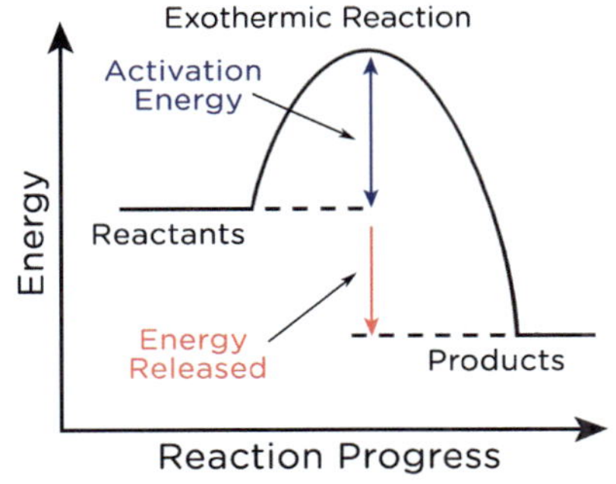

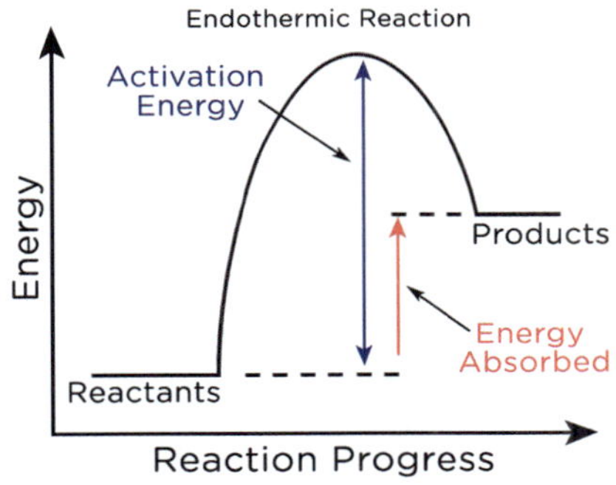

Electrolysis to extract metals 4.4.3.3

- **Metals** can be extracted from **molten compounds** by electrolysis if:
  - The metal is too reactive to be extracted by reduction with carbon.
  - The metal reacts with carbon so cannot be heated with it to extract the metal.
- **Large amounts of energy** are required to melt the compounds and produce the electrical current, which means **high costs.**
- **Aluminium** is manufactured by electrolysis of molten mixtures of **aluminium oxide** and **cryolite** using carbon graphite as the anode.
  - Cryolite lowers the melting point of aluminium oxide, so less energy is needed to melt it, reducing costs.
  - **Al^{3+} ions** are attracted to the cathode, gain electrons and form molten aluminium metal.
  - **O^{2-} ions** are attracted to the anode, lose electrons and form oxygen, which reacts with the graphite anode, burning to produce carbon dioxide.
  - The anode has to be replaced regularly.

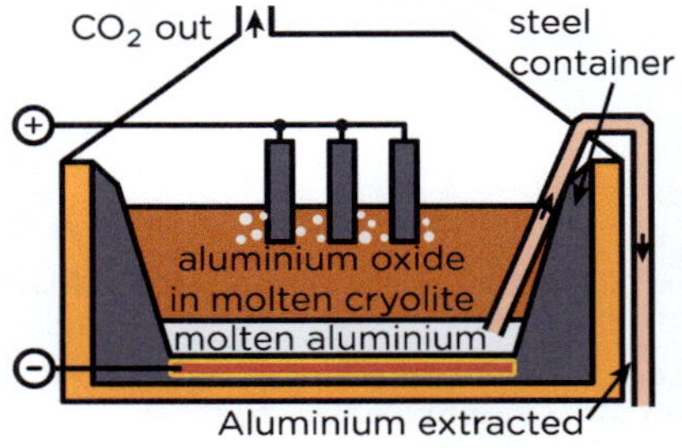

Energy transfers 4.5.1.1

- Energy is **conserved** in reactions. The amount of energy in the universe at the end of a reaction is the same as before the reaction takes place.
- If a reaction transfers energy to the surroundings, the product molecules must have less energy than the reactants, by the amount transferred.
- **Exothermic reaction**: a reaction that transfers thermal energy to the surroundings, causing the temperature of the surroundings to **increase**, such as in combustion, neutralisation and many oxidation reactions.
  - Useful for hand-warmers and self-heating cans.
- **Endothermic reaction**: a reaction that takes in energy from the surroundings, so the temperature of the surroundings **decreases**, such as in thermal decompositions and the reaction of citric acid and sodium hydrogen carbonate.
  - Useful for sports injury packs.

SNAPREVISE

Cells and batteries 4.5.2.1

- **Cells** contain chemicals that react to produce **electricity**.
  - The voltage produced by a cell is dependent upon several factors including the type of **electrode** and **electrolyte**.
  - A simple cell can be made by connecting two different metals in contact with an electrolyte.
  - The greater the difference in the reactivity of the metals, the greater the voltage produced.
  - Cells can be portable and relatively cheap, but many contain toxic chemicals that can harm the environment.
- **Batteries** consist of two or more cells connected in series to provide a
- In **non-rechargeable cells** and batteries, eventually, one of the reactants is used up so the reactions stop, such as in alkaline batteries.
- **Rechargeable cells** and batteries can be recharged because the chemical reactions can be reversed by an external electrical current supply, such as in mobile phones.

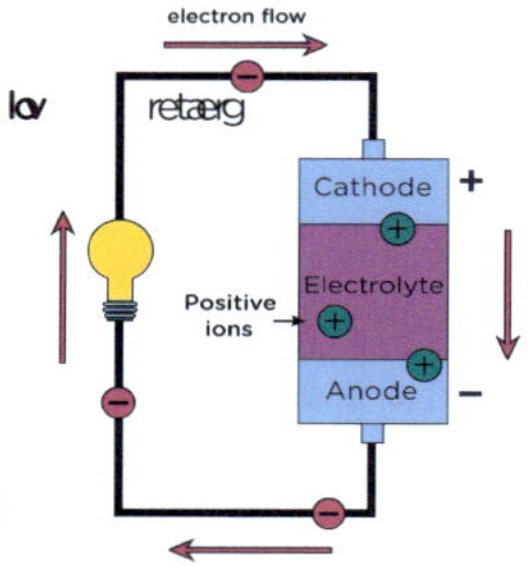

Fuel cells 4.5.2.2

- **Fuel cells** are supplied by an **external source** of **fuel** (e.g. hydrogen) and oxygen/air.
- The fuel is **oxidised electrochemically** within the fuel cell to produce a **potential difference (voltage)**.
  - The overall reaction in a **hydrogen fuel cell** involves the oxidation of hydrogen to produce **water**.
    - $Hydrogen + Oxygen \rightarrow Water$
    - $2H_2 + O_2 \rightarrow 2H_2O$
    - Excess fuel is reused.
- Hydrogen fuel cells offer a potential **alternative** to rechargeable cells and batteries as the reaction is very **efficient** and only releases water.
  - Hydrogen fuel cells can be used to power electrical devices or power motors in vehicles.
  - However, they are very **expensive**, hydrogen gas is highly **flammable** and difficult to store.
  - **Hydrogen production from fossil fuels**, or from the electrolysis of water using electricity generated from fossil fuels, produces CO_2.

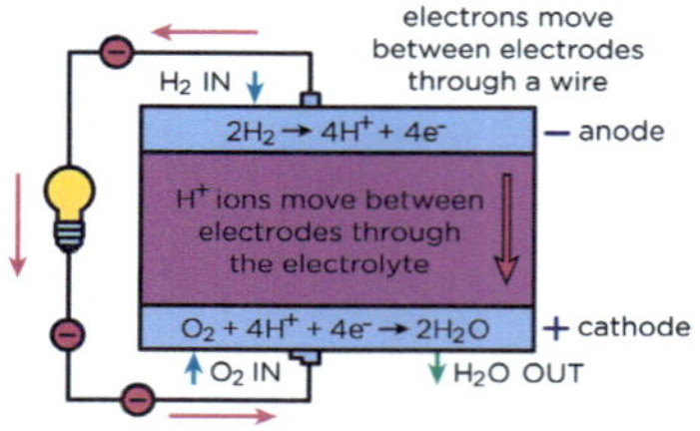

Energy changes in reactions 4.5.1.3

- Energy must be **supplied** to **break bonds** in the reactants.
- Energy is **released** when **bonds form** in the products.
- These energies can be calculated from **bond energies**.
- $\boldsymbol{Overall\ energy\ change\ of\ reaction =}$ $\boldsymbol{Energy\ needed\ breaking\ bonds\ in\ reactants -}$ $\boldsymbol{energy\ released\ making\ bonds\ in\ products}$
  - In an **exothermic reaction**, the energy released from forming new bonds is greater than the energy needed to break existing bonds.
  - In an **endothermic reaction**, the energy needed to break existing bonds is greater than the energy released from forming new bonds

Calculating the overall energy change of a reaction

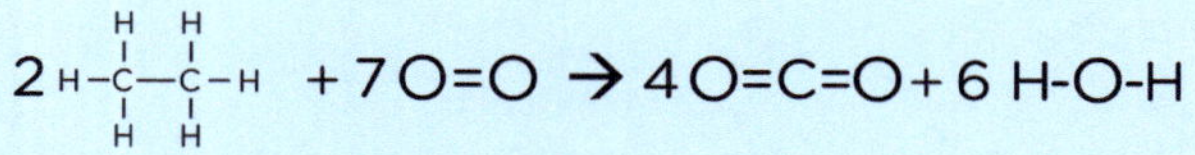

Bond energies: C—H (412 kJ), O=O (496 kJ), C=O (743 kJ), O—H (463 kJ)

Step	Example
Calculate the total bond energy of the reactants.	$[12(\text{C-H}) + 7(\text{O=O})]$ $[12(412) + 7(496)]$ $= [8416]$
Calculate the total bond energy of the products.	$[8(\text{C=O}) + 12(\text{O-H})]$ $[8(743) + 12(463)]$ $= [11500]$
Minus the energy released by making bonds in the products by the energy needed to break bonds in the reactants.	$[8416] - [11500] = -3084\ kJ$ An exothermic reaction

Rate of reaction 4.6.1.1

- The rate of a reaction **changes** during a reaction.
  - Most reactions are fastest at the start, slow down and eventually stop as reactants are used up.
  - As the rate changes, we measure the mean rate over time.
- $\boldsymbol{Mean\ rate\ of\ reaction = \frac{Quantity\ of\ reactant\ used\ OR\ product\ formed}{Time\ taken}}$
  - The quantity of reactant or product can be measured by the mass in grams, by a volume in cm^3 or by moles.
  - The units of rate of reaction may be given as **g/s, cm³/s** or **mol/s**.
- **Reaction rate graphs**:
  - Quantity of reactant used or product formed on the y-axis. Time on the x-axis.
  - The **steeper the gradient**, **the faster the reaction**.
  - Most slopes curve as the reaction slows down.
  - Tangents to the curve (straight lines that just touch a point on the curve) are used to measure the rate at a point in time by calculating their gradient.
  - $\boldsymbol{Rate\ at\ point\ X = Gradient\ of\ tangent = \frac{Change\ in\ y}{Change\ in\ x}}$

Calculate the rate at time X

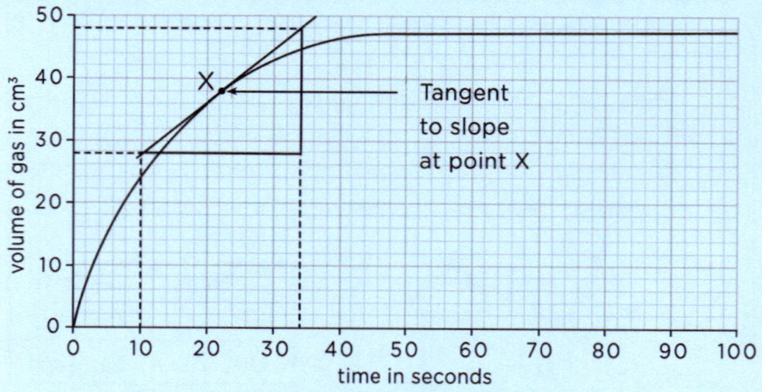

Step	Example
Calculate the change in x.	$34\ s - 10\ s = 24\ s$
Calculate the change in y.	$48\ cm^3 - 28\ cm^3 = 20\ cm^3$
Substitute into the formula.	$\frac{20\ cm^3}{24\ s} = 0.83\ cm^3/s$

Factors affecting rate 4.6.1.2

- **Higher temperatures = faster rate.**
  - Particles have more energy.
- **Higher pressure of reacting gases = faster rate**.
  - Reactant particles are closer together.
- **Higher surface area of solid reactants = faster rate**.
  - More surface particles available.
- **Higher concentration of reactants in solution = faster rate**.
  - More particles and closer together.
- **Presence of catalysts = faster rate**.
- Most factors, except for temperature, have a proportional effect on the rate, so if they double, the rate doubles.
- A small increase in temperature has a big effect on the rate of reaction.

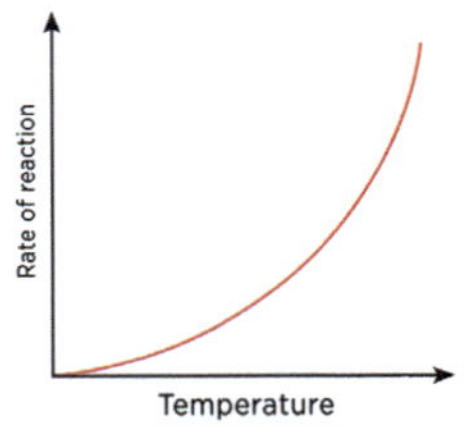

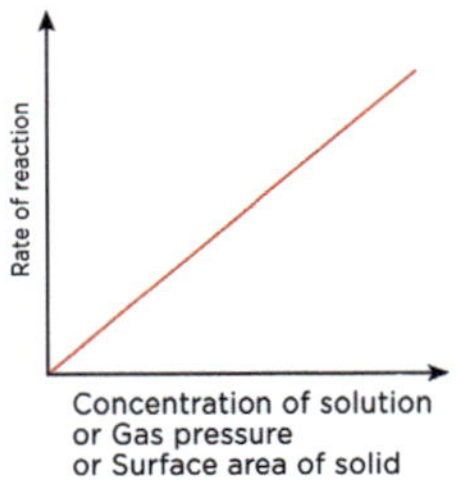

- The rate of reaction can be investigated **experimentally** upon changes in reactant concentration:
  - Measuring gas volume produced over time.
  - Measuring changes in colour using a colorimeter
  - Recording turbidity by placing the conical flask on a piece of paper marked with a cross, and timing how long it takes until you can no longer see the cross through the reaction mixture.

Volume of gas formed

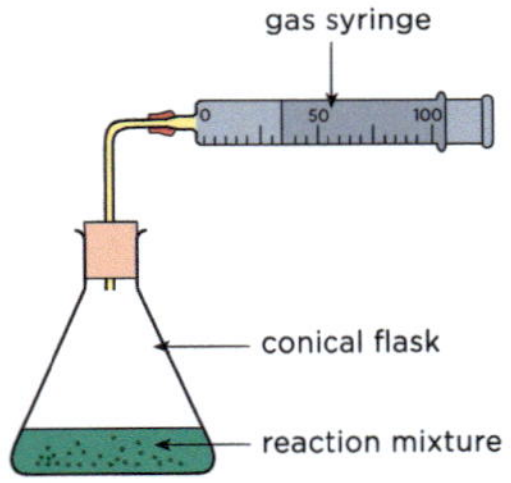

Mass of gas formed

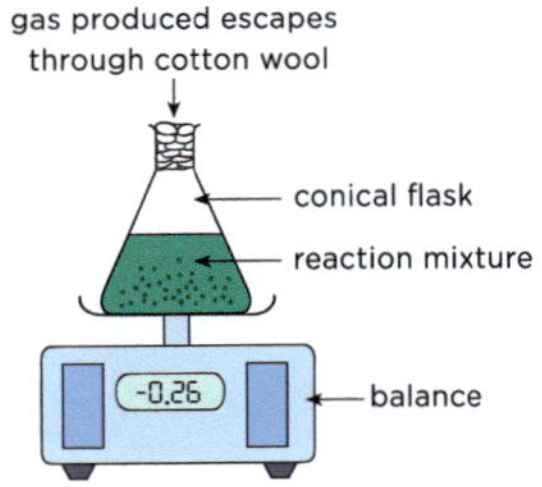

Collision theory 4.6.1.3

- The factors affecting **rate of reaction** can be explained by **collision theory**, as chemical reactions only occur from **successful collisions** when reacting particles collide with each other and with **sufficient energy**.
- The minimum amount of energy that particles must have to react is called the activation energy.
- Increasing the concentration of reactants in solution, pressure of reacting gases, or surface area of solid reactants increases the **frequency** of collisions and so increases the rate of reaction.
- Increasing temperature increases the **frequency** and **energy** of collisions, which increases the rate of reaction.

Catalysts 4.6.1.4

- **Catalysts** increase the rate of reactions by providing an **alternative pathway** for the reaction that has a **lower activation energy**.
- Catalysts are not used up during the reaction, so they are absent from chemical equations and can be reused.
- Different reactions need different catalysts. Enzymes act as catalysts in biological systems.

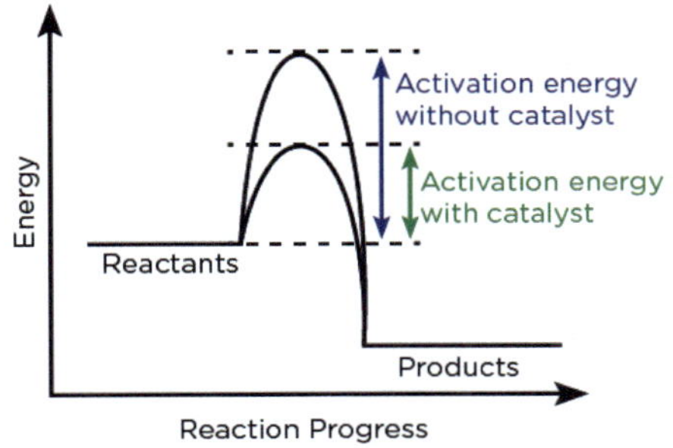

Reversible reactions 4.6.2.1-3

- In some reactions, the products can react to produce the original reactants: $A + B \rightleftharpoons C + D$
- **Equilibrium** is reached when the **forward** and **reverse reactions** occur at the **same rate**, taking place in a closed system that prevents the escape of reactants and products.
- The **direction** of reversible reactions can be changed by changing the **conditions**, such as temperature.
- If a reversible reaction is **exothermic** in one direction, it is **endothermic** in the opposite direction, and the same amount of energy is transferred in each case.

Le Chatelier's principle 4.6.2.4-7

- **Le Chatelier's principle** can be used to predict the effect of **changing conditions** on a **system at equilibrium**.
  - If a change is made to any of the conditions, the system responds to **counteract** the change until equilibrium is reached again.
  - This affects the relative amounts of all the reactants and products.
- A **change in concentration** of one of the reactants or products:
  - If the concentration of a reactant is increased, more products will be formed.
  - If the concentration of a product is decreased, more reactants will react.
- A **change in temperature** of a system at equilibrium:
  - If temperature is increased, the amount of products increases for an endothermic reaction and decreases for an exothermic reaction.
  - If temperature is decreased, the amount of products decreases for an endothermic reaction and increases for an exothermic reaction.
- A **change in pressure** for gaseous reactions:
  - If pressure is increased, equilibrium shifts towards the side with the smaller number of molecules as shown by the symbol equation.
  - If pressure is decreased, equilibrium shifts towards the side with the larger number of molecules as shown by the symbol equation.

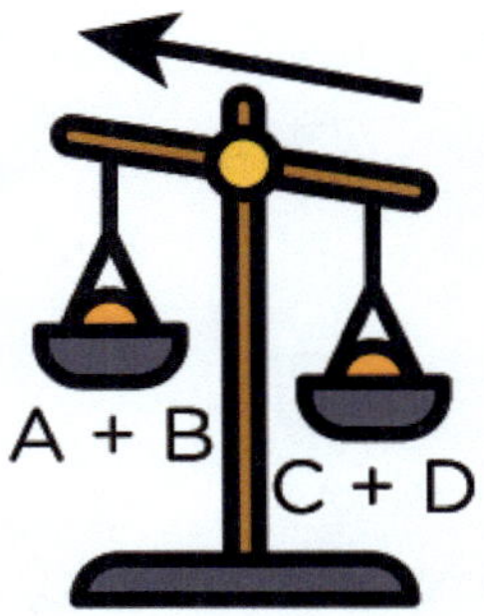

Hydrocarbons and crude oil 4.7.1.1

- **Crude oil** is a **finite resource** found in rocks. It is the remains of an ancient biomass (consisting mainly of **plankton** that was buried in mud).
- Crude oil is a **mixture** mostly made up of hydrocarbons.
- **Hydrocarbons** are molecules made only of **hydrogen** and **carbon**.
    - Most of the hydrocarbons in crude oil are alkanes, e.g. methane, ethane, propane, butane.
    - The general formula for the homologous series of alkanes is C_nH_{2n+2}

Name	Molecular formula	Molecular structure
Ethane	C_2H_6	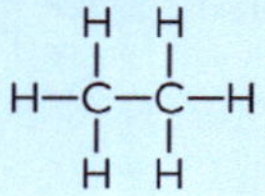

Fractional distillation 4.7.1.2

- The vast array of natural and synthetic carbon compounds occurs due to the ability of carbon atoms to form families of similar compounds.
- Hydrocarbons from crude oil can be separated into **fractions**, each containing molecules with **a similar number** of **carbon atoms**.
- It relies on **evaporating** crude oil at high temperatures and **condensing fractions** in the **fractionating tower/column**.
- The fractions can be processed to produce **fuels** (such as petrol, diesel oil and kerosene) and **feedstock** for the **petrochemical industry** (to produce useful solvents, lubricants, polymers and detergents).

Diagram	Notes
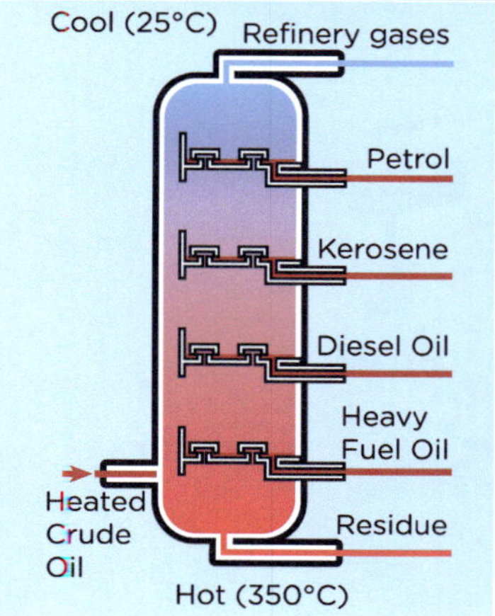	Gases are extracted at the top and can be made into liquefied petroleum gases Lighter molecules condense higher up the column Larger, heavier molecules condense at the bottom

Properties of hydrocarbons 4.7.1.3

- As the molecular size of alkanes increases**:**
    - **Boiling points** increase.
    - **Viscosity** increases.
    - **Flammability** decreases.
- **Shorter alkanes are more in demand as fuels** because they flow more easily, are more flammable and burn with a cleaner flame.
- **Combustion** of hydrocarbon fuels **releases energy**.
    - Carbon and hydrogen are **oxidised.**
    - **Complete combustion** produces carbon dioxide and water. E.g. $2C_2H_6 + 7O_2 \rightarrow 6H_2O + 4CO_2$
    - **Incomplete combustion** produces water, carbon monoxide and carbon as soot.

Alkenes 4.7.2.1

- **Alkenes** are hydrocarbons with a **double carbon-carbon bond**, e.g. ethene (2 carbons), propene (3 carbons), butene (4 carbons), pentene (5 carbons).
    - The general formula for alkenes is C_nH_{2n}.
    - They are **unsaturated** because they contain two fewer hydrogen atoms than alkanes with the same number of carbon atoms.
    - They are **more reactive** than alkanes.
- Alkenes are used to produce **polymers** and as starting materials to produce many other chemicals.

Name	Molecular formula	Molecular structure
Propene	C_3H_6	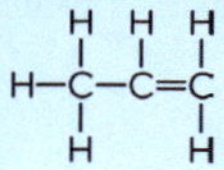

Tests for alkenes 4.7.1.4

- **Alkenes** react with **bromine water**, causing a **colour change** from **orange to colourless** (as bromine molecules are used up).

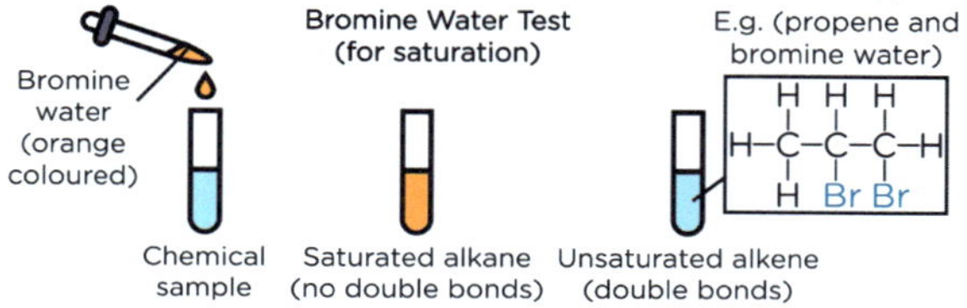

Cracking 4.7.1.4

- Alkanes can be broken down (cracked) by **thermal decomposition** to produce **smaller, more useful molecules** (**alkenes** and **smaller alkanes**).
- Modern life depends on the use of hydrocarbons, e.g. for fuel.
- **Cracking:**
    - Heat the alkanes to **vaporise** them.
    - Pass them over a hot catalyst (**catalytic cracking**) OR mix with steam and heat to very high temperatures (**steam cracking**).
    - E.g. $C_6H_{14} \rightarrow C_4H_{10} + C_2H_4$

Reactions of alkenes 4.7.2.2

- **Functional groups** determine the reactions of organic compounds, such as the **C=C group** in alkenes.
- Alkenes burn in air with **smoky flames** due to **incomplete combustion** with oxygen**.**
- Alkenes react with hydrogen, steam and halogens by the **addition** of atoms across the C=C double bond, making it a single carbon-carbon bond and turning it into a **saturated** molecule.

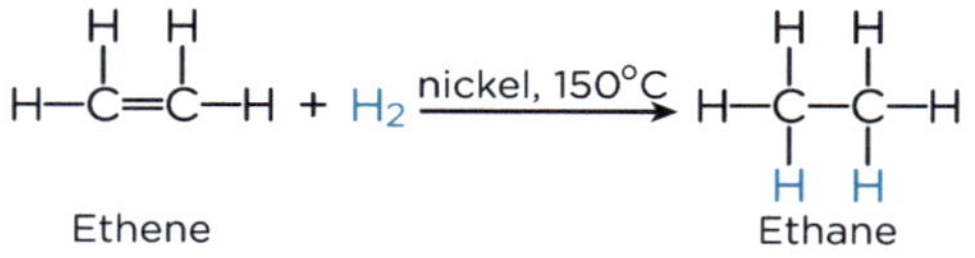

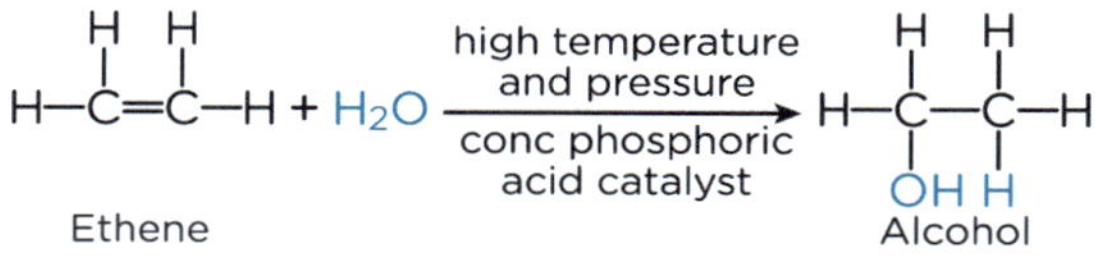

Alcohols 4.7.2.3

- Contain the functional group **-OH**.
- Examples include methanol (1 carbon), ethanol (2 carbons), propanol (3 carbons) and butanol (4 carbons).
- Alcohols burn in air via **complete combustion** to form CO_2 and H_2O in a good supply of oxygen:
    - $C_2H_5OH + 3O_2 \rightarrow 2CO_2 + 3H_2O$
- Alcohols react with an **oxidising agent** to form **carboxylic acids**:
    - $Ethanol \xrightarrow{oxidising\ agent} Ethanoic\ acid$
- **Alcohols react with sodium** to produce **hydrogen gas**.
- **Alcohols do not react with water**, but small alcohol molecules do dissolve to form a neutral solution of pH 7, whilst most other organic liquids separate into layers.
- Alcohols have many uses such as fuels, solvents, and ethanol in alcoholic drinks.

Name	Molecular formula	Molecular structure
Ethanol	CH_3CH_2OH OR C_2H_5OH	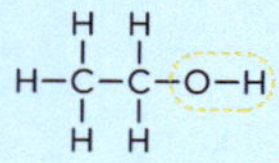

Fermentation 4.7.2.3

- **Ethanol** is made by **fermentation** of sugars:
    1. Sugars are dissolved in water.
    2. Yeast is added.
    3. The mixture is kept warm (at about 30°C) and air is kept out of the mixture (anaerobic).
- $\textbf{Glucose} \xrightarrow{yeast} \textbf{ethanol} + \textbf{carbon dioxide}$
- Fermentation also produces **carbon dioxide**, which can be tested for by using **limewater**, which turns **cloudy**.

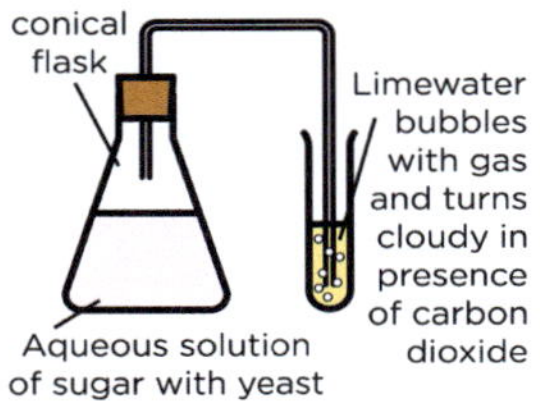

Carboxylic acids 4.7.2.4

- Contain the functional group **-COOH**.
- Examples include methanoic acid (1 carbon), ethanoic acid (2 carbons), propanoic acid (3 carbons) and butanoic acid (4 carbons).

Name	Molecular formula	Molecular structure
Ethanoic acid	CH_3COOH	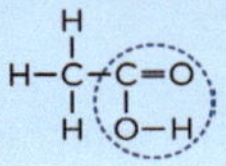

- Carboxylic acids react slowly with metal **carbonates** to form a **salt**, **water** and **carbon dioxide**, so the reaction fizzes.
- React with alcohols in the presence of an **acid catalyst** to form **esters** such as **ethyl ethanoate**, which is used as a solvent in nail varnish.
- Esters have the functional group **-COO-** and are found naturally in fruit.

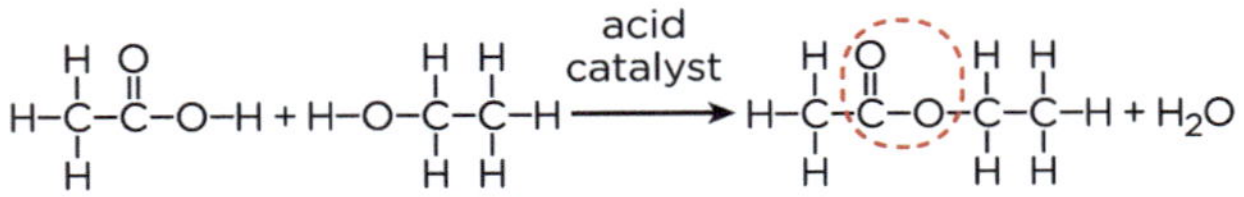

- Carboxylic acids are **weak acids** and dissolve in water to form **slightly acidic solutions** as they only **partially ionise**, producing some **H+ ions**, which lower the pH**.**
    - $CH_3COOH \xrightarrow{H_2O} CH_3COO^- + H^+$

Addition polymers 4.7.3.1

- **Alkenes** can be used to make **polymers**, such as poly(ethene) and poly(propene), by **addition polymerisation**.
- Many **small molecules** (**monomers**) join to form very **large molecules** (**polymers**).
- No other molecules are formed so it is a very efficient reaction, and the **repeating unit** has the same atoms as the monomer.

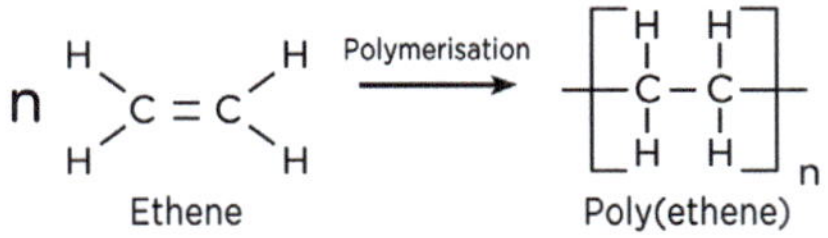

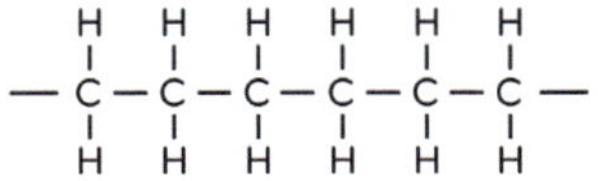

Amino acids 4.7.3.3

- **Amino acids** contain a **-COOH** group and an **-NH₂** group.
- Amino acids react by **condensation polymerisation** to produce **polypeptides.**
- Different amino acids can be combined in the same chain, producing **proteins.**

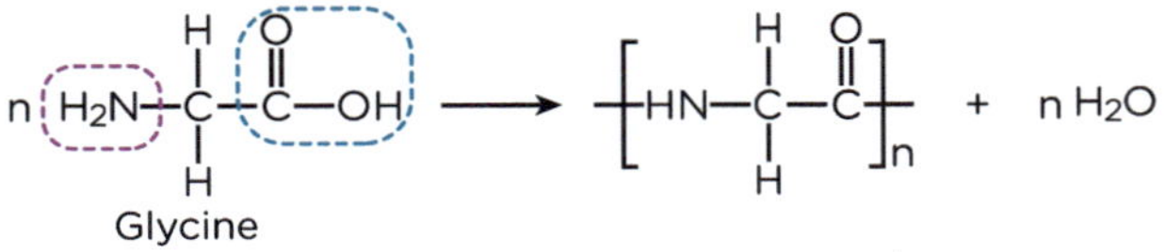

Pure substances 4.8.1.1

- A pure substance is a **single element** or **compound**, not mixed with any other substance.
- Pure elements and compounds **melt and boil at specific temperatures**, which can be used to distinguish pure substances from impure mixtures.
    - Impurities lower the melting point, raise the boiling point and cause substances to change state over a range of temperatures rather than at a single specific temperature.
    - Water has a boiling point of 100°C and a melting point of 0°C.
    - Saltwater freezes at lower temperatures below 0°C, depending on how much salt is dissolved, so is used to stop ice forming on roads in winter.
- In everyday language, a pure substance can refer to natural substances without additives, such as pure orange juice.

Condensation polymers 4.7.3.2

- **Condensation polymerisation** involves joining **monomers** with **two functional groups**, with the loss of small molecules such as water.
- The simplest condensation polymers are produced from two different monomers with **two of the same functional groups on each monomer**.
    - **Polyesters** are made from molecules with two **-COOH** groups reacting with molecules with two **-OH** groups, such as ethanediol and ethanedioic acid.
    - Polyesters can also be formed from monomers that each contain one **-COOH** and one **-OH** group.
    - **Polyamides** are made from molecules with two **-COOH** groups reacting with molecules with two amine functional groups (**-NH$_2$**).

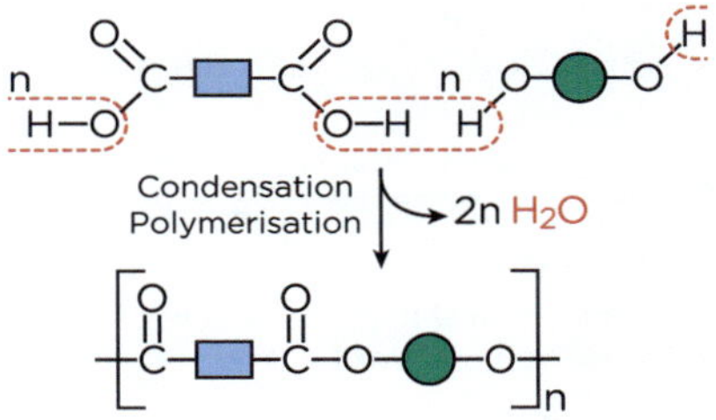

DNA 4.7.3.4

- **DNA (deoxyribonucleic acid)** is a large molecule essential for life.
- DNA encodes **genetic instructions** for the development and functioning of living organisms and viruses.
- Most DNA molecules are two polymer chains that form a **double helix**.
- DNA polymers are made up from different combinations of four different monomers called **nucleotides** (A, T, C and G).
- Other naturally occurring polymers important for life include **proteins** (from amino acid monomers), **starch** and **cellulose** (from glucose monomers).

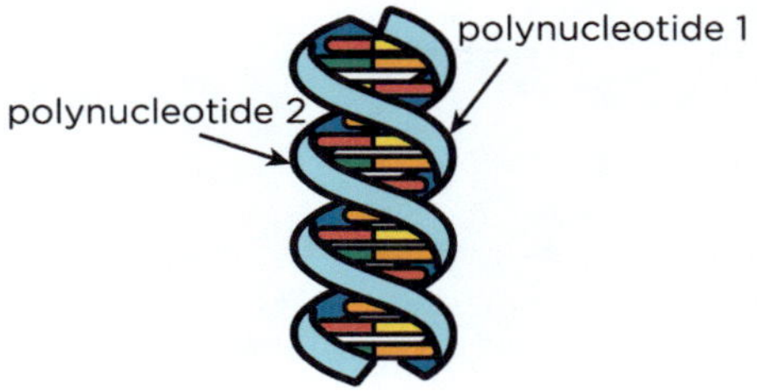

Chromatography 4.8.1.3

- Chromatography can be used to separate and identify the substances in mixtures.
- It involves a **stationary phase** and a **mobile phase**:
  - Substances with a stronger attraction to the mobile phase move quickly and travel further.
  - Substances with a stronger attraction to the stationary phrase move slowly and will not travel as far.
  - This causes the substances in a mixture to separate into different spots.
  - A pure compound will produce a single spot in all solvents.
- **Paper chromatography**:
  - Stationary phrase = **chromatography paper**.
  - Mobile phase = **solvent**, such as water.
    1. A line is drawn with **pencil**.
    2. Small amounts of each substance are **spotted** on the pencil line.
    3. The paper is hung in a **beaker** of the **solvent** so that the line and spots are above the level of the solvent.
    4. The solvent soaks up the paper over a few minutes.
    5. Paper is removed and the level reached by the solvent is marked as the **solvent front**.
    6. Paper is left to **dry**.
- The **R_f value** is the ratio of the distance moved by a compound to the distance moved by the solvent:
  - $R_f = \dfrac{\textit{distance moved by substance}}{\textit{distance moved by solvent}}$
  - R_f values can be used to identify substances as different compounds have different R_f values, the same compound will always have the same R_f value in the same solvent, but different R_f values in different solvents.

Calculating R_f values

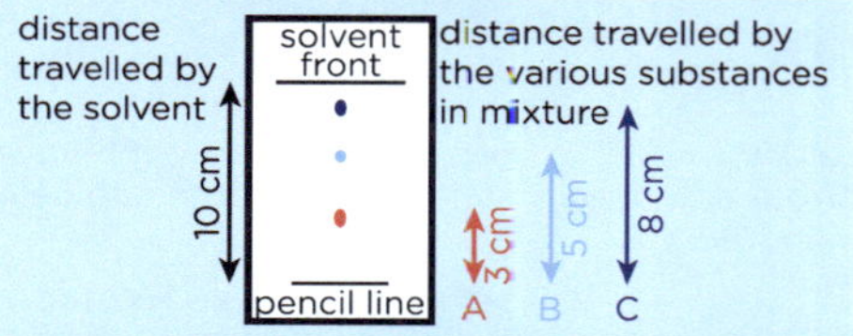

Step	Example
Substitute values into the formula.	$R_f of\ A = \frac{3}{10} = 0.3$ $R_f of\ B = \frac{5}{10} = 0.5$ $R_f of\ C = \frac{8}{10} = 0.8$

Identifying common gases 4.8.2.1-4

- **Hydrogen test**:
  - Hold a **burning splint** at the open end of a test tube of the gas.
  - Hydrogen burns rapidly with a **squeaky pop sound**.
- **Oxygen test**:
  - Insert a **glowing splint** into a test tube of the gas.
  - The **splint relights** in oxygen.
- **Carbon dioxide test**:
  - Bubble the unknown gas through an aqueous solution of **calcium hydroxide (limewater)**.
  - Limewater turns **cloudy** (milky).
- **Chlorine test**:
  - Damp litmus paper is bleached white in the presence of chlorine gas.

Flame tests 4.8.3.1

- Used to **identify metal cations**.
- Mixtures of the ions may mask the distinctive colours.

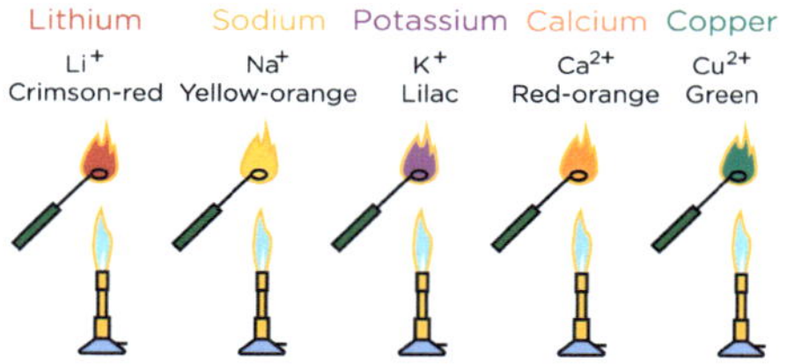

Metal hydroxides 4.8.3.2

- **Sodium hydroxide solution** can be mixed with solutions of unknown substances to **identify some metal cations**, which form as coloured **precipitates.**
  - e.g. $2NaOH(aq) + CuSO_4(aq) \rightarrow Na_2SO_4(aq) + Cu(OH)_2(s)$
  - Only the **aluminium hydroxide** precipitate **dissolves** in **excess sodium hydroxide solution**.

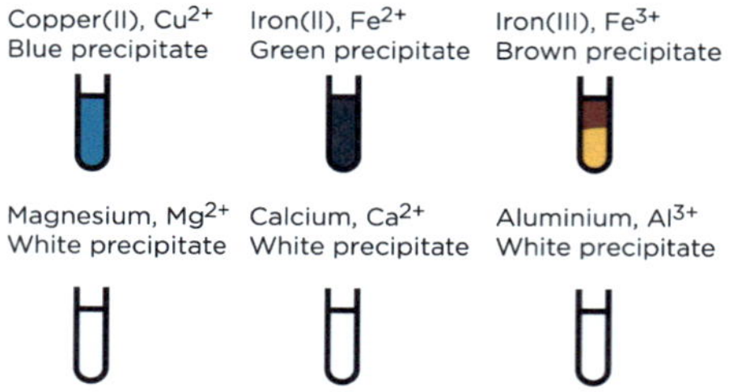

Formulations 4.8.1.2

- A formulation is a **mixture** designed as a useful product with **particular properties**, such as fuels, cleaning agents, medicines, alloys, paints, fertilisers and foods.
- Formulations are made by mixing the components in **carefully measured amounts**, in which each chemical has a specific purpose, to ensure that the overall product has the required properties.

Identifying other common compounds with negative ions 4.8.3.3-5

- **Carbonates test**:
  - React with **dilute acids** to form **carbon dioxide gas**, which can be identified **with limewater**.
- **Sulfates**:
  - Sulfate ions, in solution with **barium chloride solution** in the presence of **dilute hydrochloric acid**, produce a **white sulfate precipitate**.
- **Halides**:
  - Halide ions in solution produce **precipitates** with **silver nitrate solution** in the presence of **dilute nitric acid**.

Instrumental methods 4.8.3.6-7

- Elements and compounds can be detected and identified using **instrumental methods**, which are **sensitive**, **rapid**, and more **accurate** than the chemical tests.
- One example is **flame emission spectroscopy**, a more sophisticated flame test.
  - Used to analyse **metal ions** in **solutions**.
  - Sample is put into a flame and the wavelength of light given out is passed through a **spectroscope**.
  - The output is a **line spectrum** that can be analysed to identify the metal ions in the solution and measure their concentrations.

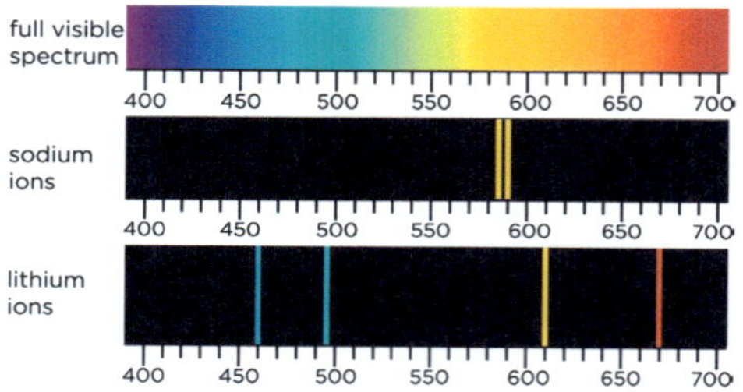

The atmosphere 4.9.1.1

- For 200 million years, the **proportions** of different **gases** in the **atmosphere** have been much the same as they are today:
  - About four-fifths (approx. 80%) **nitrogen (N_2)**.
  - About one-fifth (approx. 20%) **oxygen (O_2)**.
  - Small proportions of various other gases, including **carbon dioxide (CO_2)**, **water vapour** and **noble gases**.

Human contributions 4.9.2.2

- Some human activities **increase** the **amounts of greenhouse gases** in the **atmosphere**, including CO_2 and CH_4.
  - **Burning of fossil fuels** produces CO_2.
  - **Deforestation** means less CO_2 is absorbed for photosynthesis.
  - **Animal farming** produces CH_4 as a product of animal digestion and manure decomposition.
  - **Decomposition of waste in landfill** produces CH_4.
- Based on **peer-reviewed evidence**, many **scientists** believe this will increase the temperature of the Earth's atmosphere at the surface, and that **global warming** will result in **global climate change**.
- It is difficult to model such **complex systems** as global climate change, leading to **simplified models**, and **speculation** and **opinions** presented in the media, which may only be biased or based on parts of the evidence.

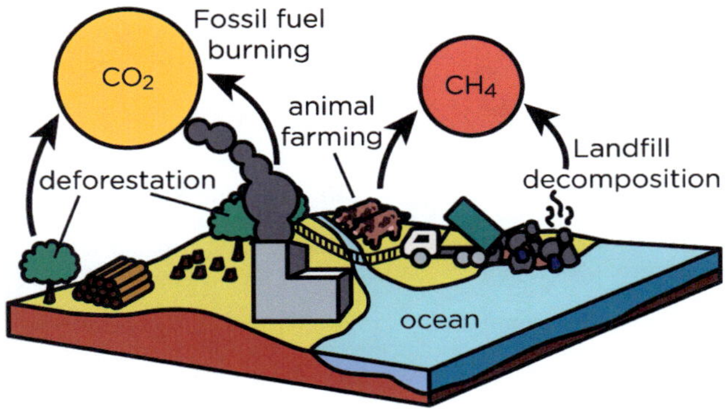

The greenhouse effect 4.9.2.1

- **Greenhouse gases** in the atmosphere **maintain temperatures** on Earth high enough to **support life**.
- The gases include **water vapour**, **CO_2** and **CH_4**.
  1. The sun gives off electromagnetic radiation in the ultraviolet, visible and infrared regions, much of which passes through the atmospheric gases to Earth.
  2. The Earth also gives off radiation, however at a longer wavelength and in the infrared region as the Earth is much cooler than the Sun.
  3. Greenhouse gases absorb long-wavelength infrared radiation given off by the Earth but not by the Sun.

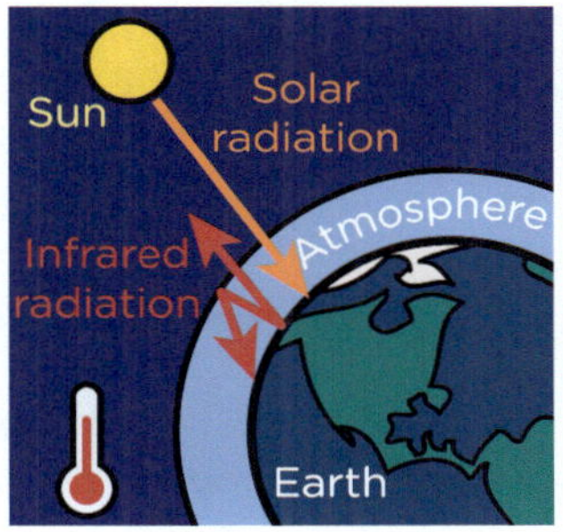

The early atmosphere 4.9.1.2

- Evidence for the early atmosphere is limited because of the time scale of **4.6 billion years**.
- Earth's early atmosphere may have been similar to how its neighbouring planets **Mars and Venus** exist today, consisting **mainly of CO_2** with **little or no O_2 gas**.
- One theory suggests that during the first billion years of the Earth's existence, there was **intense volcanic activity** that released gases that formed the early atmosphere:
  - **Water vapour**, which condensed to form the oceans.
  - **CO_2**, which also dissolved in the oceans and precipitated as carbonate sediments, reducing the amount of atmospheric CO_2.
  - **N_2**, which gradually built up in the atmosphere.
  - Small proportions of **methane (CH_4)** and **ammonia (NH_3)**.

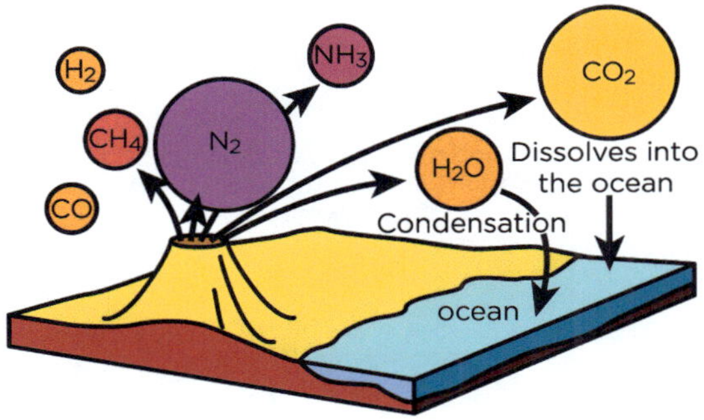

How the atmosphere changed 4.9.1.3-4

- **Plants and algae** produced the **O_2** that is now in the atmosphere by **photosynthesis**, **decreasing CO_2 levels**.
  - $\textit{Carbon dioxide} + \textit{water} \xrightarrow{light} \textit{glucose} + \textit{oxygen}$
  - $6CO_2 + 6H_2O \xrightarrow{light} C_6H_{12}O_6 + 6O_2$
- Algae first produced oxygen about **2.7 billion years ago**.
- Plants evolved over the next billion years, and the percentage of O_2 eventually increased to a level that **enabled animals to evolve**.
- CO_2 was also decreased by the formation of **sedimentary rocks**, such as limestone:
  - Some CO_2 dissolved in oceans to form insoluble carbonate compounds that became sediment.
  - Some CO_2 dissolved in oceans to form compounds that became part of the shells and skeletons of sea animals. Upon death, these shells and skeletons became sediment.
  - Over millions of years, the sediment became sedimentary rocks.
- The formation of carbon **fossil fuels** decreased the levels of CO_2 in the atmosphere:
  - Crude oil and natural gas – formed from dead plankton in the ocean being compressed in the mud over millions of years.
  - Coal – formed from dead plants in swamps being compressed over millions of years.

Climate change, pollution, and sustainability

SNAPREVISE

Climate change 4.9.2.3-4

- An increase in average global temperature is a major cause of climate change.

Effect	Environmental implications
Rising sea levels	**Warm water expands** and the **polar ice caps and glaciers will melt**. This may cause **flooding** of coastal regions and islands and **increase coastal erosion**.
More frequent and severe storms	There is evidence of **more rainfall** in the most severe storms; however, there is mixed evidence as to whether the number of hurricanes is increasing or not.
Changes in rainfall patterns	Rainfall may **increase in some parts of the world**, such as northern Europe, causing flooding. Rainfall may **decrease in hot regions near the equator**, leading to drought.
Shortage of fresh water	**Water stress affects all living creatures**, and more **droughts** will affect humans, plants, and animals, and so **will affect food chains**.
Changes in wildlife	**Earlier flowering** and **earlier rise from hibernation**. Some **species may migrate** further north as temperatures rise and the number of some animals will fall as there are **fewer suitable places to live**, such as for polar bears.
Changes to food production	Changes in **temperature**, **rainfall**, **drought**, **flooding** and the **distribution and number of pests** may affect the capacity of some regions to grow food.

- The **carbon footprint** is the total amount of CO_2 and other greenhouse gases emitted over the full life cycle of a product, service or event.
- Carbon footprints can be reduced by **reducing greenhouse gas emissions**, though it may be expensive:
  - **Alternative energy sources** (e.g. solar energy) or carbon-neutral fuels (e.g. biodiesel).
  - **Carbon capture** and storage.
  - Using **energy-efficient products**.
  - **Reforestation**.

Pollution 4.9.3.1-2

- Fuel combustion produces gases and atmospheric pollutants:
  - **Gases**: CO_2, water vapour, carbon monoxide (CO), sulfur dioxide (SO_2) and oxides of nitrogen.
  - **Particulates**: solid particles (e.g. soot) and unburned hydrocarbons.
- **CO** – **toxic**, colourless, odourless gas, so is not easily detected. Produced from incomplete combustion.
- **SO_2 and oxides of nitrogen** – cause **respiratory problems** in humans and cause **acid rain**. Produced from sulfur impurities in fuels and from reaction of nitrogen with oxygen at the very high temperatures used for combustion.
- Particulates cause global dimming and health problems.

Potable water 4.10.1.2

- Water of appropriate quality is essential for life and is called **potable** when it is **safe to drink** but still contains **dissolved substances**, unlike chemically **pure water**.
- For humans, drinking water should have sufficiently low levels of dissolved salts and microbes.
- The methods used to produce potable water depend on available supplies of water and local conditions.
- In the UK, rain provides fresh water with low levels of dissolved substances, which collects in the ground and in reservoirs, lakes and rivers.
- **Freshwater and groundwater treatment to produce potable water**:
  1. An **appropriate freshwater source** is chosen.
  2. Water is **filtered to remove solids**, through filter beds.
  3. **Water is sterilised to kill microbes** using sterilising agents such as chlorine, ozone, or ultraviolet light.
- **Desalination of saltwater** can be done if supplies of fresh water are limited, by **distillation** or by processes that use membranes (such as **reverse osmosis**). However, these processes require a lot of energy to remove the large amounts of sodium chloride.
- **Water samples can be analysed and purified**.
  1. **pH** can be measured.
  2. Evaporation using distillation to investigate **dissolved solids** left behind. **Impurities in water** cause the **boiling point to increase** past that of pure water at 100°C.

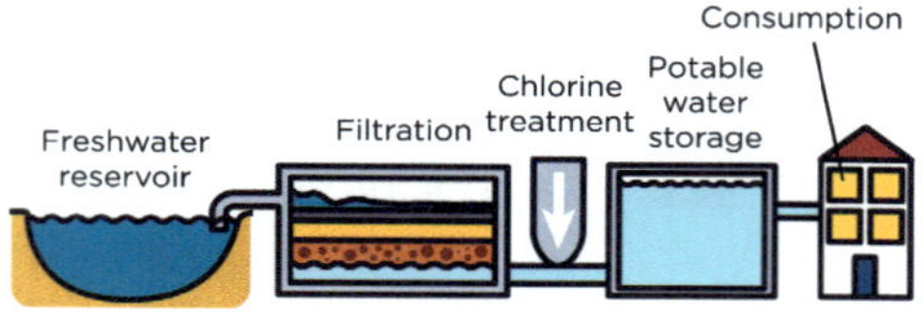

Wastewater treatment 4.10.1.3

- **Urban lifestyles, agricultural and industrial processes produce large amounts of wastewater** that must be treated before being released into the environment to remove organic matter, and harmful microbes and chemicals.
- **Sewage treatment** includes:
  1. **Screening** and **grit removal** to remove large solids.
  2. **Sedimentation** to produce **sewage sludge** and **effluent.**
  3. **Aerobic biological treatment** of effluent in aeration tanks post-sedimentation allows good bacteria to kill harmful bacteria before returning the treated water to the environment.
  4. **Anaerobic digestion** of sewage sludge produces methane for burning for heat and energy.
- Obtaining potable water from groundwater is relatively easy.
- Obtaining potable water from saltwater is less favourable as it requires a lot of energy.
- Obtaining potable water from wastewater is the most difficult as this contains the largest amount of harmful substances that must be removed.

Sustainable development 4.10.1.1

- Humans use the **Earth's resources** to provide **warmth**, **shelter**, **food and transport.**
  - **Natural resources** provide food, timber, clothing and fuels.
  - Some natural resources have been supplemented or replaced by **agricultural** and **synthetic** products. E.g. natural fertilisers such as manure are being replaced with synthetic alternatives using nitrogen in the air.
  - **Finite resources** from the earth, oceans and atmosphere are processed to provide materials and energy.
- Chemistry plays an important role in **improving agricultural and industrial processes** to provide **new products** such as new medicines, new materials (e.g. polyesters and microfibre) and better fertilisers, and in sustainable development.
- **Sustainable development** is that which meets the needs of current generations without compromising the ability of future generations to meet their own needs, which may involve switching from finite resources to **renewable resources**.

Alloys and reducing environmental impact

Alternative metal extraction methods 4.10.1.4

- Metal ores are a **finite resource**.
- Copper ores are becoming scarce.
- **Copper** can be extracted from **low-grade ores** by methods that avoid traditional mining methods, such as digging, moving and disposing of large quantities of rock.
  - **Phytomining** uses **plants** to absorb metal compounds from metal-rich soil through their roots. The plants are harvested and burned to produce ash rich in the metal compounds.
  - **Bioleaching** uses **bacteria** that absorb metal compounds and produce **leachate** solutions containing the metal compounds.
- The metal compounds are processed to obtain the metal. For example, copper can be extracted from solutions of copper compounds using **electrolysis** or **scrap iron** in a displacement reaction.

Phytomining of Copper

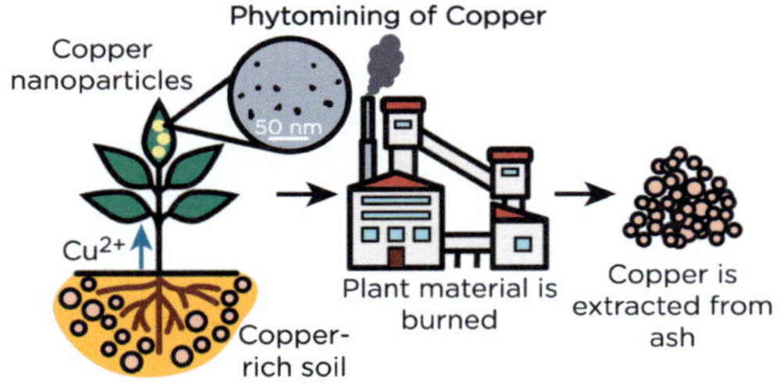

Corrosion 4.10.3.1

- Corrosion is the **destruction of materials by chemical reactions** with substances in the environment.
- Many metals corrode when they come into contact with **oxygen and water**, such as in the **rusting** of iron.
- **Protective coatings prevent corrosion** by applying a layer that acts as a barrier, such as painting, greasing, plastic coating, or electroplating. This barrier prevents the metal from coming into contact with air and water.
- Some metals, such as copper and aluminium, form their own **oxide coatings** that protect the metal from further corrosion.
- **Sacrificial protection** is when the protective coating is a more reactive metal that corrodes in its place, e.g. a protective layer of zinc is used to galvanise iron.

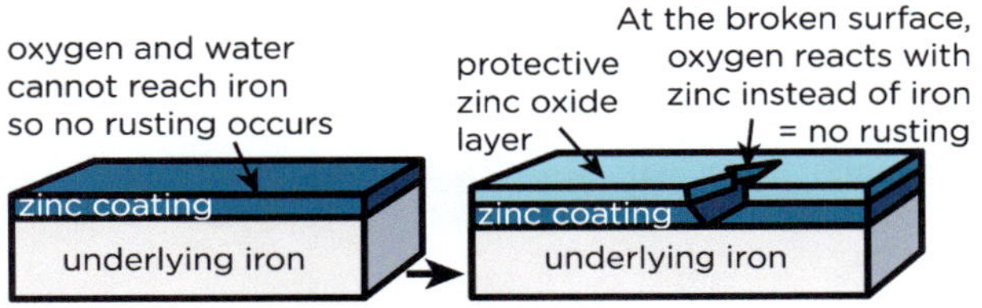

Sacrificial protection in the galvanising of iron

Alloys 4.10.3.1

- Most metals in everyday use are **alloys**, such as **bronze** (an alloy of copper and tin) used for statues, or **brass** (an alloy of copper and zinc) used for doorknobs.
- Metals are usually shiny, strong and malleable, with high melting points and high conductivity.
- Alloys of gold with silver, copper and zinc, are usually used for jewellery as pure gold would lose its shape too easily. The proportion of gold is measured in **carats**, where 24-carat gold is 100% pure gold, and 18 carats is 75% gold.
- Aluminium alloys are low density, useful for cans and foils.
- **Steel** is an alloy of iron with specific amounts of carbon and other metals.
  - **High carbon steel** is strong but brittle, often used for tools such as saw blades.
  - **Low carbon steel** is softer and more easily shaped, useful for car bodies.
  - **Stainless steels** containing chromium and nickel are hard and resistant to corrosion, useful for cutlery.

pure metal - easier for the layers to slide over each other

alloy - more difficult for the layers to slide over each other

Life cycle assessments 4.10.2.1

- Carried out to assess the **environmental impact** of products in each of these stages:
  - **Extraction and processing** of raw materials.
  - **Manufacture and packaging** of product.
  - **Use and operation** during product's lifetime.
  - **Disposal** at the end of its useful life.
  - **Transport and distribution** at each stage.
- It is fairly easy to quantify the use of raw materials, water, energy sources and the production of some wastes.
- It is difficult to assign numerical values to pollutant effects, which rely on value judgements, so LCA is not a purely objective process.
- **Selective or abbreviated LCAs** can be devised to evaluate a product but can be misused to reach desirable or pre-determined conclusions (e.g. in support of claims for advertising purposes).
- LCA for plastic shopping bags:
  - Crude oil is used as a raw material and is a finite resource. Processing crude oil requires a lot of energy.
  - Cheap to manufacture a large quantity.
  - Can be reused many times as they last a long time, which has environmental benefits.
  - Do not biodegrade, may take centuries to degrade in landfill.
- LCA for paper shopping bags:
  - Making paper from trees requires much less energy than making plastics from crude oil.
  - It is more expensive to make bags from paper.
  - Do not last as long as plastic bags so can only be used a few times before breaking.
  - Biodegrade easily.

Reducing use of resources 4.10.2.2

- Reducing the use of limited/finite resources, energy sources and waste by reusing and recycling can decrease environmental impacts.
- Metals, glass, building materials, clay ceramics and most plastics are produced from **limited raw materials**. Much of the energy for the processes comes from limited resources.
- Obtaining raw materials from the Earth by quarrying and mining causes environmental impacts.
- Non-reusable products made of glass and metals can be **recycled** through **crushing**, **melting**, **and reforming/recasting** into different products**.**
  - The amount of separation required for recycling depends on the material and the properties required of the final product.
  - E.g. some scrap steel can be added to iron from a blast furnace to reduce the amount of iron that needs to be extracted from iron ore.
- Some products, such as glass bottles, can be **reused**.

The Haber Process 4.10.4.1

- This process is used to manufacture ammonia (NH_3), which can be used to produce nitrogen-based fertilisers.
- The raw materials are purified nitrogen and hydrogen:
  - **Nitrogen** is purified from the air.
  - **Hydrogen** is made by reaction of steam with methane from natural gas or other sources.
- $Nitrogen + Hydrogen \rightleftharpoons Ammonia$
- $N_2 \quad + \quad 3H_2 \quad \rightleftharpoons \quad \mathbf{2NH_3}$
  - The forward reaction is exothermic.
  - 4 reactant molecules are producing 2 molecules of product.

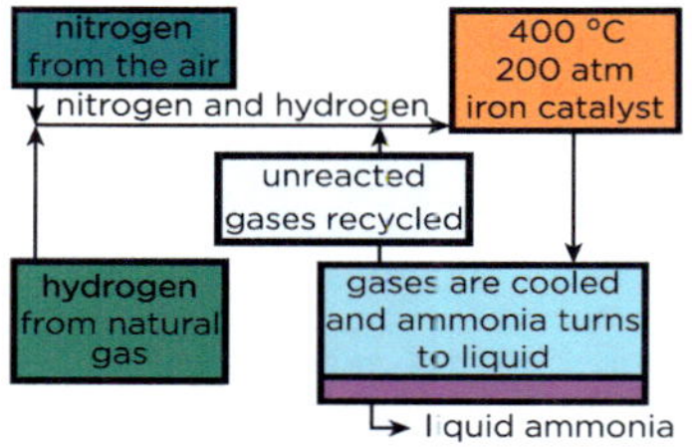

- The reaction is **slow** and **reversible**.
- A catalyst, high temperature and pressure are used to ensure a good yield of ammonia is produced at a good rate. There is a **trade-off** between rate of production and position of equilibrium.
  - **Temperature (450°C)**:
    - The forward reaction is **exothermic** so the lower the temperature, the higher the yield, as equilibrium will shift further to the right.
    - However, the higher the temperature, the faster the rate of reaction as there are more frequent successful collisions of particles with the required activation energy.
    - The higher the temperature, the higher the cost to produce the thermal energy.
  - **Pressure (200 atm)**:
    - There are fewer gas molecules of products than reactants so the higher the pressure, the higher the yield as equilibrium shifts further to the right.
    - The higher the pressure, the faster the rate of reaction as the particles are closer together and so there are more frequent successful collisions.
    - The higher the pressure, the higher the cost of expensive apparatus to withstand the pressure and energy to compress the gases.
  - **Catalyst (iron)**:
    - The reaction is faster with a catalyst, but this does not change the yield.
    - Iron is relatively cheap.

Types of polymer 4.10.3.3

- Polymer properties depend on what monomers they are made from and the conditions under which they are made.
- They are usually relatively flexible and weak, with low conductivity.
- Two different types of poly(ethene) are produced from ethene.
  - **LD poly(ethene)** is soft and flexible so used for cling film and bags. It is **formed at high temperature and pressure** (200°C and 2000atm) with traces of oxygen as a catalyst.
  - **HD poly(ethene)** is hard and strong so used for buckets and water pipes. It is **formed at much lower temperature and pressure** (60°C and 2atm) with a Ziegler-Natta catalyst.
- The atoms within polymer chains are joined together by covalent bonds.
  - **Thermosoftening polymers** melt when they are heated as the individual polymer chains are not joined together. E.g. poly(ethene), PVC.
  - **Thermosetting polymers** do not melt when they are heated, remaining hard as the polymer chains are joined to each other by covalent bonds called cross-links. E.g. superglue, epoxy resins.

Tangled web of polymer chains are not fixed together, allowing melting

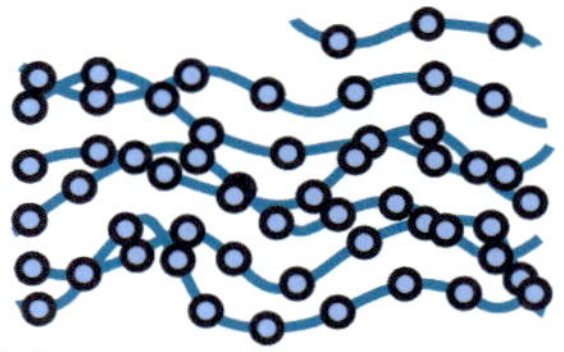

Thermosoftening polymer

Chains are cross-linked by strong covalent bonds, preventing melting

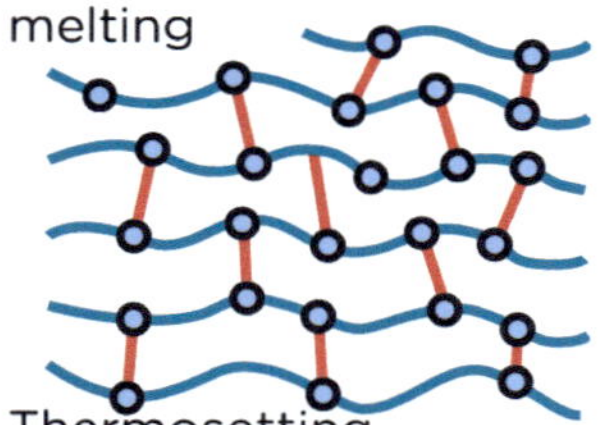

Thermosetting polymer

NPK fertilisers 4.10.4.2

- Water-soluble salt compounds containing **nitrogen (N)**, **phosphorus (P)** and **potassium (K)** in specified ratios are used as fertilisers to **improve agricultural productivity**.
- The salts can be **mined** (e.g. potassium chloride, potassium sulfate).
- **Phosphate rock** (containing calcium and phosphorus) is mined but cannot be directly used as a fertiliser as it is insoluble. The soluble salt can be formed when the **rock reacts with acids**.
  - $\boldsymbol{Phosphate\ rock + Nitric\ acid \rightarrow Calcium\ nitrate}$
  - $\boldsymbol{Phosphate\ rock + Sulfuric\ acid \rightarrow Single\ Superphosphate\ (calcium\ phosphate + calcium\ sulfate)}$
  - $\boldsymbol{Phosphate\ rock + Phosphoric\ acid \rightarrow Triple\ Superphosphate\ (calcium\ phosphate)}$
- Ammonia can be used to manufacture ammonium salts and nitric acid. Ammonium nitrate is made from the reaction of ammonia with nitric acid.

Ceramics, glass, and composites 4.10.3.3

- **Clay ceramics**, including pottery and bricks, are made by shaping wet clay and then heating in a furnace or kiln.
  - Opaque, hard and strong under compression, but brittle.
  - Unreactive, with low conductivity.
  - Resistant to heat with a high melting point.
- **Glass**
  - Transparent, weak, and brittle, with a high melting point and low conductivity.
  - **Soda-lime glass** is made by heating a mixture of sand, sodium carbonate and calcium carbonate (limestone), and is commonly used for windows and glass bottles.
  - **Borosilicate glass** is made from sand and boron trioxide, and melts at higher temperatures, making it useful for cookware and laboratory glassware.
- Most **composites** are opaque and made from two materials, involving a matrix/binder that binds together fibres/fragments of another material (the reinforcement).
  - **Concrete** – a matrix of cement and water is reinforced with sand and crushed rock.
  - **Fibreglass** – a polymer matrix is reinforced with glass fibres.
  - **Carbon fibre** – a polymer matrix is reinforced with carbon fibres or carbon nanotubes.
- They are very strong with high melting points and low conductivity, but are brittle.

Contents - Physics

SNAPREVISE

Systems and energy

SNAPREVISE

Energy stores and systems 4.1.1.1

- A system is an object or a group of objects, such as a kettle filled with water.
- Energy is stored in a system and can take numerous forms.

Types of Energy Store	
Energy	**Description**
Kinetic	The energy that causes an object to move.
Thermal	The energy that causes objects to become hotter.
Electric	The energy transferred by an electric current.
Chemical	The energy stored in batteries and fuels.
Nuclear	The energy stored in nuclei to hold atoms together.
Gravitational Potential	The energy an object gains as it travels upward away from the Earth.
Elastic Potential	The energy an object gains as it is stretched or compressed.
Magnetic Potential	The energy an object gains due to the magnetic attraction or repulsion it is experiencing.

- Changes that occur in a system will change how the energy is stored in it.

Energy calculations 4.1.1.2-3

- Energy is measured using the unit Joules, $\mathbf{J}$.
- The kinetic energy of a moving object is $\mathbf{0.5 \times mass \times (speed)^2}$.
  - This can be written as $E_k = \frac{1}{2}mv^2$.
  - E_k is the kinetic energy in $\mathbf{J}$, m is the object's mass in $\mathbf{kg}$ and v is its speed in $\mathbf{m/s}$.
- The elastic potential energy stored in a spring that has been stretched is given by $\mathbf{0.5 \times spring\ constant \times (extension)^2}$.
  - This can be written as $E_e = \frac{1}{2}ke^2$.
  - E_e is the elastic potential energy in $\mathbf{J}$, k is the spring constant of the spring in $\mathbf{N/m}$ and e is the extension of the spring in $\mathbf{m}$.
- The gravitational potential energy stored in an object raised above ground level is given by **mass × gravitational field strength × height**.
  - This can be written as $E_p = mgh$.
  - E_p is the gravitational potential energy in $\mathbf{J}$, m is the mass of the object in $\mathbf{kg}$, g is the gravitational field strength in $\mathbf{N/kg}$ and h is the height raised in $\mathbf{m}$.
- The energy transferred due to a temperature change is given by **mass × specific heat capacity × temperature change**.
  - The specific heat capacity of a substance is the energy to raise the temperature of one kilogram of the substance by one degree Celsius.
  - This equation can be written as $\Delta E = mc\Delta\theta$.
  - ΔE is the thermal energy transferred in $\mathbf{J}$, m is the mass of the object heated or cooled in $\mathbf{kg}$, c is its specific heat capacity of the object in $\mathbf{J/kg\,°C}$ and $\Delta\theta$ is the temperature change in $\mathbf{°C}$.

Power 4.1.1.4

- Power is the rate at which energy is transferred or at which work is done.
- Power is measured in Watts, $\mathbf{W}$. One Watt is the power that would transfer one Joule of energy in one second.
- The power of a process can be calculated as **energy transfered ÷ time** or **work done ÷ time**.
  - This can be written as $P = \frac{E}{t}$ or $P = \frac{W}{t}$.
  - P is the power in $\mathbf{W}$, E is the energy transferred in $\mathbf{J}$ and t is the time taken in $\mathbf{s}$.
- If two processes transfer the same amount of energy, then the one that completes the process in less time has a greater power.

Energy resources 4.1.3

- Energy resources are used for transport, heating and electricity generation.
- Most forms of transport, such as cars and planes, are designed to run on fuel. Some cars and trains can run on electricity instead.
- A renewable energy resource is one that can be replenished as it is used.

Types of energy resource		
Non-renewable		
Resource	**Description**	**Uses**
Fossil fuels (coal, oil, and natural gas)	Stores of energy found underground, which take millions of years to form.	Transport, electricity, heating
Nuclear power	The process of extracting the nuclear energy in uranium and plutonium.	Electricity
Renewable		
Resource	**Description**	**Uses**
Bio-fuel	The energy gained from burning waste products, such as wood.	Electricity, heating
Wind	The energy generated from wind turning a wind turbine.	Electricity
Hydro-electricity	The energy generated from water flowing downhill, often from a high lake behind a dam and turning a turbine.	Electricity
Geothermal	The energy generated using the heat inside the Earth.	Electricity, heating
Tidal	The energy generated from water flowing through a turbine as the tides change.	Electricity
Solar	The energy gained from sunlight through the use of solar panels.	Electricity
Wave	The energy gained from water waves flowing through a turbine.	Electricity

- Approximately 70% of the UK's energy was generated by fossil fuels in 2015, but this value is decreasing.

Conservation and dissipation of energy 4.1.2.1

- The principle of conservation of energy states that energy cannot be created or destroyed, only transferred.
- Energy can be transferred from one form to multiple others in a system. Dissipated or wasted energy is the energy that has transferred into a form that isn't useful.

- Heat losses can often be reduced using thermal insulation.
  - Thermal conductivity is the rate at which heat is transferred through a material.
  - Insulators have very low thermal conductivities.
- Ways of reducing energy losses are present in many parts of everyday life.
  - Buildings use thick, insulating walls and double glazed windows to keep heat inside.
  - Cars are streamlined to reduce heat lost to air resistance.

Efficiency 4.1.2.2

- The efficiency of an energy transfer is a unitless number that describes the proportion of energy that is transferred to a useful form. It can be written as a decimal or a percentage.
- Efficiency can be calculated as **useful output energy ÷ total input energy**.
- Efficiency can also be calculated as **useful output power ÷ total input power**.
- Efficiency can be increased by reducing energy losses.
  - Reducing the effects of friction through lubrication, reducing heat loss through insulation or reducing the effects of air resistance through streamlining will reduce the energy dissipated to the surroundings.

Energy and the environment 4.1.3

- Fossil fuels will eventually run out in the next 100 years, meaning we will eventually have to switch to renewable energy resources.
- A nuclear power plant can generate much more energy than a fossil fuel power station. The resources for it are expected to last for thousands of years despite being non-renewable.
- The burning of fossil fuels causes carbon dioxide to be released into the environment, contributing to global warming.
  - Nuclear power produces no pollutant gases. However, it does produce radioactive nuclear waste, which needs to be stored safely.
  - Coal will also release sulfur dioxide when burned, which is a cause of acid rain.
  - Bio-fuels are carbon neutral, as the carbon dioxide they release is the same as that taken in before their use as a fuel.

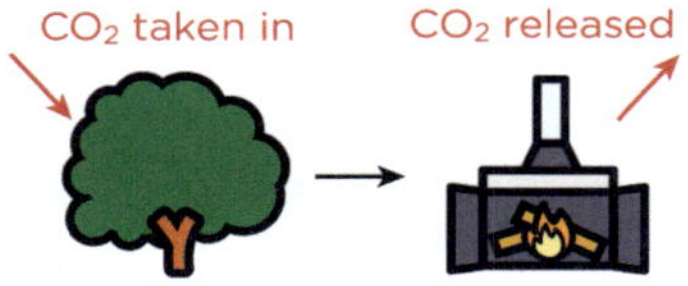

- Some power stations can have a negative effect on the areas in which they are constructed.
  - Wind turbines can be loud and potentially harmful to birds.
  - Hydro-electric dams will cause a new lake to form behind them. This can destroy natural habitats and force people to move homes.

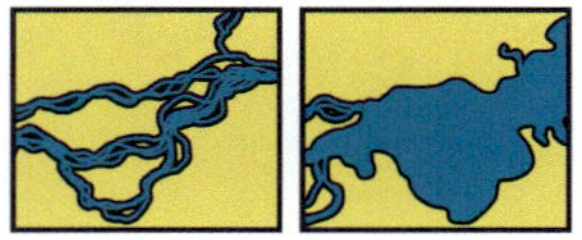

- Renewable energy resources, such as wind and solar, are entirely weather-dependent. Many countries have systems that switch from these resources to fossil fuels when renewable energy isn't available.

Circuit diagrams 4.2.1.1

- Circuit diagrams use symbols and lines to show the components in a circuit and how they are connected.

Symbol	Component	Symbol	Component
	Switch (open)		Switch (closed)
	Cell	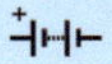	Battery
	Ammeter		Voltmeter
	Resistor		Fuse
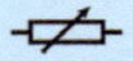	Variable resistor		Thermistor
	Lamp	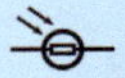	Light-dependent resistor (LDR)
	Diode		Light-emitting diode (LED)

- A fuse will melt when the current is greater than its rating, stopping a current from flowing in that branch of the circuit.

Charge and current 4.2.1.2

- Electrical charge is an intrinsic property of particles.
  - Protons have a positive charge while electrons have a negative charge.
  - Opposite charges will attract while like charges will repel.
  - Charge is measured in Coulombs, **C**.
- An electric current is a flow of electrical charge. In circuits, this is the flow of free electrons in wires and components.
  - The current will be the same at any point in a single closed loop.
  - The direction of the current is shown as the opposite to the direction of electron flow.

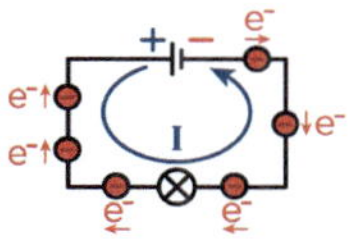

- The size of an electric current is given as the rate of flow of charge. The charge transferred by a current is given as **current × time**.
  - Current is measured in amperes, **A**.
  - This equation can also be written as $Q = It$.
  - Q is the charge in **C**, I is the current in **A** and t is the time in **s**.

Potential difference and resistance 4.2.1.3

- A current will only flow through a circuit when it has a source of potential difference (sometimes called a voltage). This will typically be provided by a cell or battery.
  - The electrons in the circuit are repelled from the negative terminal of the cell and attracted towards the positive terminal.
  - Potential difference is a measure of the electrical work done to move charge carriers through the circuit. It is measured in volts, **V**.
- Resistance is a measure of how difficult it is to form a current for a particular potential difference.
  - Resistors are used in circuits to decrease the current through it or certain parts of it.
  - Resistance is measured in Ohms, **Ω**.
- Current, potential difference and resistance in a component are related by the equation **potential difference = current × resistance**.
  - This can also be written as $V = IR$.
  - V is the potential difference across the component in **V**, I is the current through it in **A**, and R is the resistance of it in **Ω**.

Types of resistor 4.2.1.4

- An ohmic conductor is one that has constant resistance. This means the current through the conductor is proportional to the potential difference across it.
  - Most wires and standard resistors behave as ohmic conductors, so long as their temperatures are kept constant.
  - Variable resistors are ohmic conductors that can have the value of their resistance manually changed.
- The resistance of a filament lamp increases as the current through it increases. This is because the current is causing the filament in the lamp to heat up.

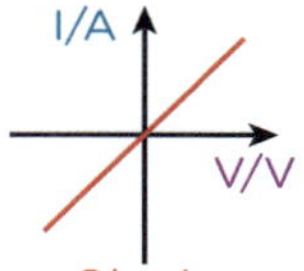

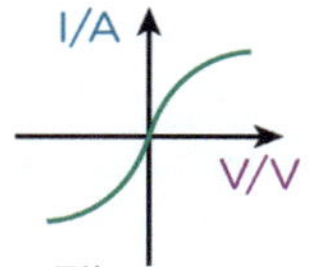

- A diode is a component that only allows current to flow in a single direction.
  - This is because its resistance is extremely high if the potential difference across it is below +0.7 V.
  - An LED is a diode that emits light when a current flows through it.

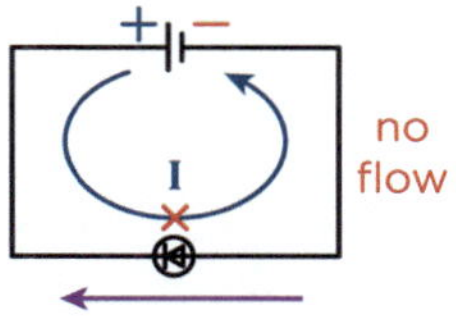

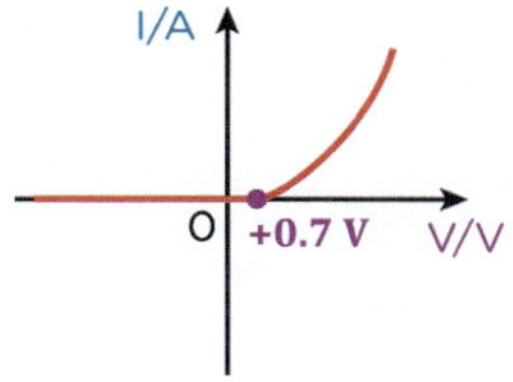

- The resistance of a thermistor decreases as its temperature increases. They can be used in circuits that react to temperature changes, such as thermostats.
- The resistance of an LDR decreases as the light intensity upon it increases. They can be used in circuits that react to changes in brightness in the surroundings, such as automatic lights.

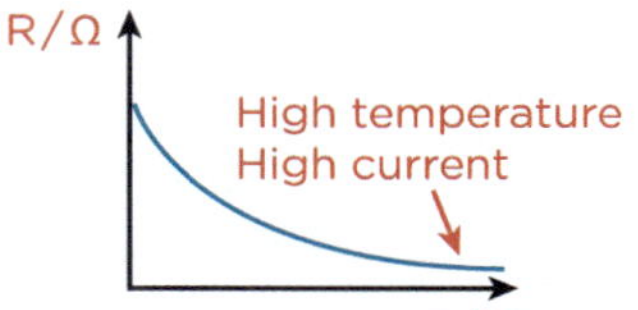

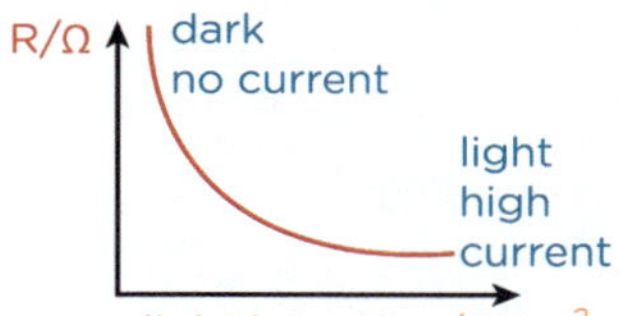

Circuits and domestic electricity

Measuring resistance 4.2.1.4

- The current through a component can be measured using an ammeter.
  - This must be connected in series with the component.
  - Ammeters have very low resistance so that they don't change the current in the circuit.
- The potential difference across a component can be measured using a voltmeter.
  - This must be connected in parallel with the component.
  - Voltmeters have very high resistances so that very little current flows through them.
- The resistance of a component can be found by measuring the current through it and potential difference across it.
  - A variable resistor can also be used to vary the current through the component.
  - By taking potential difference readings for multiple currents, it can be determined how the resistance changes for non-ohmic conductors.

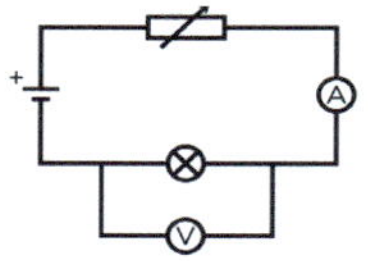

Series circuits 4.2.2

- Components connected in series are all part of the same branch of a circuit.
- The current through each component will be the same.
- The potential difference will be split between components dependent on their resistances.
  - The total potential difference across the components must be equal to that of the power supply: $V_{supply} = V_1 + V_2$.
  - When connecting cells and batteries in series, the power supply is the sum of their potential differences as long as they are all directed the same way.
- The total resistance, in Ω of two components connected in series is given as $V_{total} = R_1 + R_2$. Connecting resistors in series will increase the total resistance and reduce the current through them.

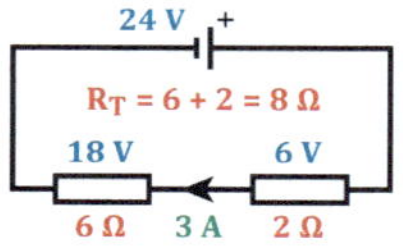

Parallel circuits 4.2.2

- Components connected in parallel are all on separate branches that meet at the same point.
- The potential difference across each component will be the same.
- The current will be split between the branches dependent on their resistances. The current through each component on the same branch will be the same.
- The total resistance of two components connected in parallel will be less than that of the smaller of their resistances.
- Connecting resistors in parallel will reduce the total resistance of the circuit and increase the total current flowing.

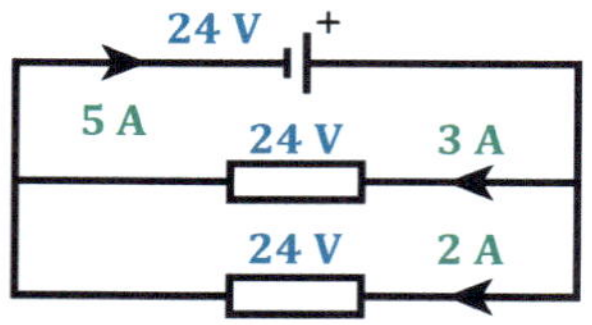

Electrical power 4.2.4.1

- The power of an electrical appliance is given as **power = potential difference × current**.
  - This can be written as $P = VI$.
  - P is the power of the appliance in **W**, V the potential difference across it in **V** and I the current through it in **A**.
- This can be combined with the equation for resistance to give **power = (current)^2 × resistance**, or $P = I^2R$, where R is the resistance of the appliance in Ohms, **Ω**.
- Most household appliances have a power rating, which can be used to determine the current that should flow through it from mains electricity.

Electrical energy transfers 4.2.4.2

- Batteries and cells do work to move electrons around a circuit.
  - This transfers the chemical energy in the battery to electrical energy in the circuit.
  - Electrons will collide with atoms in a resistor, causing electrical energy to be transferred to thermal energy as the resistor becomes hot.
- The energy transferred by electrical work to a component is given as **charge × potential difference**.
  - This can be written as $E = QV$.
  - E is the energy transferred in **J**, Q the charge that flows through the component in **C** and V the potential difference across it in **V**.
- The electrical energy transferred to an appliance is dependent on its power and the time it is turned on for. This is because **energy transfer = power × time** or $E = Pt$.
- Appliances will transfer energy from mains electricity or batteries to other forms.
  - Kettles will transfer energy to heat in water.
  - Motors will transfer energy to kinetic energy for rotation.

AC and DC currents 4.2.3.1

- A direct potential difference provides a direct current, which always flows in the same direction.
- An alternating potential difference causes an alternating current, which is constantly changing direction.
  - The number of times the current changes direction per second is its frequency.
  - Frequency is measured in Hertz, **Hz**. **1 Hz** is 1 cycle per second.
- UK mains electricity is supplied as an AC current of around **230 V** and **50 Hz**.

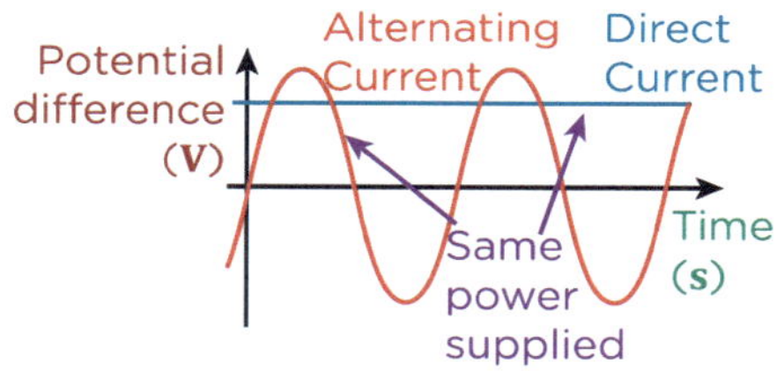

Three-core cables 4.2.3.2

- Most electrical appliances connect to a wall socket using cables containing three wires:
  - A live wire, which carries an alternating potential difference of **230 V** from the mains supply.
  - A neutral wire, which completes the circuit and has a potential difference of close to **0 V**.
  - The earth wire, which has a potential difference of **0 V**. It is a safety wire which only carries current in case of a fault.

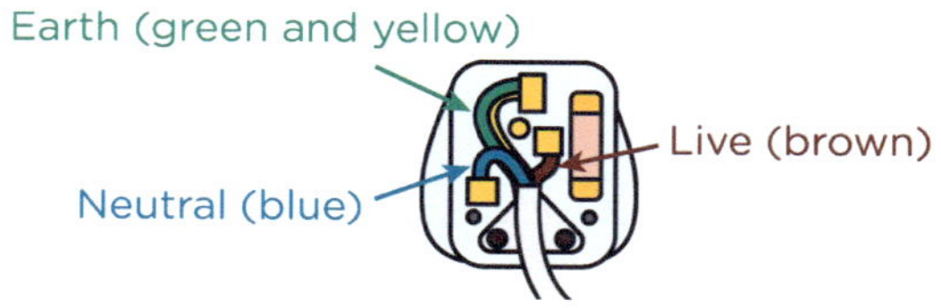

- There is a large potential difference between us and the live wire, so touching it would cause a current to flow through us and give us an electric shock.
- If the live wire touches a metallic appliance, then the earth wire is used to carry the resulting current away.

The National Grid 4.2.4.3

- The National Grid transfers electricity from power stations to consumers safely and efficiently.
  - Electricity is produced by generators in power stations at a high current.
  - Step-up transformers will raise the potential difference and lower the current.
  - This is transferred through long, overhead transmission cables. The low current means little energy is lost to heating in the cables.
  - A step-down transformer reduces the potential difference so it is suitable for domestic use.

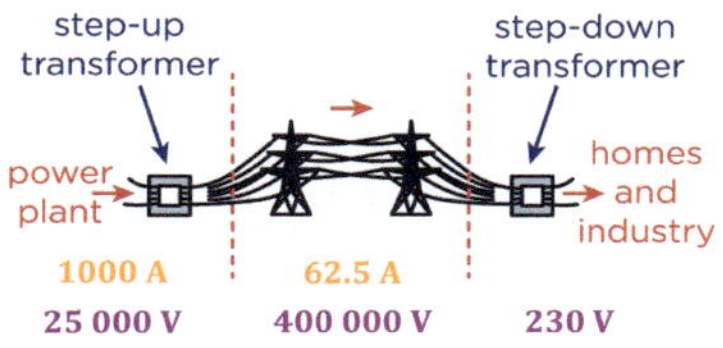

- The transformers change potential difference using the equation **primary potential difference × primary current = = secondary potential difference × secondary current**

Static charge 4.2.5.1

- When certain insulating materials are rubbed together, electrons will transfer from one material to the other.
  - This produces a static charge in both objects.
  - The object which gains electrons becomes negatively charged while the object which loses electrons becomes positively charged. These charges are equal and opposite.

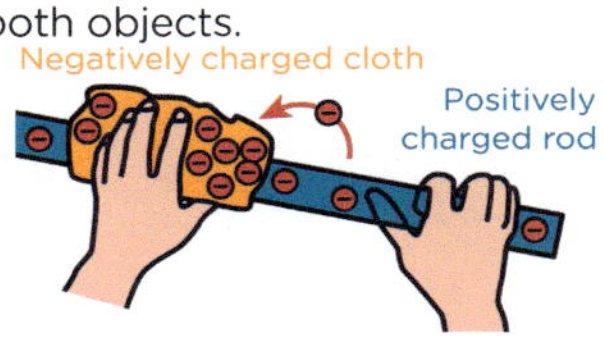

- Two charged objects will attract each other when they have opposite charges and repel each other when they have like charges.
- A spark is produced when a current flows from a charged object to an earthed metal object.
- Thunder clouds are examples of static electricity on a large scale.
  - Clouds gain charge when ice crystals in them rub together.
  - The bottom of the cloud gains a large negative charge.
  - Lightning is a spark between the cloud and the Earth due to a potential difference of millions of volts between them.

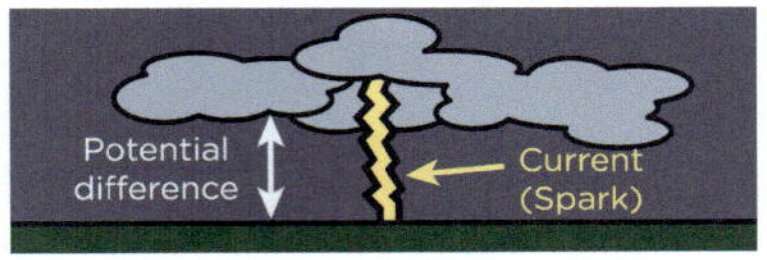

Electric fields 4.2.5.2

- A charged object will create an electric field around itself.
  - This field is strong close to the object and weakens with distance from the object.
  - Increasing the charge of the object will also increase the strength of the field.
- A charged object in the field will experience a non-contact force.
  - This will be an attractive force for opposite charges and repulsive for like charges.
  - The strength of the force is dependent on the strength of the field.
- Electric fields can be shown using field lines.
  - The field lines point in the direction of the force that a positively charged object would experience in the field.
  - The field lines get further apart with distance from the object because the field becomes weaker.

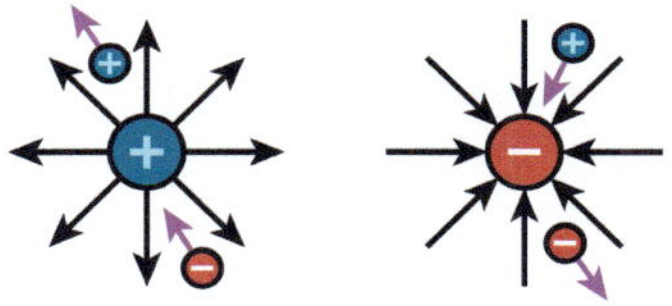

Density 4.3.1.1

- The density of an object is given as $\textbf{density} = \textbf{mass} \div \textbf{volume}$.
  - This can be written as $\rho = \frac{m}{V}$.
  - ρ is the density of an object in $\mathbf{kg/m^3}$, m is its mass in **kg** and V is its volume in $\mathbf{m^3}$.
- Density is a property of a material. We say steel is heavier than plastic because steel has a higher density.
- Density is partially dependent on the atomic mass of the molecules making up a material.
- Determining the density of irregularly shaped objects requires measuring their volume. This can be done by placing them in a measuring cylinder filled with water and measuring the change in volume.

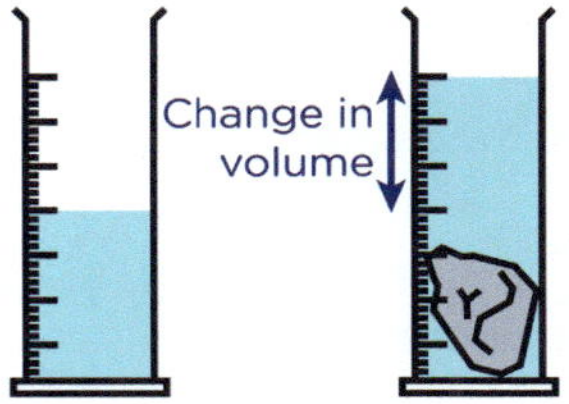

States of matter 4.3.1.1-2

- The different states of matter can be explained using particle models of atoms and molecules.
  - In a solid, the particles are all tightly packed in a rigid structure. They cannot move because of strong intermolecular forces but they can vibrate.
  - In a liquid, these forces are slightly weaker. The particles stay in contact but they can move and flow. The liquid can change shape to fit a container.
  - In a gas, the particles can freely move. They are spread out so the gas expands to fill any volume, and the forces between particles are very small.

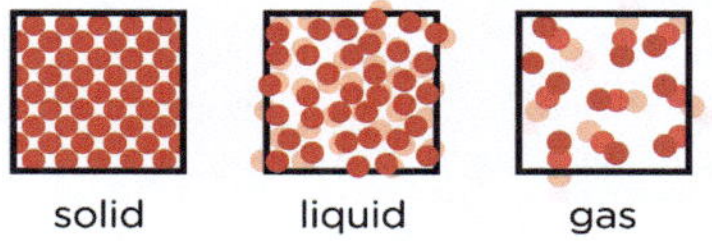

- Solids and liquids have high densities as atoms are tightly packed together. In gases, the density is much lower as the atoms or molecules are spread out.
- Substances can change state through various processes.
  - During these, mass is conserved as the number of particles doesn't change.
  - These are physical processes because they are reversible and the substance does not change.

Process	Change from...	To...
Melting	Solid	Liquid
Freezing	Liquid	Solid
Boiling/evaporating	Liquid	Gas
Condensation	Gas	Liquid
Sublimation	Solid	Gas

Internal energy 4.3.2.1

- The internal energy of a system is the total kinetic and potential energy of the particles in the system.
- Internal energy represents the energy stored in a system.
- Heating a system will increase its internal energy in one of two ways:
  - The kinetic energy of the particles increases, causing them to move or vibrate faster. This raises the temperature of the system.
  - The potential energy increases due to a change of state. The substance will change from a solid to a liquid or from a liquid to a gas.

SNAPREVISE

Specific heat capacity and latent heat 4.3.2.2-3

- The change in thermal energy associated with a temperature change in a system is given by **energy = mass × specific heat capacity × temperature change** or $\Delta E = mc\Delta\theta$.
- When heating a substance as it is changing state, its internal energy will increase but its temperature will not change. This can be noticed on a heating or cooling graph for the substance.
- The specific latent heat of a substance is the energy required to change the state of one kilogram of the substance without changing its temperature.

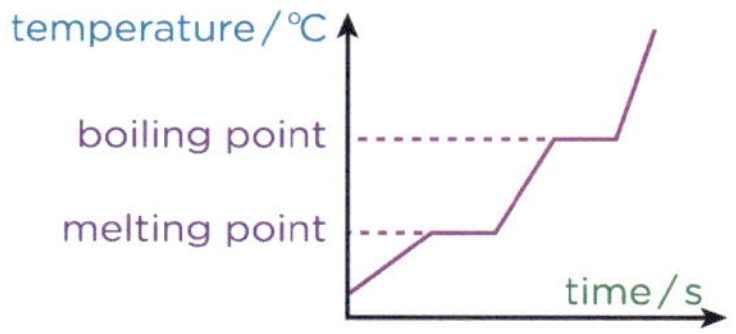

  - The specific latent heat of fusion is the specific latent heat for changing the substance from solid to liquid.
  - The specific latent heat of vaporisation is the specific latent heat for changing the substance from liquid to gas.
- The energy required to change state is given by **energy = mass × specific latent heat**.
  - This can be written as $E = mL$.
  - E is the energy required to change state in **J**, m is the mass of the substance in **kg** and L is its specific latent heat in **J/kg**.

Gas particles 4.3.3.1

- The particles in a gas move with random motion.
  - They travel in random directions with random speeds.
  - As the temperature of the gas increases, the particles gain more kinetic energy and their speeds increase.
- Gas particles will collide with each other and the walls of the container they are in.
  - No kinetic energy is lost during these collisions.
  - The collisions with the walls exert a force on them at right angles to them. This means the gas is exerting a pressure on the container.
  - Increasing the temperature of the gas without changing its volume increases this pressure, as the particles hit the walls with more force.

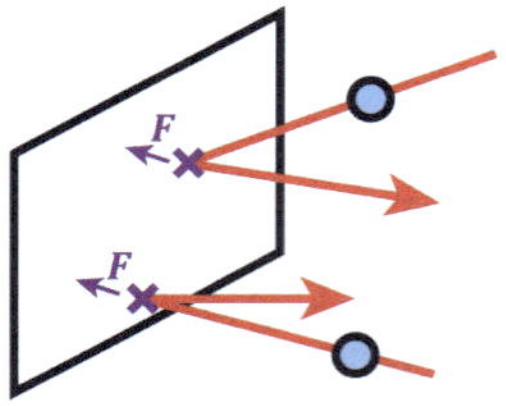

Gas pressure and volume 4.3.3.2

- If the volume of a gas increases without changing its temperature, then the pressure it exerts will decrease.
  - This is because the particles hit the walls of the container at the same speed but less frequently because of the larger space.
  - The walls will also be larger, so the force per unit area (pressure) will also decrease.
- For a gas at a fixed temperature, **pressure × volume = constant**.
  - This can also be written as $pV = \text{const}$
  - p is the pressure of the gas in Pascals, **Pa**, V is its volume in $\mathbf{m^3}$ and **const** is a constant value in $\mathbf{Pa\ m^3}$, which won't change as p and V change.

Work on gases 4.3.3.3

- Forces will transfer energy, this is called work.
- Work can be done on a gas to increase its internal energy, such as with a bicycle pump:
  - The piston in the pump does work to push gas particles into the bicycle tyre.
  - This work transfers kinetic energy from the piston to the particles.
  - This raises their kinetic energy, causing their temperature to increase.

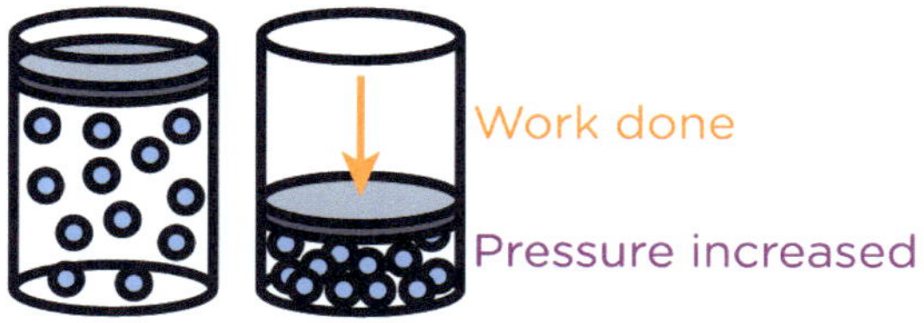

Atomic notation 4.4.1.2

- Atoms are represented using atomic notation, e.g. ${}^{56}_{26}\mathbf{Fe}$:
  - **56** is the mass number, which is equal to the total number of protons and neutrons in the nucleus.
  - **26** is the atomic number, equal to the number of protons in the nucleus.
  - **Fe** is the element the atom is of. This is determined by the atomic number.
- The number of neutrons in a nucleus can be found as **mass number − atomic number**.

Structure of the atom 4.4.1.1

- Materials are made up of atoms, which have a radius of around $\mathbf{1 \times 10^{-10}\ m}$.
- Each atom contains a nucleus, consisting of positively charged protons and uncharged neutrons.
  - The nucleus is around **1/10, 000** the size of the atom.
  - Almost all the atom's mass is contained in the nucleus.
- The nucleus is surrounded by negatively charged electrons.
  - These electrons move in set energy levels at different distances from the nucleus.
  - An electron will move further from the nucleus and increase its energy level by absorbing electromagnetic radiation.
  - It will move towards the nucleus and decrease its energy level by emitting electromagnetic radiation.

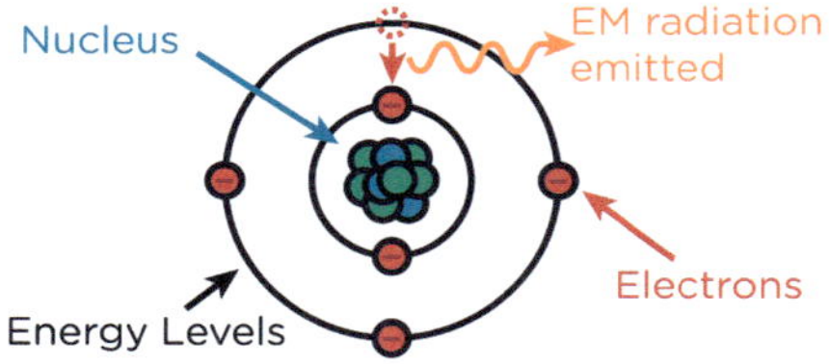

Ions and isotopes 4.4.1.2

- The number of protons in an atom is equal to the number of electrons it has.
  - Protons have equal and opposite charges to electrons.
  - So, the atom has no overall charge.
- Ions are particles that have charge due to an imbalance in proton and electron numbers.
  - Removing electrons from an atom will result in a positively charged ion.
  - Adding electrons to an atom will result in a negatively charged ion.
- Isotopes are atoms of the same element but with different masses. They will have the same number of protons and electrons but different numbers of neutrons.

${}^{4}_{2}\mathbf{He}^{-}$ (ion) ${}^{4}_{2}\mathbf{He}$ ${}^{3}_{2}\mathbf{He}$ (isotope)

Atomic models 4.4.1.3

- The idea of an atom as a tiny sphere that could not be divided was first suggested by Democritus in ancient Greece. This idea has evolved over time with new evidence.
- The discovery of the electron led J. J. Thomson to suggest the "plum pudding" model of the atom in 1904:

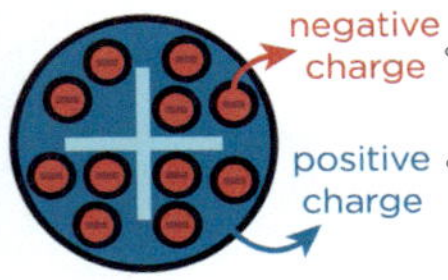

  - The atom consists of a sphere of positive charge that is evenly spread throughout.
  - Negatively charged electrons are dotted around this sphere.
- Geiger and Marsden's alpha scattering experiment led to Rutherford suggesting the nuclear model of the atom in 1911:
  - Alpha particles were fired at a thin sheet of gold foil. The plum pudding model suggested the alpha particles would pass straight through the foil.
  - Instead, a small number experience slight deflections with an even smaller number experiencing heavy deflections.

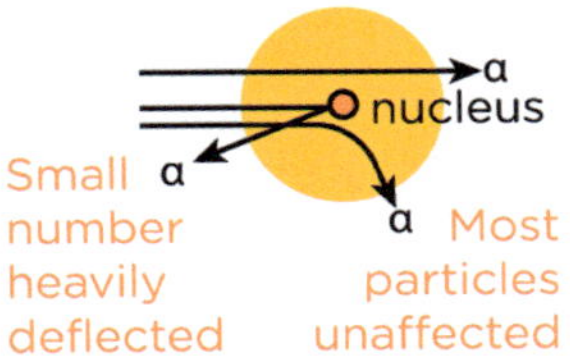

  - The nuclear model of the atom suggests the atom consists of mostly empty space. Almost all the mass and all the positive charge of the atom is contained in a very small nucleus.
- Later experiments led to the conclusion that the positive charge of the nucleus could be subdivided into smaller particles called protons.
- Niels Bohr adapted the nuclear model in 1913 to explain the role of electrons in the atom:
  - Electrons orbit the nucleus in set energy levels. These electrons emit or absorb electromagnetic radiation to change levels.
  - Bohr's theoretical calculations around these energy levels were later supported by experimental observations.
- In 1932, James Chadwick discovered that the nucleus also contained uncharged neutrons, which contribute to its mass.

Radiation and ionisation 4.4.2.1

- Certain nuclei are unstable, meaning they will undergo radioactive decay and emit radiation to become more stable.
- This radiation can ionise atoms, causing them to become ions.
- Activity is the rate of radioactive decay, measured in Becquerels (emissions per second).
- Detectors, such as a Geiger-Muller tube, can measure radioactivity by counting the number of particles entering it. This will give a count rate as the number of decays recorded per second.

Properties of radiation 4.4.2.1

- Nuclear radiation comes in multiple forms:
  - Alpha particles (α) consisting of two protons and two neutrons released from the nucleus (the same as a helium nucleus).
  - Beta particles (β) consisting of a high-speed electron. A neutron will turn into a proton to release this.
  - Gamma rays (γ) consisting of electromagnetic radiation emitted from the nucleus.
  - A neutron ($\mathbf{n}$) released from the nucleus.

Radiation	Range in air	Stopped by	Ionising power
Alpha	5 cm	Paper	Strong
Beta	Several metres	Aluminium sheet	Medium
Gamma	Near infinite	Thick lead	Weak

- Radiation is harmful to the body as it can damage cells and tissues.
  - Alpha radiation is the most damaging inside the body as it will be the most ionising.
  - Gamma radiation is the most damaging outside the body as it can penetrate the body from far away.

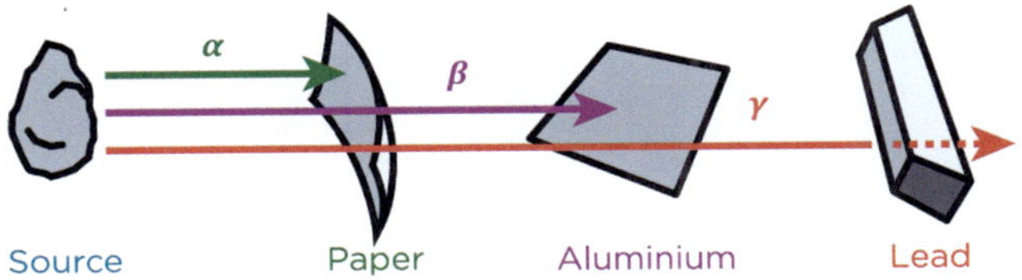

Nuclear equations 4.4.2.2

- An alpha particle can be denoted as ${}^{4}_{2}\mathrm{He}$.
  - Alpha decay will cause the atomic number of a nucleus to decrease by 2 and its mass number to decrease by 4.
  - For example, ${}^{235}_{92}\mathrm{U} \rightarrow {}^{231}_{90}\mathrm{Th} + {}^{4}_{2}\mathrm{He}$.
- A beta particle can be denoted as ${}^{0}_{-1}\mathrm{e}$.
  - Beta decay will cause the atomic number of a nucleus to increase by 1 while keeping its mass number the same.
  - For example, ${}^{99}_{43}\mathrm{Tc} \rightarrow {}^{99}_{44}\mathrm{Ru} + {}^{0}_{-1}\mathrm{e}$.
- Gamma rays are emitted after alpha or beta decays to carry away excess energy the nucleus has. This does not affect the mass or atomic number of the nucleus.

Half-lives 4.4.2.3

- Radioactive decay is a random process:
  - It is impossible to predict which nuclei in a radioactive sample will decay next or when.
  - Radioactive decay is unaffected by external physical conditions, such as temperature. Each nucleus has an equal chance of being the next to decay.
  - For a large number of radioactive nuclei, it can be calculated what proportion of nuclei will decay in a period of time.
- The half-life, $t_{\frac{1}{2}}$, of a radioactive isotope is the time it takes half the nuclei in a sample of that isotope to decay.
  - This will also be the time it takes the activity of the sample to halve.
  - Half-life will be the same for any sized sample and throughout its decay.
  - After n half-lives, the number of undecayed nuclei will be $\frac{1}{2^n}$ of its initial value.
- Half-life is a property determined by the isotope of a nucleus. The shorter the half-life, the faster an isotope will decay.

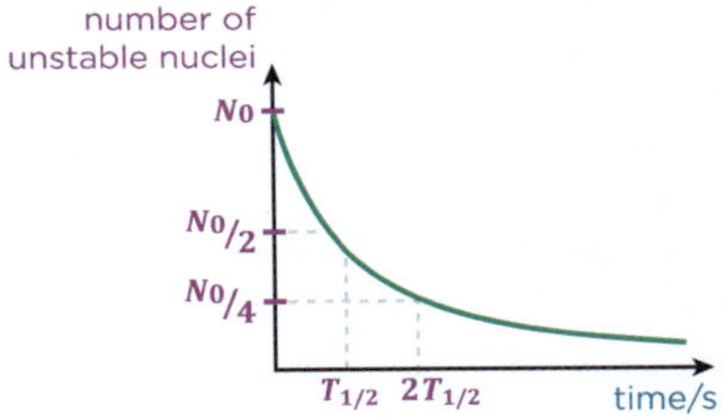

Contamination and irradiation 4.4.2.4

- Contamination is when radioactive materials are present where they are unwanted.
  - This poses a hazard as these materials will irradiate their surroundings, potentially without anyone realising this is happening.
  - Contamination can be caused by mishandling of radioactive materials or damage to nuclear power stations.
- Irradiation is the process of exposing an object to radiation.
  - This poses a hazard due to the potential damage the radiation can do to the body.
  - Irradiation can be useful in small, controlled doses.
  - Irradiation does not cause contamination.
  - Irradiation can be caused by unsafe handling of radioactive materials or exposure to contaminated materials.

Using radiation, nuclear energy, and forces

SNAPREVISE

Background radiation and dose 4.4.3.1

- There is always a small amount of background radiation around us due to:
  - Radon gas in the atmosphere and cosmic rays from space.
  - Small amounts of radioactive isotopes in rocks and building materials.
  - Man-made sources, such as nuclear power stations and weapons.
- When measuring activity, a background count should be taken to distinguish the activity from a sample from background radiation.
- The radiation dose a person receives is measured in sieverts, **Sv**:
  - A dose of **10 mSv** or lower will not cause immediate harm but could increase the risk of cancer.
  - A dose of **1000 mSv** will not be fatal but can make people unwell for some time.
  - A dose of around **4000 mSv** will be fatal.
- Background radiation alone will give extremely small doses. The exact dose a person receives will depend on location and occupation.

Uses of radiation 4.4.3.2-3

- The hazards and uses associated with radioactive isotopes depend on their half-lives:
  - Short half-lives mean isotopes are dangerous for a short period of time but are safe in the long term.
  - Long half-lives mean isotopes cause little irradiation but could cause damage through long-term exposure.
- Radioactive isotopes can be used as radioactive tracers.
  - Technetium-99 or another radioactive liquid is injected into the body and absorbed by an organ or system. The radiation it emits is detected outside the body.
  - Gamma emitters should be used as they cause minimal damage from inside the body. They should also have short half-lives so they can be detected but don't cause long-term damage.

- Radiation can be used in cancer treatment:
  - Intense gamma radiation can be directed at a tumour from outside the body to kill cancerous cells.
  - An alpha or beta emitter can be injected into the body to supply radiation directly to the tumour.

Nuclear fission 4.4.4.1

- Nuclear fission is the process of a large, unstable nucleus splitting into two smaller nuclei.
  - These two nuclei are similar in size but rarely identical.
  - Gamma rays will also be released after the fission reaction, along with two or three neutrons.
- Fission rarely happens spontaneously. It is typically induced by a neutron colliding with the unstable nucleus. The neutrons released in the fission reaction can then collide with other unstable nuclei to cause a chain reaction.

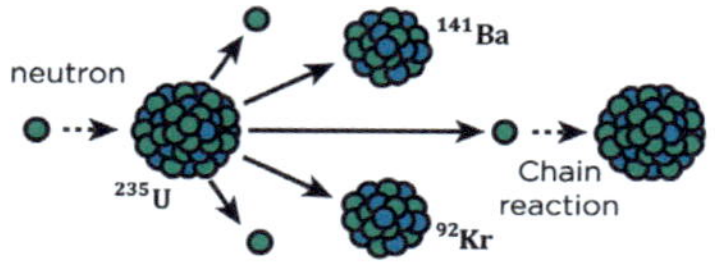

- A large amount of energy is released in the reaction:
  - The smaller nuclei gain kinetic energy due to their electrostatic repulsion.
  - This energy is transferred to the internal energy of atoms the nuclei collide with, raising the temperature of the system.

Nuclear reactor 4.4.4.1

- A nuclear reactor harnesses the energy released by fission:
  - Fuel rods of uranium-238 and uranium-235 are lowered into a reactor. Neutrons released from one rod cause a fission reaction of uranium-235 in another.
  - Control rods made of boron absorb neutrons released during fission to control the rate of chain reactions. The further the rods are lowered the slower the rate will be.
  - A thick concrete shield prevents neutrons and other radiation from escaping the reactor.

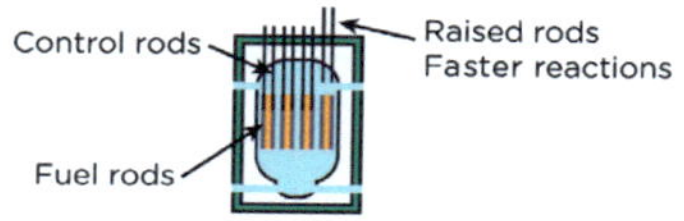

- Failing to control the chain reaction will cause energy to be released at an extremely fast rate. This is the principle used in a nuclear bomb.

Nuclear fusion 4.4.4.2

- Nuclear fusion is the process of joining together two small nuclei into a larger nucleus.
- This is extremely difficult to achieve but happens continuously in stars.
- The fusion reaction causes a large amount of energy to be released. This is what causes the star to be hot and bright.

Scalars and vectors 4.5.1.1

- Quantities can be scalars or vectors:
  - Scalars only have size.
  - Vectors have both size and direction.
- Vector quantities can be represented as arrows:
  - They point in the direction of the vector.
  - Their length represents the size of the vector.

Defining forces 4.5.1.2

- A force is a push or pull that one object performs on another, which can:
  - Change the direction an object is moving in.
  - Change the speed of an object.
  - Deform an object and change its shape.
- Contact forces act between objects that are physically touching. Non-contact forces act between objects that are physically separated.
- A force is a vector quantity that is measured in Newtons, **N**.

Contact forces	
Force	**Description**
Friction	The force a surface performs on an object moving along it to try and stop it.
Air resistance	The force that acts on an object moving through air to try and slow it down.
Drag	The force a fluid performs on an object moving through it to try and slow it down. Air resistance is a form of drag that acts on objects moving through air.
Tension	The force a rope exerts on an object when it is pulled.
Normal contact force	The force caused by a surface pushing against an object in contact with it.
Non-contact forces	
Force	**Description**
Gravitational force	The force that causes Earth to pull objects downwards and the Sun to keep planets in orbit.
Electrostatic force	The force that causes charged objects to attract or repel each other.
Magnetic	The force that pulls magnetic materials, such as iron or steel, towards magnets.

Gravity 4.5.1.3

- Large objects, such as the Earth, will produce a gravitational field.
  - Masses inside the gravitational field will experience a force called weight.
  - Weight will pull the mass towards the centre of the field. On Earth, this will pull masses down toward its surface.
  - Weight will act through a single point in the object called its centre of mass.
  - Smaller objects also produce gravitational fields, but the forces from these are too small to be noticed.
- The weight of an object can be measured using a spring balance.

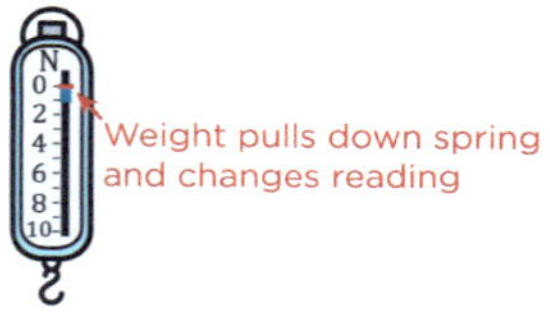

Calculating weight 4.5.1.3

- The weight an object experiences depends on mass and gravitational field strength.
  - Gravitational field strength is the force a **1 kg** object would experience at a point in a gravitational field, given in **N/kg**. This will depend on location in the field and what is producing the field.
  - Mass is how much matter makes up an object. An object's mass will be the same in any gravitational field at any point in the universe.
- The weight an object experiences is given by **weight = gravitational field strength × mass**.
  - This can be written as $W = mg$.
  - W is the weight an object experiences in **N**, m is its mass in **kg** and g is the gravitational field strength in **N/kg**.
- On the Earth's surface, the gravitational field strength has a constant value of **9.8 N/kg**.
  - This means that on Earth, mass is proportional to weight.
  - However, on other planets, the weight of an object will change while its mass will not.

Resultant force 4.5.1.4

- A resultant force is a single force that has the same effect on an object as the multiple forces acting on it.
- For two forces acting in a straight line:
  - If they are acting in the same direction, then the resultant will be the sum in that direction.
  - If they are acting in opposite directions, then the resultant will be their difference in the direction of the larger force.

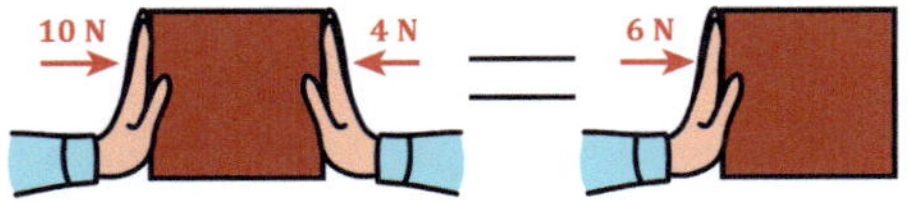

Free body diagrams 4.5.1.4

- A free body diagram shows the forces acting on an object:
  - Arrows are used to signify the forces and their directions.
  - The resultant force in the horizontal and vertical directions can be found by finding then adding or subtracting the forces in those directions.
  - If two forces acting in opposite directions have the same size, then they will cancel each other out.

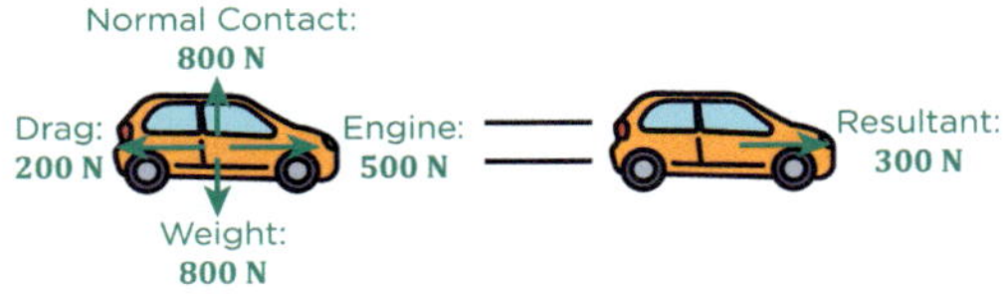

Resolving forces 4.5.1.4

- Resolving a force is the process of splitting a force into two perpendicular components. The resultant of these two components will be the original force.
  - Draw the original force as a vector arrow in the correct direction and to a suitable scale.
  - Draw a horizontal line from the start of the vector to a point that lines up vertically with its end.
  - Draw a vertical line from this point to the end of the vector.
  - Measure the lengths of the horizontal and vertical lines to determine the size of these components.

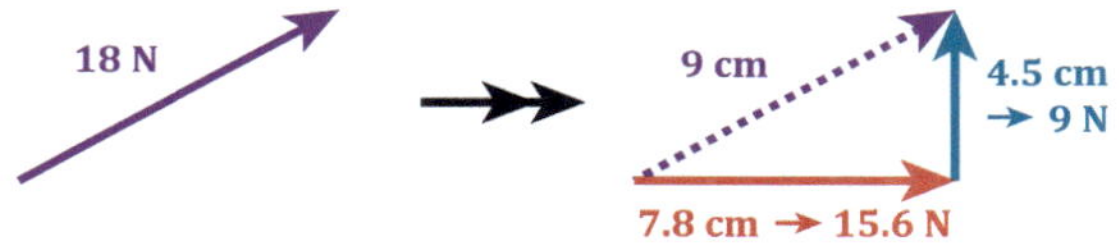

Work done 4.5.2

- A force does work on an object when it causes the object to move.
- The work done by a force is given by **work = force × distance moved (in the direction of the force)**
  - This can be written as $W = Fs$.
  - W is the work done in **J**, F is the magnitude of the force doing the work in **N** and s is the distance the force causes an object to move in **m**.
  - This equation assumes the object is moving in the direction of the force. No work is done if the object is stationary or the force is perpendicular to the direction the object is moving in.

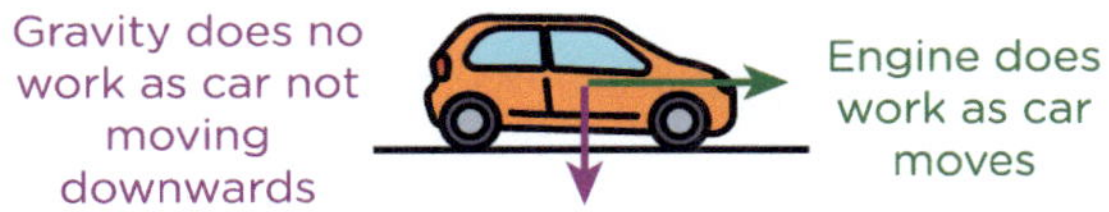

- Work is measured in Joules, **J**.
  - One joule is the work done by a **1 N** force to move an object **1 m**.
  - The units joules and newton-metres, **Nm**, are the same.

Energy transfer from work 4.5.2

- An energy transfer will occur when a force does work. This is why work and energy have the same unit.
- Lifting an object will cause work to be transferred to gravitational potential energy.
- Holding a heavy object stationary in the air will cause you to get tired as your muscles transfer energy, but they do no work.
- Pushing or pulling an object will cause work to be transferred to kinetic energy.
- If you are doing work against friction, then this work will be transferred to thermal energy in the object. This is why objects heat up when we rub them together.

Deformation 4.5.3

- A single force will only cause a stationary object to move. To deform (change the shape of) an object, multiple forces must be used:
  - Two forces pulling in opposite directions can stretch an object.
  - Two forces pushing in opposite directions can compress an object.
  - Two forces pushing in one direction at the ends of an object and one pushing in its centre can bend it.

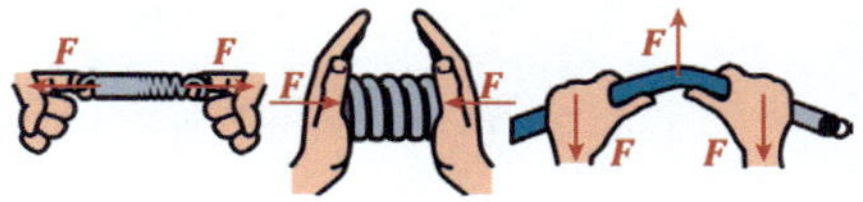

- Stretches can be elastic or inelastic:
  - An object will return to its original length after an elastic deformation.
  - An object will be permanently stretched after an inelastic deformation.

Extending springs 4.5.3

- The force required to stretch a spring is given by **force = spring constant × extension**.
  - The spring constant, or stiffness, of a spring determines how difficult it is to stretch. It is the force required to stretch the spring by **1 m**, with its value given in **N/m**.
  - This equation can also be written as $F = ke$.
  - F is the force causing the extension in **N**, k is the spring constant in **N/m** and e is the extension in **m**.
  - This equation can also be applied when e instead represents the distance the spring has been compressed.
- This equation will only apply to springs that have not been stretched beyond their limit of proportionality.
  - This is the extension after which force is no longer proportional to extension.
  - Inelastic deformation starts after this point.

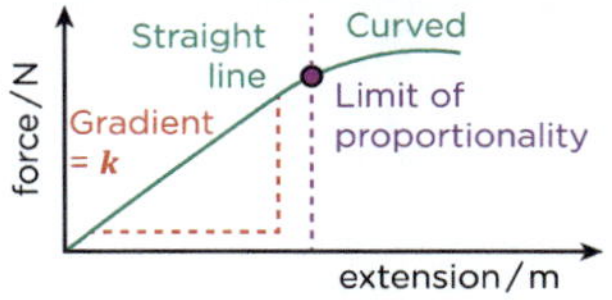

Elastic potential energy 4.5.3

- The work done to stretch a spring means energy is stored in a spring as elastic potential energy, given by

elastic potential energy $= \frac{1}{2} \times$ **spring constant** $\times$ **(extension)**^{2}

or $F = \frac{1}{2}ke^2$.

- No energy is stored in objects that deform inelastically. Instead, the work done on them causes them to heat up.

Moments 4.5.4

- The moment of a force is the turning effect it causes.
- The moment can be calculated as **moment = force × distance**.
  - This can be written as $M = Fd$.
  - M is the moment of the force in $\mathbf{Nm}$, F is the force in $\mathbf{N}$ and d is the perpendicular distance from the line the force acts on to the pivot of the object it is acting on in $\mathbf{m}$.
- Levers help to improve the moment from a force by allowing it to act far from a pivot. They are used to lift heavy objects that are close to the pivot and so the moment of their weight is small.
- Gears will exert contact forces on each other of equal magnitude. The radius of the gear determines the turning effect this force produces.

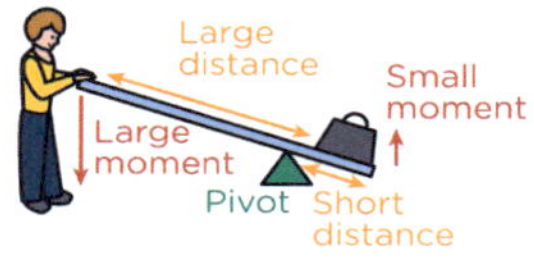

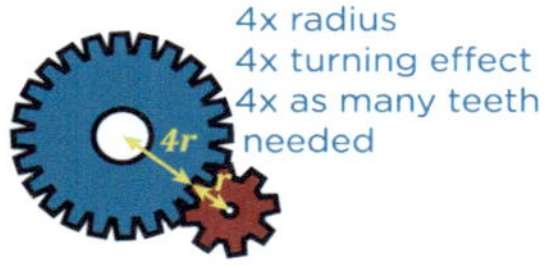

Resultant moment 4.5.4

- Moments can be directed clockwise or anticlockwise about a pivot.
  - The resultant moment is the difference between the total clockwise and anticlockwise moment. An object will turn in the direction of the resultant moment.
  - If the resultant moment is zero (meaning the clockwise and anticlockwise moments are equal) then the object doesn't turn and is in equilibrium. This is the principle of moments.
- Cranes and other machinery that could topple use counterweights to balance the moment from their load.

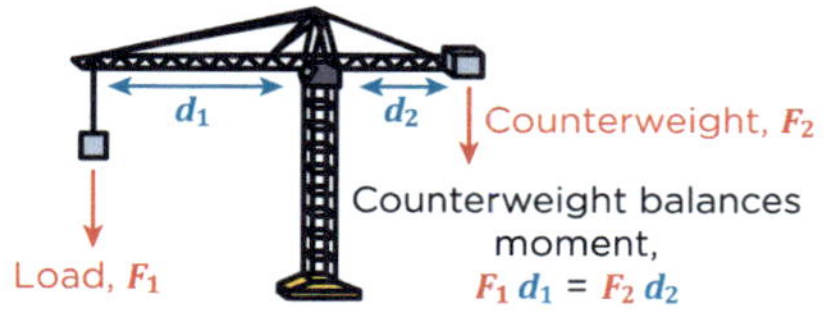

Fluid pressure 4.5.5.1.1

- A fluid is a substance that can flow, it is a liquid or a gas.
- Fluid in a container will exert a force on the walls of the container, at right angles to each wall.
- The pressure a force exerts on a surface is given by **pressure = force normal to a surface ÷ area of the surface**.
  - This can be written as $p = \frac{F}{A}$.
  - p is the pressure in pascals, $\mathbf{Pa}$, F is the force normal to a surface in $\mathbf{N}$ and A is the area of the surface in $\mathbf{m^2}$.

Column pressure 4.5.5.1.2

- As an object falls to a lower depth in a liquid, the pressure the liquid exerts on it increases. This is because there is a greater weight of liquid above the object.
- The pressure an object experiences at the bottom of a column of water is given by **pressure = height of column × density of liquid × gravitational field strength**.
  - This can be written as $p = h\rho g$.
  - p is the pressure in $\mathbf{Pa}$, h is the height of the column in $\mathbf{m}$, ρ is the density of the liquid in $\mathbf{kg/m^3}$ and g is the gravitational field strength in $\mathbf{N/kg}$.

Upthrust 4.5.5.1.2

- The pressure on the bottom surface of a submerged object will be greater than the pressure on the top surface. This pressure difference results in a force called upthrust.
  - Upthrust will try to push the object upwards to the surface of the liquid.
  - The size of the upthrust force is equal to the weight of the fluid that has been displaced by the object.
- An object will float if the upthrust force is greater than its weight.
  - Objects with densities greater than that of the liquid will sink.
  - Objects with densities less than that of the liquid will float on the liquid's surface, partially submerged. How much of the object is submerged depends on how dense it is compared to the liquid.

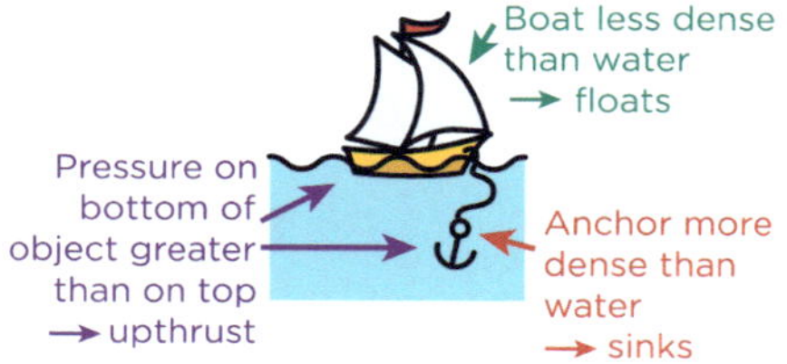

Distance and displacement 4.5.6.1.1

- Distance is a scalar quantity that describes how far an object moves or how far apart two objects are.
- Displacement is a vector quantity measured as a straight line from a start point to a finish point.

Atmospheric pressure 4.5.5.2

- Air particles are pulled towards the Earth by its gravitational field. This forms a layer of air around the Earth called the atmosphere.
- Atmospheric pressure is the pressure air molecules exert on a surface as they collide with it.
- Atmospheric pressure decreases with height above the Earth's surface.
  - This is because the air density decreases, and so there are fewer air molecules.
  - This means collisions between air molecules and surfaces happen less frequently, so the force exerted by the molecules is smaller.

Speed and velocity 4.5.6.1.2-3

- Speed is a scalar quantity that describes how fast an object is moving (or increasing the distance it has travelled).
- The constant speed and the distance travelled by an object are related by the equation **distance travelled = speed × time**.
  - This can be written as $s = vt$.
  - s is the distance travelled in $\mathbf{m}$, v is the speed in $\mathbf{m/s}$ and t is the time in $\mathbf{s}$.
  - This equation can also be used to calculate the average speed of a complete journey.
- Velocity is a vector quantity, given as an object's speed in a particular direction.

Example speeds 4.5.6.1.2

Motion	Typical speed
Walking	$1.5\ \mathrm{m/s}$
Running	$3\ \mathrm{m/s}$
Cycling	$6\ \mathrm{m/s}$
Car (on a motorway)	$30\ \mathrm{m/s}$
Train	$60\ \mathrm{m/s}$
Jet plane	$200\ \mathrm{m/s}$
Sound wave	$330\ \mathrm{m/s}$

- Few objects move at a constant speed. They will have small variations in speed during their motion. This also applies to sound waves and wind.
- The average speed at which people travel by walking, running or cycling is affected by numerous factors:
  - Age and fitness.
  - How far they are travelling.
  - The terrain they are travelling on.

Circular motion, acceleration, and terminal velocity

SNAPREVISE

Circular motion 4.5.6.1.3

- When an object travels in a circle:
  - It is travelling at a constant speed.
  - The direction it is travelling in is constantly changing.
  - As a result, its velocity is constantly changing.
- Examples of objects that travel in circles are:
  - Satellites in orbit.
  - Cars travelling around bends.
  - Planes banking to change direction.
  - Fairground rides, such as Ferris Wheels.

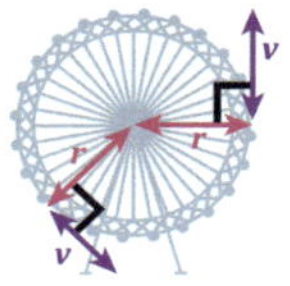

Distance-time graphs 4.5.6.1.4

- A distance-time graph shows how the distance travelled by an object changes with time.
- The speed of the object can be found by calculating the gradient of the graph.
  - A steeper gradient means a greater speed.
  - If the graph is horizontal, then the object is not moving.
- The distance-time graph for an accelerating object will be curved. The speed at a point in time can be found by measuring the gradient of the tangent to the graph at that point.

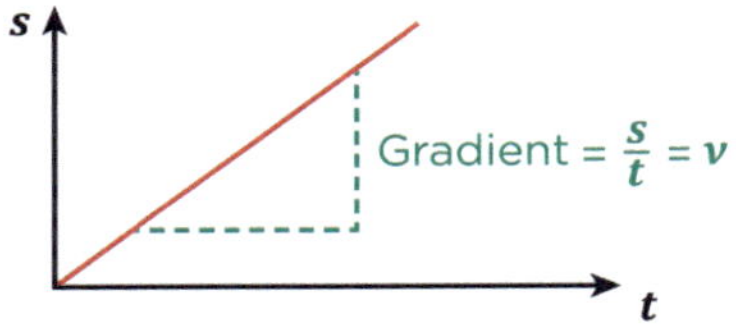

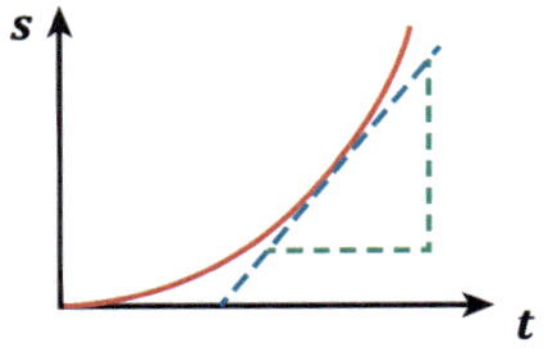

Acceleration 4.5.6.1.5

- Acceleration is the rate at which an object's speed is changing.
- An object that is speeding up is accelerating. An object that is slowing down is decelerating.
- The average acceleration of an object is given by **acceleration = change in velocity ÷ time**.
  - This can be written as $a = \frac{\Delta v}{t}$.
  - a is the average acceleration in $\mathrm{m/s^2}$, Δv is the change in velocity in $\mathrm{m/s}$ and t is the time in s.

Velocity-time graphs 4.5.6.1.5

- A velocity-time graph shows how the velocity of an object changes with time.
- The acceleration of the object can be found by calculating the gradient of the graph.
  - A steeper gradient means a greater acceleration.
  - If the graph is horizontal, then the object is moving at a constant velocity.
- The area under a velocity-time graph gives the distance travelled by an object.
  - For straight graphs, this can be calculated as the area of multiple triangles and rectangles.
  - For curved graphs, this distance can be estimated by counting the squares under the graph.

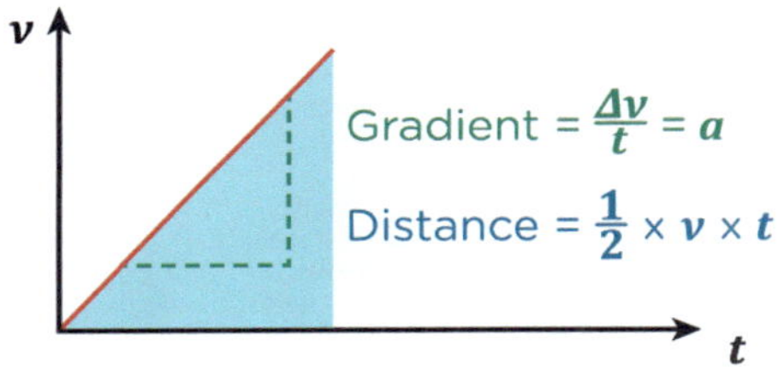

Distance = 52 x 50 m/s x 5s
= 13000 m

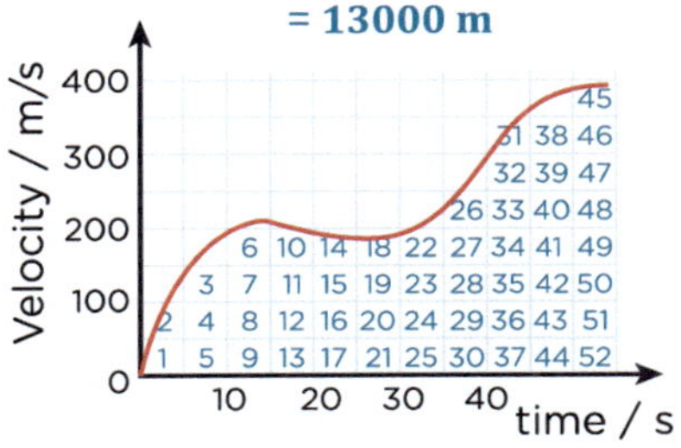

The distance each square represents is the velocity its height represents multiplied by the time its width represents

Uniform acceleration equation 4.5.6.1.5

- For an object that has constant acceleration, the following equation holds: $(\textbf{final velocity})^2 - (\textbf{initial velocity})^2 = 2 \times$ **acceleration × distance travelled**.
  - This can be written as $v^2 - u^2 = 2as$.
  - v is the final velocity in $\mathrm{m/s}$, u is the initial velocity in $\mathrm{m/s}$, a is the constant acceleration in $\mathrm{m/s^2}$ and s is the distance travelled in m.

Acceleration due to gravity 4.5.6.1.5

- Any object that is falling, with the only force affecting it being gravity, will have an acceleration of $9.8\ \mathrm{m/s^2}$.
- When an object is falling through a fluid:
  - It will initially accelerate downwards because of gravity.
  - This motion will cause air resistance or drag forces to affect it.
  - Eventually, the drag forces will equal the gravitational force and the object will stop accelerating. The constant speed it now travels at is its terminal velocity.
- The terminal velocity and the time it takes to reach it can be decreased by:
  - Increasing the surface area of the object, such as by using a parachute.
  - Increasing the thickness of the fluid, such as by falling in water rather than air.

Terminal velocity graph and forces 4.5.6.1.5

- As a parachutist falls through the air:
  - Their downward velocity will initially increase rapidly due to acceleration from gravity.
  - As air resistance starts to affect them, this acceleration will start to decrease. However, their velocity is still increasing as their weight is greater than the drag forces.
  - The air resistance will increase with their speed, to a point where it is equal to their weight. The parachutist now falls at a constant terminal velocity.
  - When the parachutist opens their parachute, the increase in surface area causes a sudden increase in air resistance. The parachutist rapidly decelerates as a result.
  - This air resistance decreases as the parachutist slows down. Eventually, it matches the weight again and the parachutist falls at a slower terminal velocity.

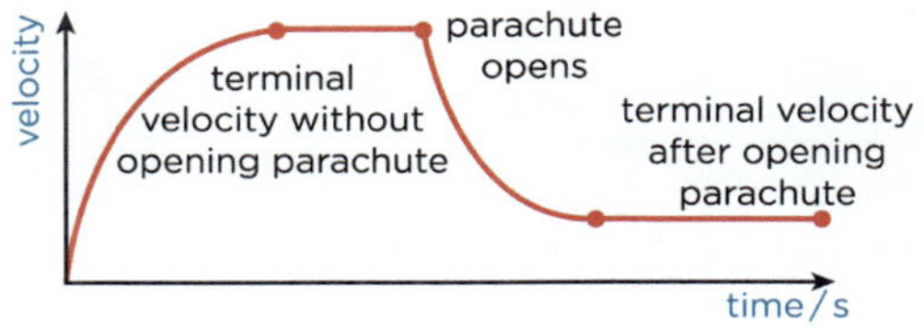

Newton's laws, stopping distance, and momentum

SNAPREVISE

Newton's First Law 4.5.6.2.1

- Newton's first law states that if the resultant force on an object is zero then it will experience no acceleration. This means the object will either:
  - Remain stationary.
  - Travel at the same, constant velocity.

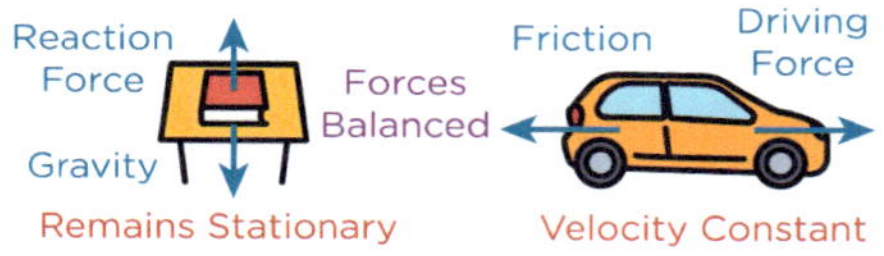

- Inertia is the tendency of an object to remain at rest or continue moving with uniform motion.

Newton's Second Law 4.5.6.2.2

- Newton's second law states that the acceleration of an object is proportional to the resultant force acting on it and inversely proportional to its mass.
- This law can be written as the equation **resultant force** $=$ **mass** $\times$ **acceleration**.
  - This can also be written as $F = ma$.
  - F is the resultant force in $\mathbf{N}$, m is the mass in $\mathbf{kg}$ and a is the acceleration in $\mathbf{m/s^2}$.
- The inertial mass of an object is a measure of how difficult it is to move or change the velocity of an object. It can be calculated as **inertial mass** $=$ **force** $\div$ **acceleration** or $m = \frac{F}{a}$.

Newton's Third Law 4.5.6.2.3

- Newton's third law states that if an object exerts a force on another object, that object will exert an equal and opposite force, of the same type, on the first.
- Examples of Newton's third law in action:
  - When an object is pulled towards Earth by gravity, the object is also pulling the Earth towards it.
  - When two charges repel or attract, they both experience the same force towards or away from each other.
  - When you stand on a floor, the floor exerts an upward reaction force that is equal to your weight pushing down on it.

Stopping distance 4.5.6.3.1

- The stopping distance of a vehicle is the distance it will travel before decelerating to a stop.
- The stopping distance will be the sum of the thinking distance and braking distance.
  - The thinking distance will be the distance travelled before the driver reacts to the need to stop.
  - The braking distance will be the distance the vehicle travels after its brakes are applied.
- The greater the speed of a vehicle, the further its stopping distance will be.

Estimating stopping distance 4.5.6.3.1

- Average stopping distances for cars at varying speeds are given in the Highway Code:
  - A car travelling at **20 mph** will have a thinking distance of around **6 m** and a braking distance of around **6 m**.
  - A car travelling at **70 mph** will have a thinking distance of around **21 m** and a braking distance of around **75 m**.
- The relationship between speed and stopping distance can be inferred from graphed data.

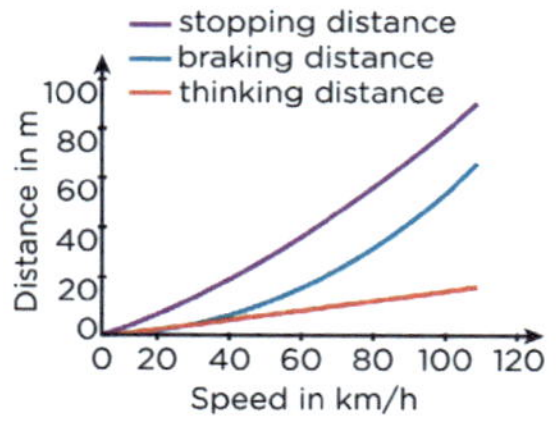

Factors affecting reaction time 4.5.6.3.2

- People's reaction times will vary. They are typically between **0.2 s** and **0.9 s**. Reaction times can be tested by asking someone to grab a ruler as it is dropped or press a timed button after a light comes on.
- A driver's reaction time will be increased by:
  - Drinking alcohol.
  - Drugs and certain medications.
  - Tiredness.
  - Becoming distracted or using a phone whilst driving.

Momentum 4.5.7.1

- The momentum of an object is calculated as **momentum** $=$ **mass** $\times$ **velocity**
  - This can also be written as $p = mv$.
  - p is the object's momentum in $\mathbf{kg\ m/s}$, m is its mass in $\mathbf{kg}$ and v is its velocity in $\mathbf{m/s}$.
- Momentum is a vector quantity. Its direction is the same as that of the object's velocity.

Factors affecting braking distance 4.5.6.3.3

- Thinking distance is changed by conditions affecting the driver while braking distance is affected by conditions affecting the vehicle or road.
- The braking distance of a vehicle will increase if:
  - The roads are slippery, icy, smooth or other conditions that will reduce the friction it causes.
  - The braking force the vehicle can provide is reduced.
  - The vehicle is not maintained well, particularly its tyres and brakes.

Braking force 4.5.6.3.4

- When a vehicle applies its brakes:
  - The brakes apply a frictional (braking) force to the wheels.
  - This frictional force does work to transfer kinetic energy away from the wheels and hence the vehicle.
  - This energy is stored in the brakes and causes them to heat up.
- At higher speeds, the braking force will need to be larger.
  - This will increase the work done by the braking force.
  - This creates a risk of the brakes overheating and the driver losing control of the vehicle.
- A **1500 kg** family car travelling on a motorway would need a braking force of **~6000 N** to come to a stop, while a **35 000 kg** truck travelling at the same speed would need a force of **~90 000 N** to stop.

Conservation of momentum 4.5.7.2

- The principle of conservation of momentum states that in a closed system, the total momentum before an event must be the same as the total momentum after an event.
- Examples of conservation of momentum.
  - When a stationary gun fires a bullet, the gun recoils because it gains momentum equal and opposite to that of the bullet.
  - If a car travelling at speed crashes into a stationary car and they stick together, they will continue moving at reduced speed. If they originally had equal and opposite momenta, they will be brought to a stop.
  - If a snooker ball strikes a second ball and stops, the second snooker ball will start travelling with the first ball's initial momentum.

Calculating change in momentum 4.5.7.2-3

- Calculations involving conservation of momentum can be solved by calculating the total momentum before and after an event and equating them.
  - If two objects are travelling in the same direction, their momenta should be added.
  - If two objects are travelling in opposite directions, then their momenta should be subtracted.

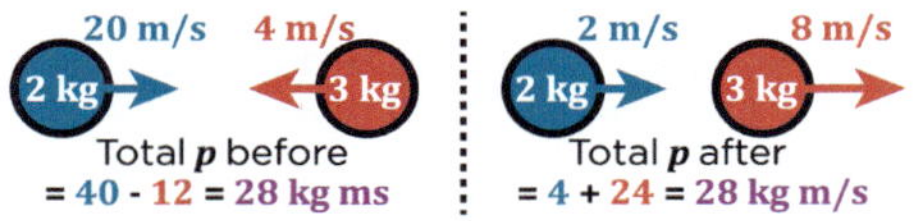

- Combining the equations $F = ma$ and $a = \frac{\Delta v}{t}$ leads to the relation between force and momentum: $F = \frac{m\Delta v}{t}$
  - F is the force causing a change in momentum in $\mathbf{N}$, m is the mass of an object in $\mathbf{kg}$, Δv is its change in velocity in $\mathbf{m/s}$ and t is the time the force is applied for in $\mathbf{s}$.
  - This equation shows that force is equal to the rate of change of momentum.
- To stop moving, a force must be applied to change momentum to zero. Increasing the time it takes to stop will reduce the rate of change of momentum and the force. This principle is applied in numerous safety features:
  - Crash mats and other cushioned surfaces.
  - Helmets, shin pads and other protective gear.
  - Seat belts and airbags in cars.
  - Crumple zones, which collapse during a collision.

Transverse and longitudinal waves 4.6.1.1

- Waves are used to transport energy or information. When a wave travels through a medium such as water or air, it is the wave and not the medium that is travelling.
- Transverse waves are caused by vibrations that are perpendicular to their energy transfer. Examples of transverse waves are light and water ripples.
- Longitudinal waves are caused by vibrations that are parallel to the direction of energy transfer.
  - Longitudinal waves consist of compressions, where matter is pushed together, and rarefactions, where it is pulled apart.
  - Sound is an example of a longitudinal wave. It is produced by a vibrating object and travels through air by creating compressions and rarefactions in it.

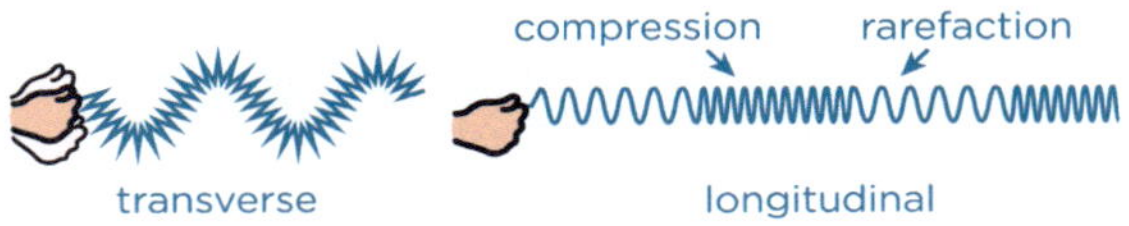

Wave properties 4.6.1.2

- The amplitude, A, of a wave is the height of a wave, measured from its peak or trough to its undisturbed position.
- The wavelength, λ, of a wave is the distance between two equivalent points on it. It can be measured as the distance between two consecutive peaks or troughs.
- The frequency, f, of a wave is the number of waves produced per second or the number of waves that pass a point in a second.
- The period, T, is the time it takes to produce one wave.
- Frequency and period are related by the equation **period = 1 ÷ frequency**.
  - This equation can be written as $T = \frac{1}{f}$.
  - T is the period in $\mathbf{s}$ and f is the frequency in $\mathbf{Hz}$.

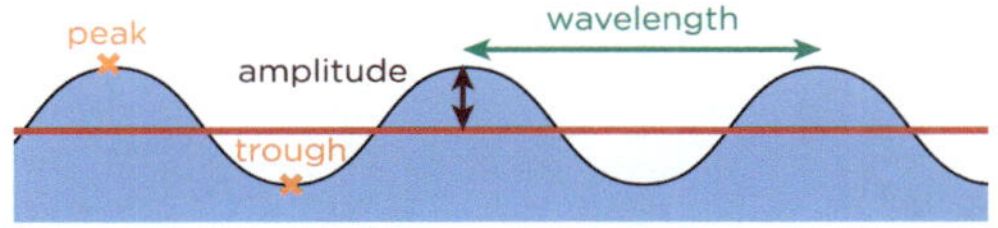

Wave speed 4.6.1.2

- Wave speed is the speed at which energy will be transferred by a wave, or the speed at which a wave moves, through a medium.
- Wave speed can be calculated as **wave speed = frequency × wavelength**.
  - This equation can be written as $v = f\lambda$.
  - v is the wave speed in $\mathbf{m/s}$, f is the frequency in $\mathbf{Hz}$ and λ is the wavelength in $\mathbf{m}$.
- Wave speeds can be determined by:
  - Measuring the wavelength and frequency of water ripples.
  - Reading the wavelength and frequency of sound waves from an oscilloscope.
  - Recording the time it takes a sound echo to return to you after reflecting off a nearby building a known distance away.

Transmission 4.6.1.2-3

- Waves can travel from one medium to another. However, when they do so:
  - Their frequency will not change.
  - Their wavelength will increase or decrease.
  - So, the wave speed will increase or decrease.
- The wavelength and speed of water ripples will decrease when they enter shallower water.
- Sound waves will travel at different speeds in different media.

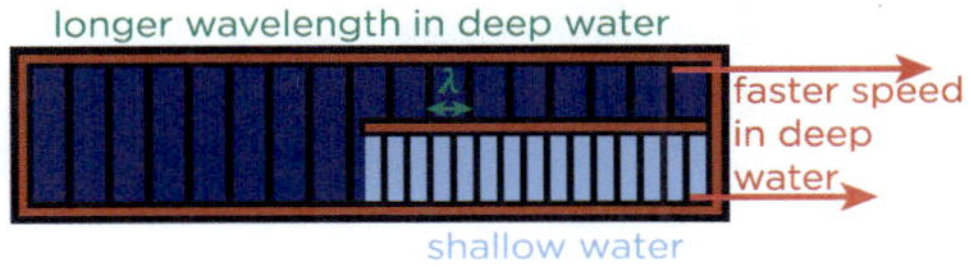

Reflection and absorption 4.6.1.3

- When a wave reaches a boundary between two media, it can be transmitted, absorbed, or reflected.
- Typically, a wave that is reflected will also partially be transmitted.
- Waves will be reflected such that **angle of incidence = angle of reflection**.
  - This equation can be written as $i = r$, where i is the angle of incidence and r is the angle of reflection.
  - These angles are measured between the path of the wave and the normal to the boundary. The normal is a line drawn at **90°** to its surface.

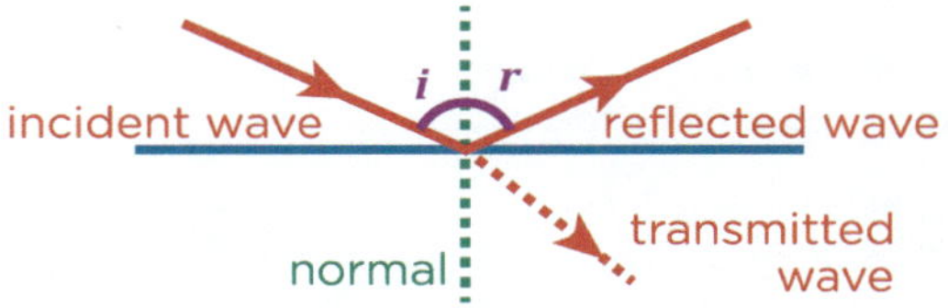

- We see an image in a mirror because reflected rays of light from an object appear to converge at a point inside the mirror.
- White and brightly coloured materials reflect a lot of light, while black and darkly coloured materials absorb a lot of light.

Sound waves 4.6.1.4

- Sound waves can travel through solids and liquids by causing vibrations in them.
- We detect sound waves using our ears:
  - When sound waves enter the ear, they cause the eardrum to vibrate.
  - This causes small bones in the ear to vibrate.
  - These connect to nerves, which send a signal to the brain, which interprets the vibrations as sound.
  - This process will only work for sound waves with frequencies between **20 Hz** and **20 000 Hz**.

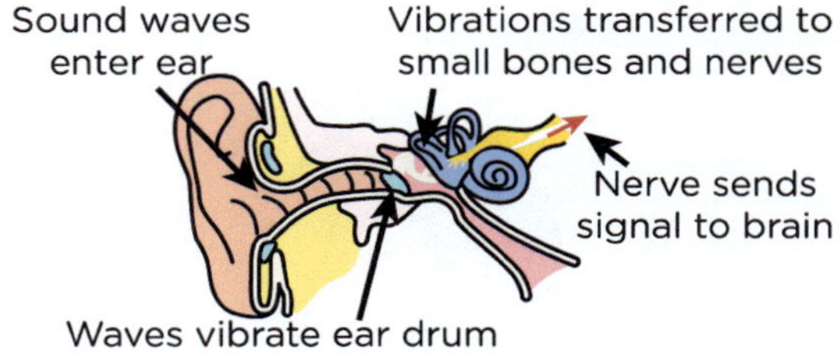

Ultrasound 4.6.1.5

- An ultrasound wave is a sound wave at a frequency above the range of human hearing.
- Ultrasound can be used for detection, such as with medical scans or sonar:
  - Ultrasound is directed as a beam.
  - The waves are partially reflected when they meet a boundary between two different media, and travel back to a detector.
  - A computer records the reflected waves' intensities and the times it took for them to return. This information is used to produce an image or determine the depth of the sea.
- Ultrasound is especially useful for foetal scanning as it does no harm to the patient or unborn baby.

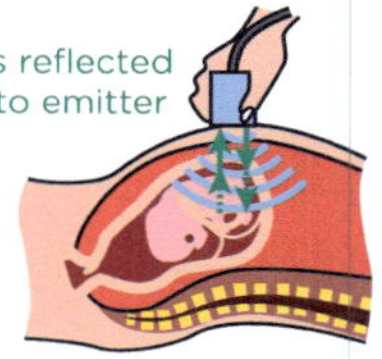

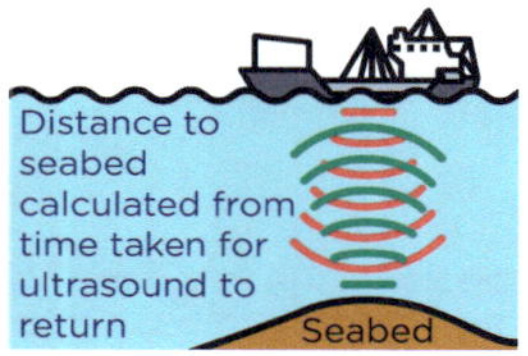

Seismic waves 4.6.1.5

- Earthquakes will produce seismic waves.
  - P-waves are longitudinal seismic waves. They will travel through solids and liquids at different speeds.
  - S-waves are transverse seismic waves. They can only travel through solids.
- The analysis of seismic waves and their reflections and transmissions inside the Earth has provided evidence to scientists about the Earth's structure and the properties of its three layers:
  - The outer layer of the Earth is the mantle. This is solid and all seismic waves can travel through it.
  - The outer layer of the core is liquid, meaning S-waves cannot travel through it.
  - The inner core is solid, meaning the P-waves that reach it will change speed.

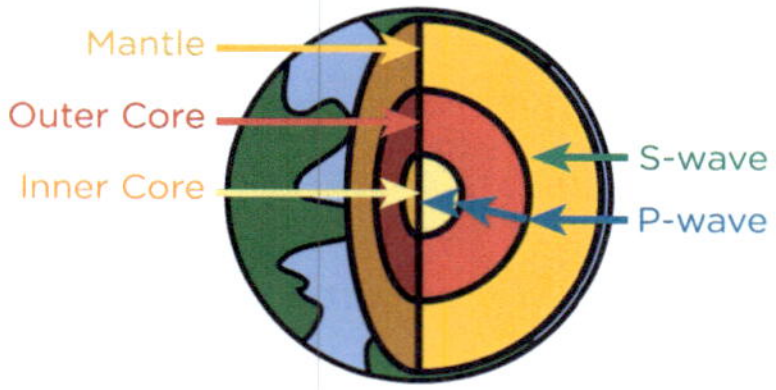

Electromagnetic waves 4.6.2.1

- Electromagnetic waves are transverse waves that transfer energy from a source to an absorber.
- The different types of electromagnetic waves form a continuous spectrum.
  - All electromagnetic waves will have the same speed in air or a vacuum.
  - This means that electromagnetic waves with larger wavelengths must have smaller frequencies.

Types of electromagnetic wave	
Wave	Approximate wavelength range
Gamma ray	10^{-12} m to 10^{-10} m
X-ray	10^{-10} m to 10^{-8} m
Ultraviolet	10^{-9} m to 10^{-7} m
Visible light	10^{-7} m
Infrared	10^{-6} m to 10^{-4} m
Microwave	10^{-4} m to 10^{-2} m
Radio wave	10^{-2} m to 10^{3} m

- Humans are only capable of seeing visible light.
  - Visible light can be split into a spectrum of colours.
  - Red light has the longest wavelength and the lowest frequency. Violet light has the shortest wavelength and the highest frequency.

Radio waves 4.6.2.3

- Radio waves can be sent and received using aerials.
  - An alternating current of high frequency in the transmitter causes electrons to oscillate up and down the aerial.
  - This causes an electromagnetic wave, consisting of electric and magnetic fields oscillating at right angles to each other and the direction of energy transfer.
  - When the wave reaches the receiving aerial, the fields cause electrons to oscillate up and down in it.
  - This produces an alternating current of the same frequency as that in the transmitter.
- Radio waves can be used to send and receive signals for TV and radio broadcasts.

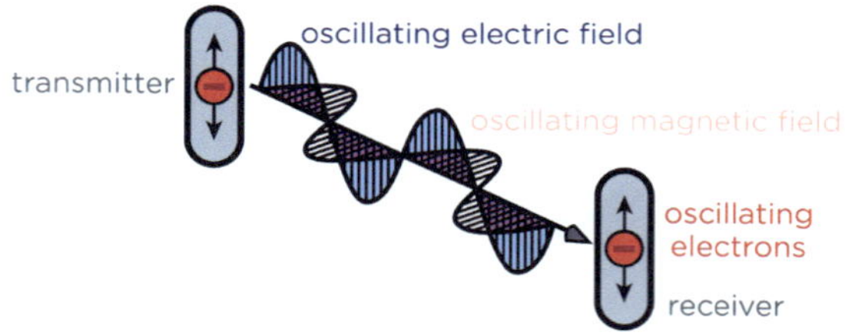

Refraction 4.6.2.2

- When an electromagnetic wave meets a surface, it can be:
  - Transmitted, causing the wave to pass through.
  - Absorbed, causing the wave to be stopped at the boundary.
  - Reflected, causing the wave to be redirected away from the boundary.
- The behaviour of the wave depends on its wavelength and the surface it is meeting.
  - Surfaces appear certain colours because those are the wavelengths of visible light that are reflected off them. All other colours are absorbed.
  - Metals reflect most waves but short wavelength waves, such as gamma waves, will pass through.
- Electromagnetic waves will change direction when transmitting into a different medium at an angle. This is called refraction.
  - Refraction can be shown on a ray diagram. A ray is a thin beam of electromagnetic waves, such as visible light.
  - The angle at which the ray enters a boundary is the angle of incidence. The angle at which it leaves is the angle of refraction. Both angles are measured against the normal, a line at **90°** to the surface.

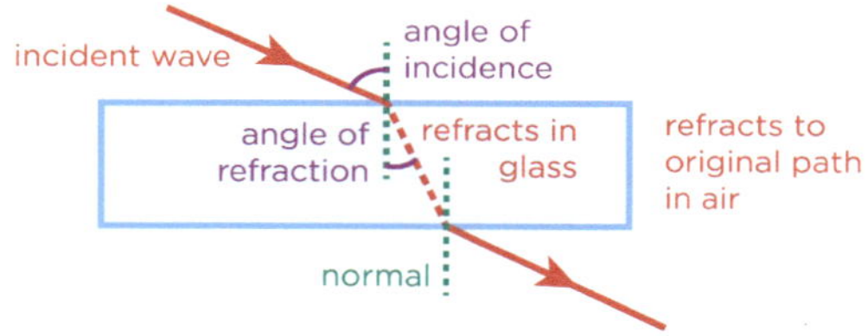

Refraction and speed 4.6.2.2

- The speed of an electromagnetic wave changes depending on the medium it is travelling through.
- Refraction is caused by light changing speed as it enters a different medium.
  - If light slows down it will bend towards the normal.
  - If light speeds up it will bend away from the normal.
- Refraction can also be observed in water waves when entering a shallower part of water.
  - The waves will slow down with shorter wavelengths.
  - The waves will change direction.

Hazardous waves 4.6.2.3

- Changes in atoms or nuclei can result in the generation of electromagnetic waves.
  - Gamma rays are generated when the nuclear energy of an atom falls.
  - Changes in atoms can be the result of them absorbing electromagnetic waves.
- Ultraviolet, X-ray and gamma electromagnetic radiation can all cause harm to the body by causing mutations to cells. This can lead to cancerous growths.
  - Ultraviolet waves can increase the risk of skin cancer or cause skin to age prematurely. Exposure to UV rays comes from the sun and tanning beds. This can be reduced by using sun cream and reducing the time spent in direct sunlight.
  - X-rays and gamma rays are commonly used in medical procedures. Doctors will limit the number of times you undergo these procedures and hospital staff take precautions against this radiation.
- The exposure people have to harmful radiations should be measured. Radiation dose is measured in sieverts, **Sv**, and depends on the type of radiation, its intensity and how long exposure is for.

Applications of EM waves 4.6.2.4

Wave	Key property	Use
Radio	Can travel long distances and reflect off the ionosphere	TV and radio Signals
Microwaves	Can easily travel through the Earth's atmosphere	Satellite communication
Microwaves	Absorbed by water to cause heating	Cooking
Infrared	Emitted by warm bodies	Heaters, cooking, and infrared cameras
Visible light	Travels at high speed in glass	Optical fibres
Ultraviolet	Absorbed by some materials and re-emitted as visible light	Energy efficient lamps
Ultraviolet	Reacts with pigments in skin	Tanning
Gamma	Penetrates skin and tissue and can be emitted by tracers	Medical imaging
X-ray	Penetrates skin and tissue but absorbed by bone	Medical imaging
Gamma/ X-ray	Damages and kills cancer cells	Medical treatments

Lenses 4.6.2.5

- Lenses use refraction to redirect light and form an image.
  - Convex lenses will cause light rays from a distant object to converge at a point to form a real image. This image can be seen by placing a sheet of paper on the other side of the lens.
  - Concave lenses will diverge light away from a point to form a virtual image. This image will make us think an object is somewhere it is not and cannot be formed on paper.
  - Convex lenses can also form virtual images of objects close to them.
- Light rays passing through the lens parallel to its principal axis will converge to a single point. This is the principal focus of the lens.
  - The focal length is the distance between the principal focus and the lens.
  - As a concave lens causes rays to diverge, the focus is instead a virtual focus that is on the same side of the lens as the original rays.

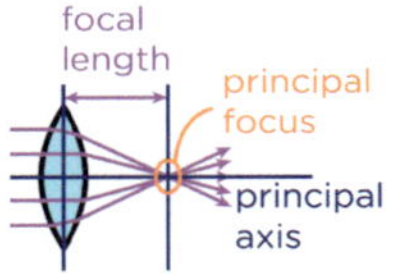

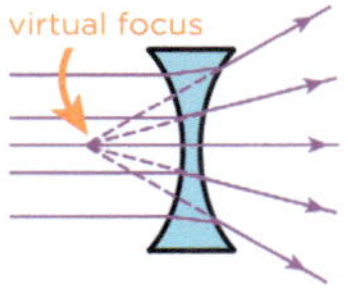

Visible light 4.6.2.6

- Visible light consists of a spectrum of different colours. Each colour corresponds to a small range of wavelengths.

- Specular reflection is when light reflects off a smooth surface. Diffuse reflection is when light reflects at different angles off a rough surface
  - Light reflects in a single direction in specular reflection to form a clear image, such as with a mirror.
  - Light will scatter after diffuse reflection. We cannot see an image but can see the colour of the surface it reflected from.
- Transparent materials will allow visible light to pass through. Translucent materials will also allow light to pass through but objects can't be as clearly seen through them, such as with frosted glass.

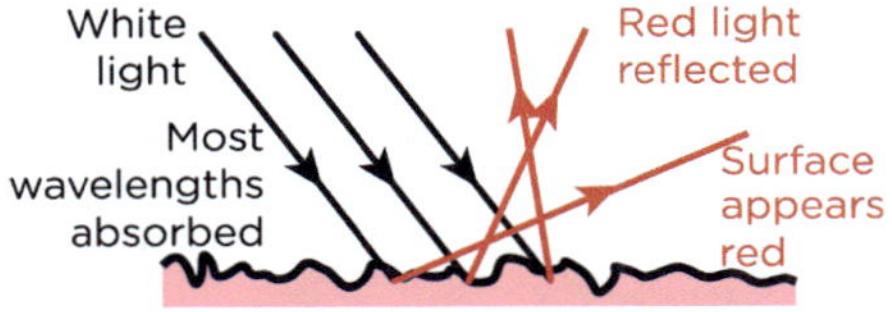

Ray diagrams 4.6.2.5

- Ray diagrams show the paths of light rays from an object to determine how and where an image forms.
  - Objects are assumed to be on the principal axis and extend a height above it.
  - The top of the image forms where rays from the top of the object converge.
- Three key rays are drawn to determine the location of an image:
  - A ray initially parallel to the principal axis to the lens, which is then redirected through its focus.
  - A ray that passes through the centre of the lens without changing direction.
  - A ray that passes through the focal point on the same side of the lens, which then travels parallel to the principal axis after reaching the lens (convex lenses only).
- The image will be:
  - Real if it is on the other side of the lens or virtual if it is on the same side of the lens as the object.
  - Inverted if the rays converge below the principal axis or upright if they converge above the principal axis.

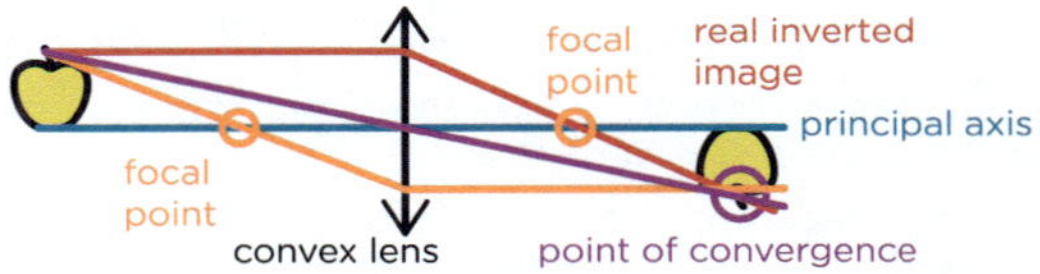

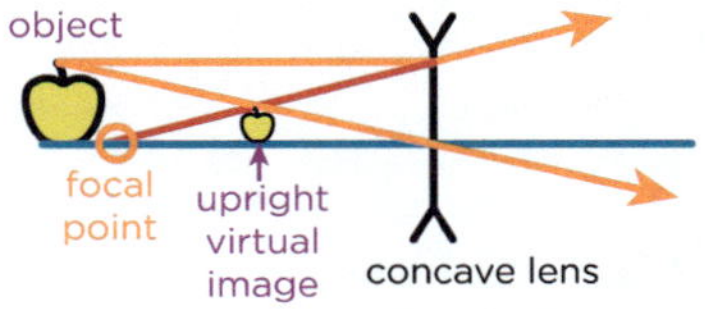

Magnification 4.6.2.5

- The magnification of a lens is a ratio of the size of the image it produces compared to the size of the object.
  - Magnification is a unitless quantity.
  - A magnification greater than 1 means the image will be larger than the object. A magnification of less than 1 means it will be smaller.
- Magnification can be calculated from a ray diagram using the formula **magnification = image height ÷ object height**.

Colour, black bodies, and magnetic fields

Seeing colour 4.6.2.6

- Light can be split into a spectrum by using a glass prism. This is because each wavelength of light refracts differently in the prism.

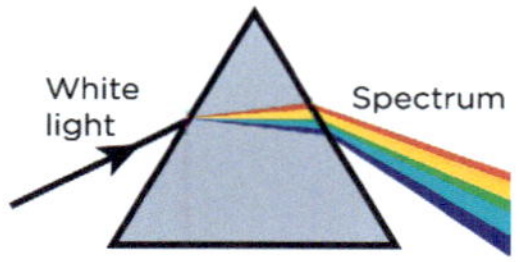

- Opaque materials are ones that won't allow visible light to pass through.
  - Certain wavelengths of light will be reflected while the rest will be absorbed. The material will appear to be a colour corresponding to the reflected wavelengths.
  - White materials will reflect all wavelengths of visible light while black materials will absorb all wavelengths.
- Colour filters are transparent materials that only allow certain wavelengths of visible light to pass through. The other wavelengths are absorbed. They are used to isolate certain colours in light.

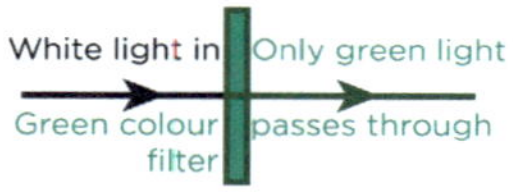

Temperature change and radiation 4.6.3.2

- If an object is at a constant temperature, then it is absorbing and emitting radiation at the same rate:
  - If it absorbs radiation faster than it can emit, then its temperature is rising, such as with an ice cube in a warm room.
  - If it emits radiation faster than it can absorb, then its temperature is decreasing, such as with a lump of hot coal in a cool room.
- The temperature of the Earth depends on how it absorbs radiation from the sun and re-emits it into space.
  - One side of Earth is facing the Sun, so it absorbs a lot of radiation. The other side faces away from the Sun, so it doesn't absorb any radiation but is still emitting it. So, the Earth's surface warms up during the day and cools at night.
  - Less radiation is incident to the Earth at its poles than on the equator. This is why the equator is very hot and the poles are very cold.

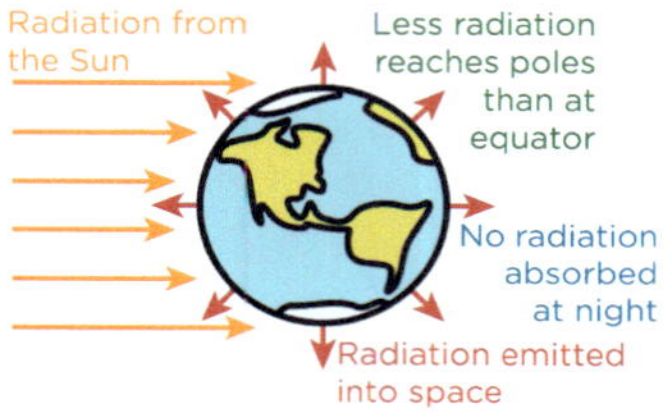

Absorption and emission of infrared radiation 4.6.3.1

- All bodies will absorb and emit infrared radiation.
  - This is true for objects of any temperature, but hotter objects will emit more radiation per second.
  - At high temperatures, the object will also emit red visible light. As the temperature increases, it also emits light of shorter wavelengths, eventually emitting white light.
- A perfect black body is an object that will not reflect or transmit any radiation directed onto it, only absorb it.
  - Black bodies are also perfect emitters of radiation as good absorbers are good emitters.
  - Perfect black bodies only exist in theory, but there are objects that absorb almost all radiation directed at them.

Magnetic poles 4.7.1.1

- Certain materials, such as iron, can experience magnetic forces. These are non-contact forces.
- Magnetic forces are strongest near magnetic poles.
  - Poles are labelled north or south depending on the direction they would eventually face if the magnet could freely turn.
  - Every magnet must have one of each pole. Both poles are as strong as each other.
  - Like poles will experience a repulsive force when brought near each other while unlike poles will attract.
- Permanent magnets are those that produce magnetic fields. Induced magnets are materials that become magnets when in another magnetic field.
  - The poles of the induced magnet will always be so that it feels an attractive force in the field. Repulsive forces can only be experienced by two permanent magnets.
  - When an induced magnet leaves the magnetic field, it will lose its magnetism very quickly.

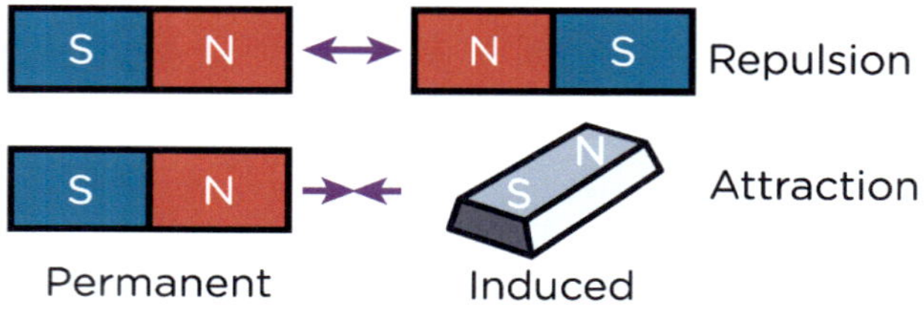

Magnetic fields 4.7.1.2

- A magnetic field is the region around a magnet where other magnets or magnetic materials will experience a force.
- Magnetic fields can be visualised using field lines:
  - The lines all point from a north pole to a south pole. This represents the direction of the force a north pole would experience in the field.
  - The strength of the field is indicated by how close together field lines are. They will be closest near to the poles of the magnet.
  - Field lines should not cross or touch each other.

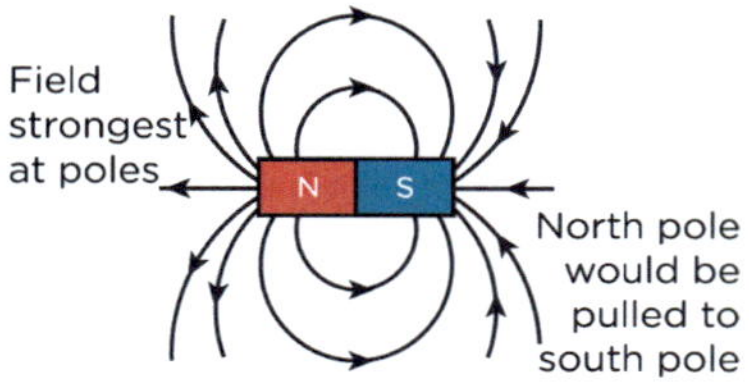

Compasses 4.7.1.2

- There is a permanent magnetic field around the Earth. Its poles align with the geographical North and South Poles.
- A compass contains a small permanent magnet that can freely rotate so that it aligns with the Earth's magnetic field.
- The North pole of the compass will point north due to an attractive force. This means the north pole of the Earth's magnetic field is actually at the South Pole.

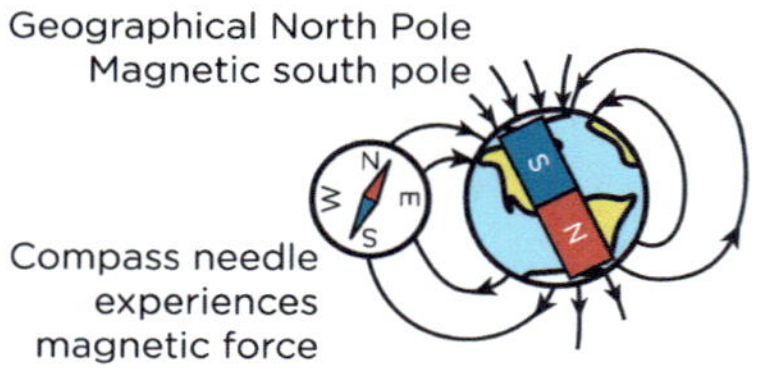

Field around a wire 4.7.2.1

- A magnetic field is produced when a current flows through a conducting wire. This field takes a circular shape.
- The field is strongest close to the wire. Increasing the current also increases the strength of the field.
- The direction of the field can be determined using the right-hand grip rule.
  - Hold out your right hand and point your thumb so that it points in the direction of the current.
  - Curl your fingers. The direction they point in is the direction of the magnetic field.

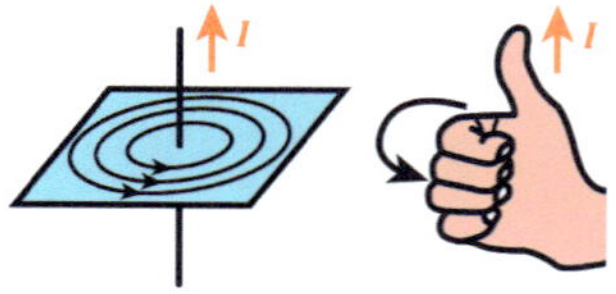

Solenoids 4.7.2.1

- A solenoid consists of a wire coiled into numerous loops.
  - The magnetic fields from each loop on the coil combine to form a field similar in shape to a bar magnet outside the coils and uniform inside them.
  - The strength of this field can be increased by increasing the current or using more loops on the coil.

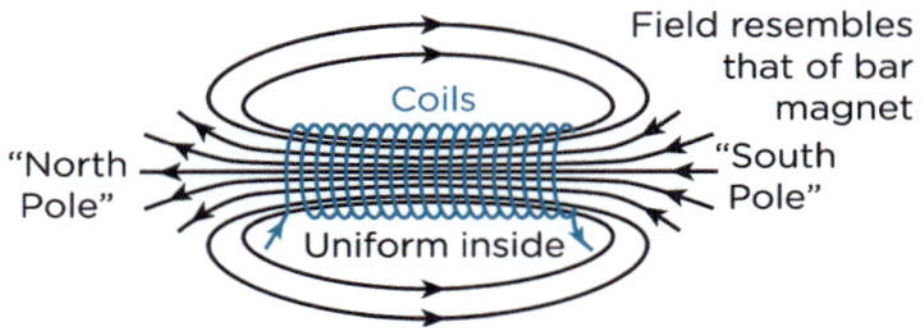

- An electromagnet is a solenoid with an iron core within the coil.
  - The iron core further increases the strength of the magnetic field.
  - Electromagnets are useful as their strong magnetic field can be switched on or off very quickly.

The motor effect 4.7.2.2

- When a conductor carries a current through a magnetic field, it will experience a force. This is called the motor effect.
  - The magnet also experiences an equal and opposite force.
  - These forces are due to the fields from the magnet and conductor squashing against each other.
- The direction of the force on a wire can be determined using Fleming's Left-Hand Rule. This is done by holding your thumb, first finger and second finger out at right angles to each other:
  - Your first finger should point in the direction of the field.
  - Your second finger should point in the direction of the current in the wire.
  - Your thumb will then point in the direction of the force.

- The magnitude of the force on a wire at right angles to the field is given by **force = magnetic flux density × current × length**.
  - Magnetic flux density is a measure of a magnetic field's strength or how close together its field lines are. It is measured in Tesla, **T**.
  - This equation can also be written as $F = BIL$.
  - F is the force the wire experiences in **N**, B is the magnetic flux density of the field in **T**, I is the current in the wire in **A** and L is the length of the wire within the field in **m**.

Electric motors 4.7.2.3

- An electric motor uses the motor effect to convert electrical energy to kinetic energy through rotation:
  - A rectangular coil of wire is placed in a magnetic field so that it can freely rotate around a pivot.
  - When a current flows through the coil, the two sides of the coil experience vertical forces in opposite directions.
  - This causes the coil to rotate.
- The coil receives its current from a circuit connected to it with a split-ring commutator.
  - This rotates while always maintaining a connection through the use of two carbon brushes.
  - The split ring switches brush periodically so the current reverses and the forces on the coil are always in the same direction.

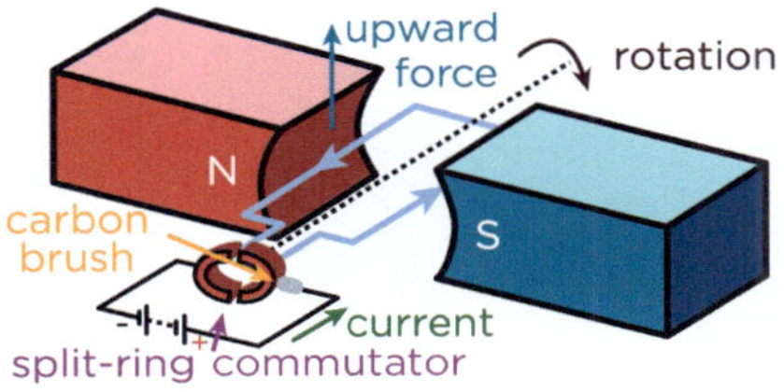

Loudspeakers 4.7.2.4

- A loudspeaker or pair of headphones generates sound waves using the motor effect.
  - An alternating current flows through a coil in a magnetic field, causing the coil and magnet to experience a force.
  - The coil pulls on a cone, which generates vibrations in the air as a sound wave.
  - Variations in the frequency and size of the current change the motion of the cone, creating different sound waves.

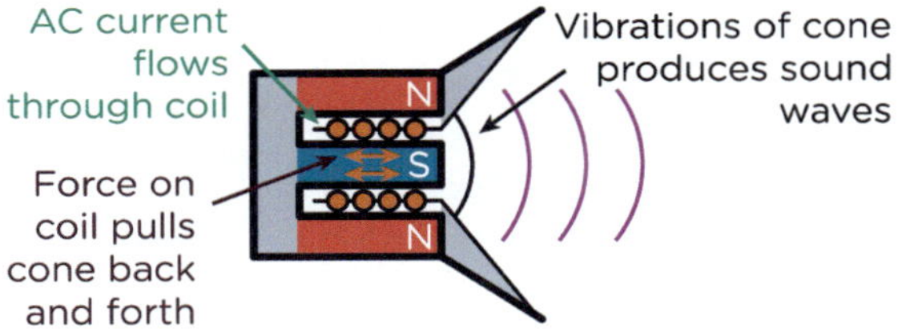

The generator effect 4.7.3.1

- A potential difference is induced in a conductor when it moves relative to a magnetic field or there is a change in the field.
  - A current is induced if the conductor is connected to a complete circuit.
  - This is called the generator effect and is the main method of generating electricity.
  - Reversing the motion of the conductor or the polarity of the field reverses the direction of the potential difference.
- The size of an induced potential difference can be increased by:
  - Increasing the speed of motion of the conductor or rate of change of the field.
  - Using a stronger magnetic field.
  - Using a longer length of conductor or coiling it.
- A magnetic field will be induced around the conductor due to the current flowing through it. This field opposes the change causing the generator effect.

Applying the generator effect 4.7.3.2-3

- An alternator uses the generator effect to produce an alternating current.
  - A coil turns in a magnetic field, inducing a potential difference in it.
  - The coil connects to a circuit using a pair of slip rings, inducing a current.
  - The strength and direction of the current vary with time. It will be strongest when the coil is perpendicular to the field.
  - Increasing the speed of rotation increases both the peak potential difference and frequency.

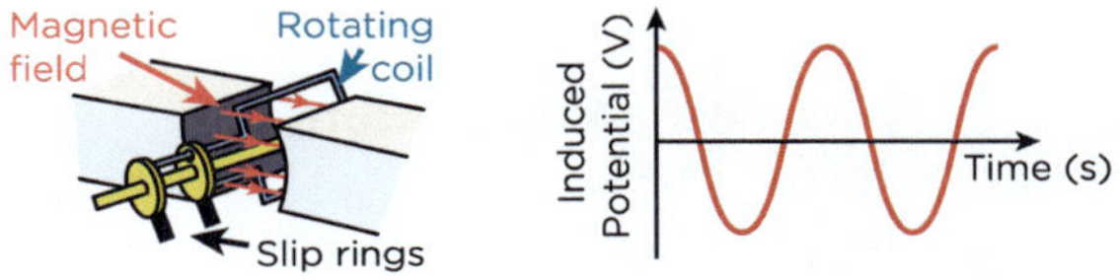

- A dynamo functions similarly to an alternator but uses a slip ring communicator instead of a pair of slip rings. So, it will instead produce a varying direct current.
- Microphones contain a coil that vibrates around a magnet when sound waves are directed at it. This generates a current that converts the sound waves to an electrical signal. This signal can be sent to a loudspeaker to project the sound.

Transformers and space

Transformers 4.7.3.4

- A transformer consists of two coils wrapped around an iron core.
  - When an alternating current flows through one coil, it induces a magnetic field around it.
  - This magnetic field is periodically changing direction and is concentrated by the iron core, so it induces an alternating current in the other coil.
  - An iron core is used as it is easily magnetised.

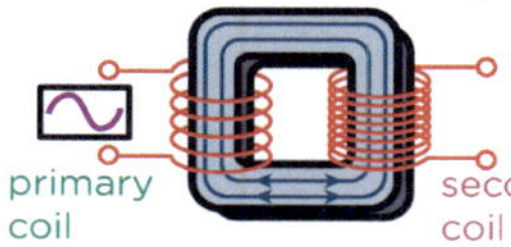

- Transformers are used to change an alternating potential difference.
  - Step-up transformers increase the potential difference by having more turns on their secondary coils.
  - Step-down transformers decrease the potential difference by having more turns on their primary coils.

Transformer equations 4.7.3.4

- The transformer equation states that the ratio of potential differences and turns in the coils of a transformer are equal:
  $\frac{V_P}{V_S} = \frac{n_P}{n_S}$.
  - V_P and V_S are the potential differences in the primary and secondary coils respectively in **V**. n_P and n_S are the number of turns in the primary and secondary coils respectively.
- If a transformer is 100% efficient, then there are no energy losses and
  power input to primary coil = power output from secondary coil.
  - This can also be written as $V_S \times I_S = V_P \times I_P$.
  - I_P and I_S are the currents in the primary and secondary coils respectively in **A**.

The solar system 4.8.1.1

- The solar system consists of:
  - A star, orbited by planets, called the Sun, which releases energy to its surroundings.
  - Four planets close to the Sun made from rock: Mercury, Venus, Earth and Mars.
  - Five planets further from the Sun made of gas: Jupiter, Saturn, Uranus and Neptune.
  - Dwarf planets further from the Sun, including Pluto.
  - Moons that orbit planets.
- The Sun is part of a group of over 200,000 million stars in a galaxy called the Milky Way.

Life of a star 4.8.1.2

- All stars start life in the same way:
  - A cloud of dust and gas, called a nebula, is pulled together by gravity. Collisions between molecules generate heat to form a ball of gas called a protostar.
  - When enough matter is pulled together, the high temperature of the star allows hydrogen to collide and fuse. The energy released from these reactions balances the gravitational forces trying to collapse the star. This is a main-sequence star.
  - When the star runs out of hydrogen to fuse, it starts to collapse under gravitational forces. This allows helium to fuse into heavier elements.
- For stars a similar size to the Sun:
  - The fusion of helium causes the star to expand into a red giant.
  - When the red giant runs out of helium to fuse it collapses into a white dwarf. The white dwarf eventually cools into a black dwarf.
- For stars much larger than the Sun:
  - Helium can fuse into even heavier elements, causing the star to expand into a red supergiant. The heaviest element made in the process is iron.
  - When the red supergiant runs out of fuel, it will collapse again. This causes the iron to fuse into even heavier elements, causing energy to be released in an explosion called a supernova. All elements heavier than iron were originally created and released in supernovae.
  - Alternatively, the star can collapse into a highly condensed ball of matter called a neutron star. Or it can collapse into a microscopic point, forming a black hole.

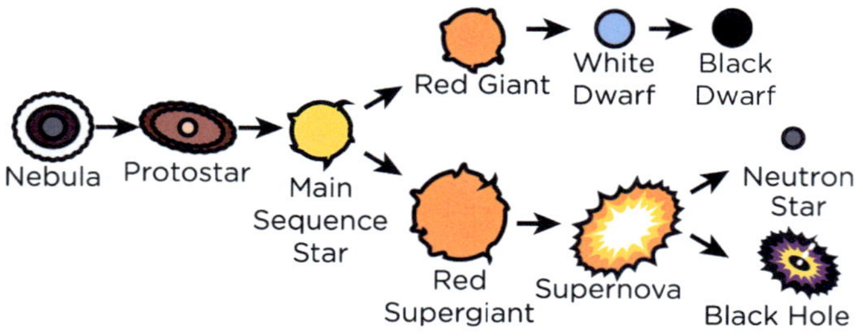

Orbits and satellites 4.8.1.3

- Planets and satellites are held in orbits by gravitational forces. Satellites experience forces with planets and planets experience forces with the Sun. Satellites can be natural, like a moon, or artificial, like the International Space Station.
- Gravitational forces keep planets and satellites travelling in circular paths.
  - The speed of the orbiting object is given by **speed = (2π × orbital radius) ÷ period of orbit**.
  - If the speed of the orbiting object changes, then its orbital radius must also change. If it doesn't, then the orbit will become unstable.

Red-shift 4.8.2

- Sounds appear to have a higher or lower pitch depending on if the source is moving towards or away from us. This is because the sound waves are being compressed or stretched respectively, changing their wavelength and frequency.
- A similar phenomenon occurs with light from extremely fast-moving sources.
  - Analysing the light from distant galaxies shows that its wavelength is longer than expected. This is called red-shift.
  - This suggests the galaxy is moving away from the Earth.
  - Furthermore, the further the galaxy is away, the greater the red-shift. This suggests the further away a galaxy is, the faster it is moving.

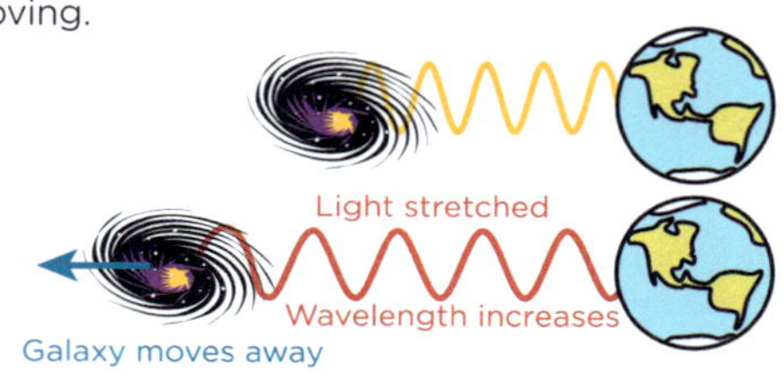

The Big Bang Theory 4.8.2

- Observations of red-shift support the Big Bang theory for the origin of the universe.
  - Matter and all space exploded from a very small, extremely hot and dense region around 13.8 billion years ago, creating the universe.
  - The extremely hot matter from this explosion eventually cooled and was pulled together by gravity, creating stars and galaxies.
  - The energy from the explosion is making the universe continue to expand, pushing galaxies apart from each other.
- It was expected that gravity would slow down the rate of the universe's expansion. However, recent observations of supernovae suggest that this rate is actually increasing. This has led to the theories of dark matter and dark energy, which influence this expansion.

Contents - Science Skills

SNAPREVISE

Scientific processes WS 1.1, 1.6

- Scientific ideas are not accepted until there is evidence to back them up.
    - Theories, theorems and experimental results are published in scientific journals.
    - These undergo peer review by the scientific community before they are accepted.
    - Scientists will also repeat experiments described in journals to confirm their results are valid.
    - Some scientific ideas considered correct today were not initially accepted until decades after they were first published, such as Darwin's theory of evolution.
- Currently accepted scientific theories and models are the ones that best fit the current evidence and knowledge of the universe. They may be disproven at some point in the future.
- Scientific ideas that are reported in popular media before verification can lead to negative opinions of them.
    - These reports are not subject to peer review so they could concern scientific ideas that turn out to be incorrect.
    - There is a risk of inaccuracies and bias in these reports.
    - More scientists are communicating directly with the public to try and stop this miscommunication.

Variables WS 2.2

- Scientific experiments are performed to determine the relationship between two or more variables.
- An independent variable is a variable that is manually changed. An experiment should have only one independent variable.
- A dependent variable is a variable that will change as a result of a change in the independent variable.
- The dependent and independent variables are measured to determine the relationship between them.
- A control variable is a variable that must be kept the same throughout the experiment to make the test fair.
- Changing a control variable will make it unclear if that change or a change in the independent variable is responsible for a change in the dependent variable.

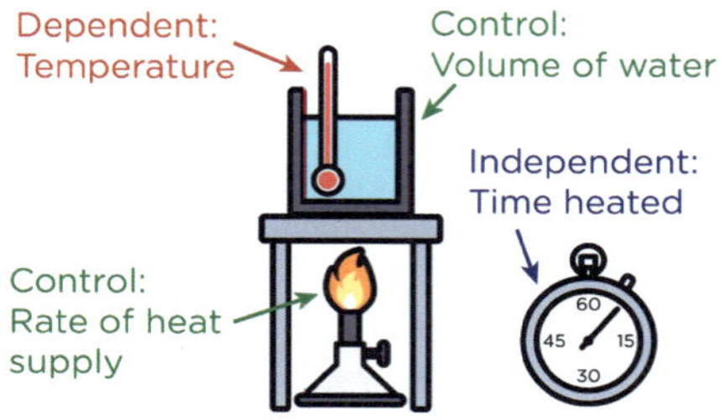

Apparatus and equipment WS 2.2, 2.3

- Diagrams can be used to show how to set up equipment for an experiment. Symbols should be 2D, simple and clear to understand.

Examples of scientific apparatus		
Apparatus	**Use**	**Symbol**
Bunsen burner	To provide a constant flow of heat to a substance.	 Heat
Beaker	To store water or other fluids. Other containers, such as canonical flasks, might be used depending on the experiment.	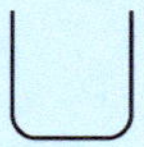
Test tube	To hold a small amount of liquid. Larger tubes for heating are called boiling tubes.	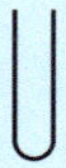
Tripod	A stand that a Bunsen burner can be placed under. Gauze can be used to place a beaker on top.	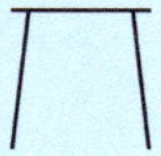
Clamp stand	A stand that can be used in conjunction with clamps and bosses to suspend test tubes and other equipment in the air.	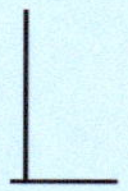
Funnel	Used to direct liquid into a test tube or another container.	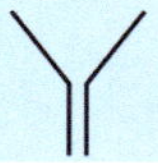

- Various equipment can be used to take measurements during experiments. More precise equipment will lead to better results.

Examples of measuring equipment	
Equipment	**Used to measure**
Ruler	Length
Measuring cylinder	Volume
Stopwatch	Time
Thermometer	Temperature
Pan balance/scale	Mass

Safe experiments WS 2.4

- Measures should be taken to ensure experiments are conducted safely.
- Sensible protective clothing should be worn.
    - Goggles or safety visors to protect the eyes from harmful substances.
    - Lab coats to protect clothing from damage or harmful substances.
    - Gloves when handling hazardous materials.
    - Long hair should be tied back.

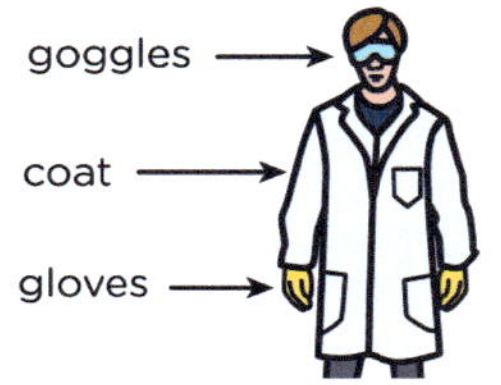

- Steps should be taken to ensure Bunsen burners are used safely.
    - They should always be placed on a heatproof mat.
    - Any heated substances or equipment should be left to cool or only handled with tongs.
    - Bunsen burners should be left on a yellow flame when not in use.
    - Gas taps should be left off when not in use.

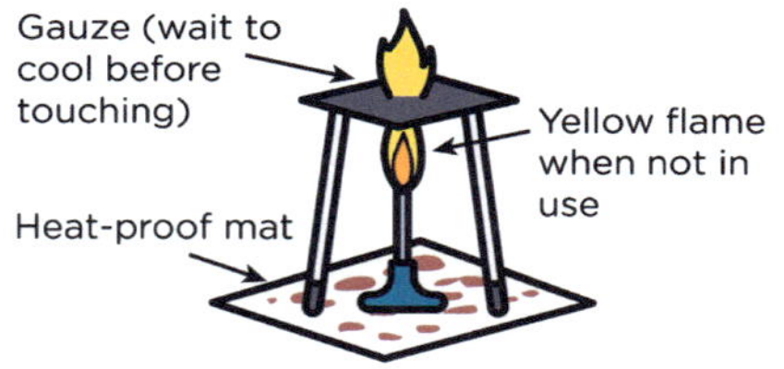

- Hazardous substances, such as chemicals or radioactive materials, should be handled with care.
    - They should be stored when not in use.
    - Containers should be correctly marked with the hazards they present (e.g. irritant).
    - Particularly dangerous substances should not be handled directly.
    - Flammable substances should be kept away from naked flames (e.g. ethanol).
- Biohazards, such as bacterial cultures, should be handled with care.
    - Aseptic techniques should be used when preparing bacterial cultures.
    - Disinfectant should be used after exposure to biohazards to prevent contamination.
    - Avoid contact with skin of stains (e.g. Toluidine blue or DCPIP).
    - Hands should be washed after handling biohazards or unsterilised samples (e.g. soil samples).
- All equipment should be checked regularly.
    - Clamps and bosses should be tightly secured.
    - Electrical equipment should be inspected to ensure they have no live wires.

Presenting data WS 3.1

- Frequency tables are used to record results from experiments.
  - The first column should be the independent variable with values in increasing order.
  - Headers should be clear and include units

Example frequency table

Independent variable, x (s)	Measured Variable, y (m)				Calculated dependent variable, y^2 (m^2)
	1	2	3	Mean	
1	1.2	1.4	1.3	1.3	1.7
2	2.8	2.6	3	2.8	7.8
3	3.7	3.2	3.8	3.6	12.7
4	4.8	4.6	4.2	4.5	20.6

- Bar charts are used to compare categoric variables to continuous variables.

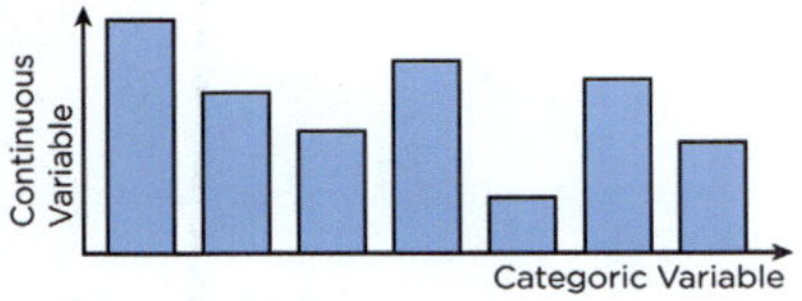

- Histograms show how a set of continuous data fits into grouped categories.
  - The height of each bar represents the frequency density.
  - The area of each bar is proportional to the number of data values in the group.
  - The bars should all be touching.

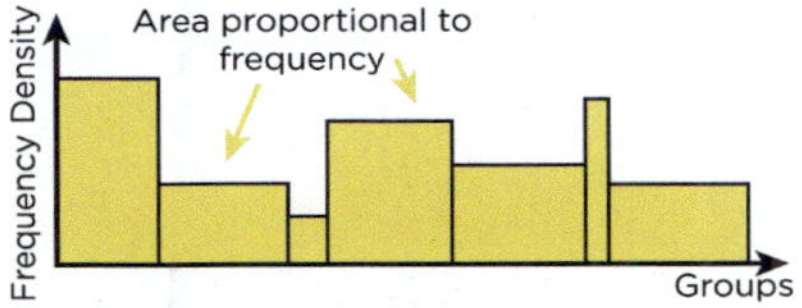

- Line graphs compare two continuous variables.
  - Recorded data is plotted onto a graph. The x and y coordinates of each point correspond to a value for the independent and dependent variable, respectively.
  - A smooth curve is drawn to show the general relationship. This should be close to as many points as possible, excluding outliers.

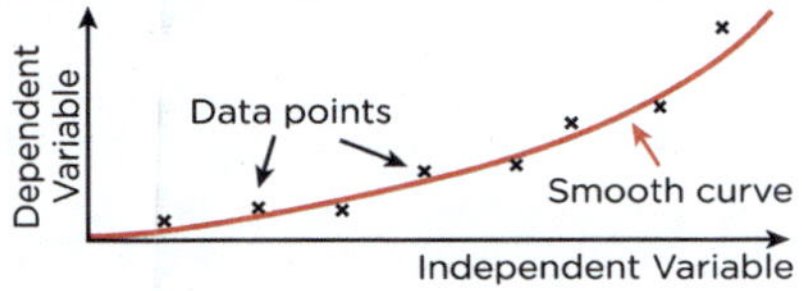

Mean and range WS 3.3

- The mean of a set of values is the sum of those values divided by the number of values there are.
  - E.g. the mean of **4, 7** and **13** is $(4 + 7 + 13) \div 3 = 8$.
  - The mean is used to calculate the average value of the results from a repeated experiment.
- The range of the set of values is the difference between the largest and smallest value.
  - E.g. the range of the values **4, 7** and **13** is $13 - 4 = 9$.
  - The range of a set of measurements can give information about the uncertainty of a repeated experiment.

Rounding and standard form WS 3.3, 4.6

- To round a value to a certain number of significant figures.
  - Identify the first non-zero digit in the value.
  - Count the number of digits after this one.
  - Identify whether to round the last digit in your count up or down, depending on if the next digit is greater than or equal to 5.
  - Remove all digits outside the count.
  - E.g. $0.00548632 = 0.00589$ to 3 significant figures.
- Calculated values should be given to a number of significant figures equal to the lowest number of significant figures from the numbers used.
  - E.g. the calculated value 583×3.4 should be given to 2 significant figures.
  - Values are rounded to the point where they should be the same as the true value rounded to that many significant figures.
- Standard form is used to write out very large or very small rounded numbers.
  - First, a number between **1** and **10** is written. The number of digits in this number is the same as the number of significant figures it has been rounded to.
  - This is then multiplied by a power of 10, which can be positive or negative depending on if the number is big or small.
  - E.g. $158000 = 1.58 \times 10^5$.
  - E.g. $0.00158 = 1.58 \times 10^{-3}$.
  - Each multiplication by 10 moves the decimal point one digit to the left or right.

Equations WS 3.3

- Equations show the relationship between scientific variables under certain conditions.
- To use an equation to find an unknown value using an equation:
  - Rearrange equation algebraically to make the unknown variable the subject.
  - Substitute in the values in the correct places, ensuring the units are the ones needed for the equation.
  - Calculate the unknown value.
- Formula triangles can be used to help understand how to rearrange equations.
  - Cover the part of the triangle for the unknown value.
  - Divide the top value by the bottom value, or multiply both of the bottom values, depending on which value is unknown.

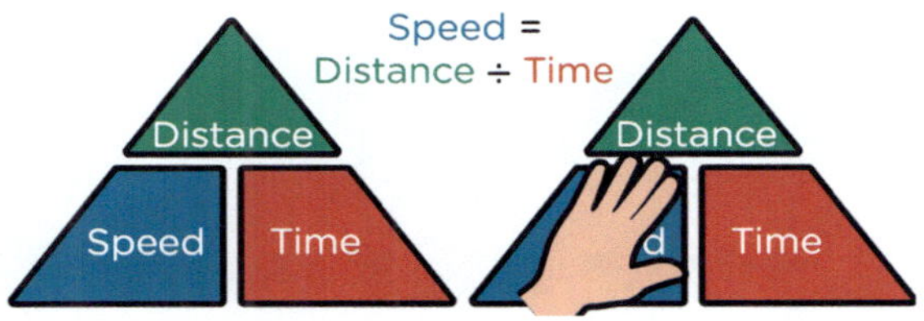

Interpreting graphs WS 1.2, 3.3

- The gradient of a straight line of best fit can give information about the relationship between two variables in a graph.
- To calculate the gradient:
  - Choose two points on the lines as far apart as possible such that their x and y values are easy to read.
  - Calculate the differences in the two x and the two y values.
  - Calculate the gradient as **difference in y ÷ difference in y**.
- A curved line of best fit has a changing gradient. The gradient at a particular point can be calculated by drawing a tangent.
  - A tangent is a straight line that only just brushes against the point on the curve.
  - The gradient of the curve is the gradient of this straight-line tangent.

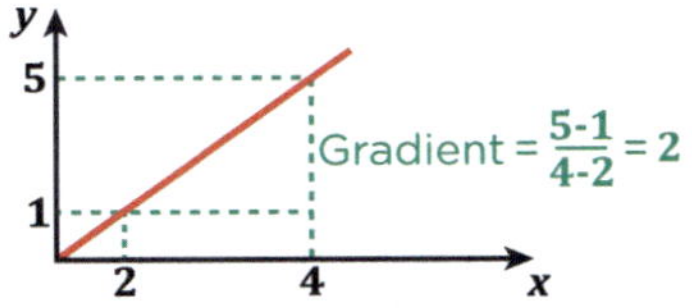

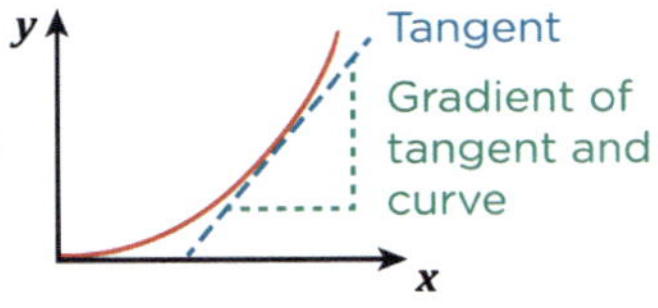

- The x or y intercept is the point where the line crosses the x or y axis.
- The area under a line graph is the value that corresponds to multiplying together the two variables shown in the graph as they are both changing.
  - For straight line graphs, this area can be calculated using the formula for the area of a rectangle or a triangle.
  - For curves, this area can be estimated by counting the squares beneath the graph.

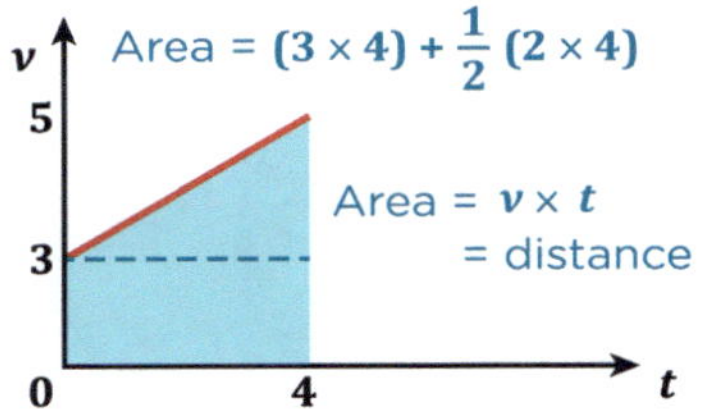

Distance = 52×50 m/s $\times$ 5s
= 13000 m

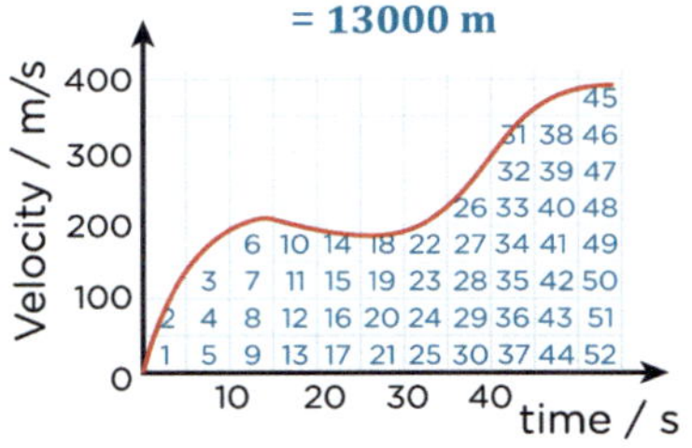

True values and units

SNAPREVIS

Uncertainty WS 3.4

- Scientific measurements often do not give the true value due to errors. For a repeated experiment, we cannot tell which measurement is closest to the true value.
- The uncertainty of a measurement is the range of values for which it suggests the true value could lie within.
  - Uncertainties are usually given as how far above or below a measured value the true value could be.
  - For example, the value 37.4 ± 2 indicates the true value could be anywhere between 35.4 and 39.4.
- The uncertainty for a repeated experiment can be measured by the range of measurements about the mean. For example, the uncertainty of the measurements $3, 4$ and 5 is 4 ± 1.

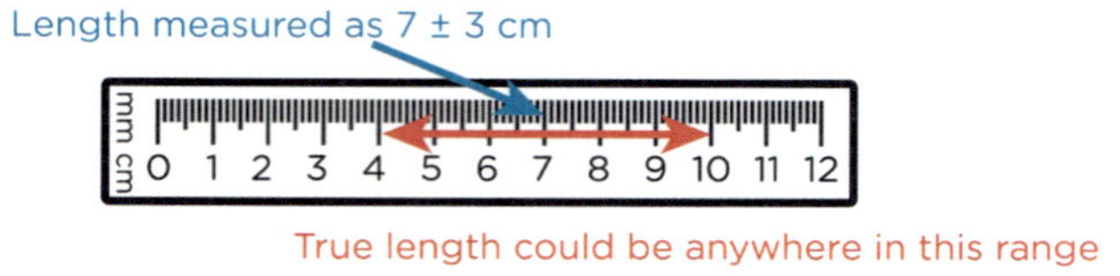

Accuracy and precision WS 3.7

- The true value of a measurement is the value that would be obtained in a perfect experiment without errors.
- The accuracy of a measurement is how close it is to the true value.
- The precision of a repeated experiment is how close together the measurements are.
- Accuracy and precision are two separate concepts. An accurate measurement is not necessarily precise and vice versa.

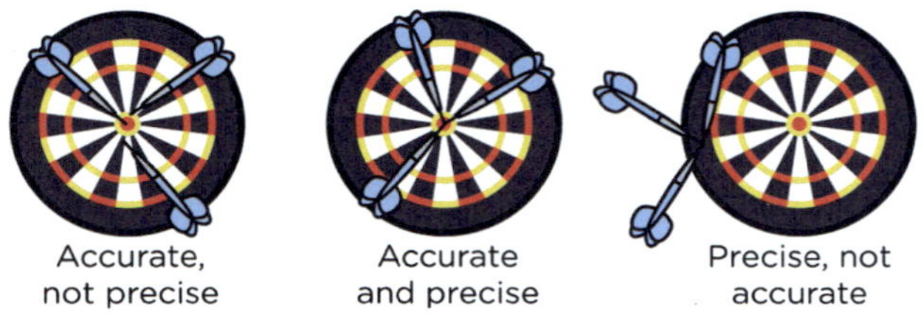

- A measurement is repeatable if the results are similar when the experiment is performed again by the same investigator, under the same conditions. This implies the measurements are precise.
- A measurement is reproducible if the results are similar when the experiment is performed again by a different investigator with different equipment. This implies the measurements are accurate.

Errors and anomalies WS 3.7

- Errors will cause measurements to differ from the true value.
  - Random errors or anomalies affect single experiments and vary unpredictably. This will reduce precision.
  - Systematic errors involve measurement results differing from the true value by a consistent amount each time. This will reduce accuracy.
- Anomalies should be identified and omitted from the results. This can be done by:
  - Repeating experiments to find values that do not match others. For example, in the measurements $3, 7, 25,$ and 8, taken under the same conditions, the value 25 would be an anomaly.
  - Plotting results and seeing which values would not fit the pattern established by the rest of the data.

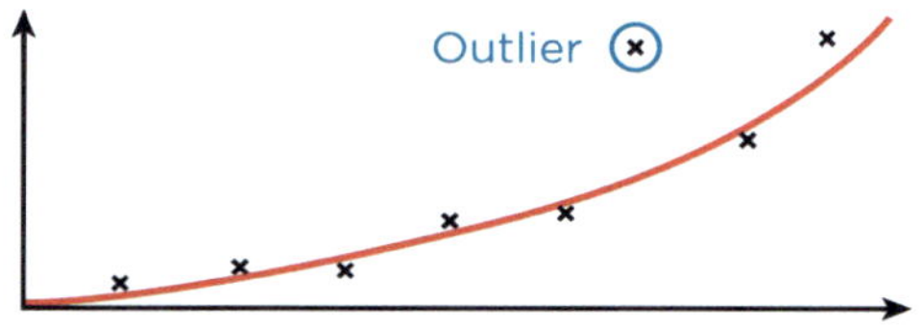

- Systematic errors are prevented through careful planning of experiments. This includes:
  - Ensuring all control variables remain unchanged during the experiment.
  - Calibrating all equipment and using it correctly.
  - Turning off equipment between measurements to prevent heating if temperature is a variable.
  - Testing equipment before an experiment.
  - Only measuring the meniscus at eye level when using a measuring cylinder.

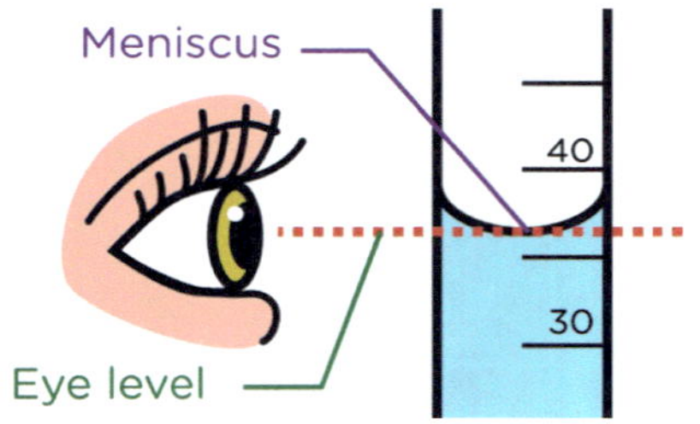

Units WS 4.3

- Measurements must be given units to indicate what they are measured in terms of.

Examples of Units		
Unit	**Symbol**	**Quantity**
Metre	m	Distance
Second	s	Time
Degrees Celsius	°C	Temperature
Litre	L	Volume
Grams	g	Mass
Joules	J	Energy
Coulombs	C	Charge

- Some units are derived as combinations of other units. For example:
  - Speed in metres per second, **m/s**.
  - Area in metres squared, $\mathbf{m^2}$.
  - Rate in grams per second, **g/s**.
  - Density in kilograms per meter cubed, $\mathbf{kg/m^3}$.

Prefixes WS 4.4

- Prefixes are added to units to indicate that they should be multiplied by a power of 10 to convert to the standard unit.
  - For example, $1\ \text{cm} = 1 \times 10^{-2}\ \text{m}$.
  - Prefixes are useful for writing out large or small values.
  - When substituting values into equations, their units must be converted to have the correct prefix first.

Prefix	Symbol	Multiplier
Tera-	T	10^{12}
Giga-	G	10^{9}
Mega-	M	10^{6}
Kilo-	k	10^{3}
Centi-	c	10^{-2}
Milli-	m	10^{-3}
Micro-	µ	10^{-6}
Nano-	n	10^{-9}